WE MAKE SHIPS

WE MAKE SHIPS

TOM PICKARD

SECKER & WARBURG
LONDON

First published in Great Britain 1989
by Martin Secker & Warburg Limited
Michelin House, 81 Fulham Road,
London SW3 6RB

Pickard, Tom, 1946–
We make ships
1. Great Britain. Shipbuilding industries
I. Title
338,4'762382'00941

ISBN 0 436 36960 5

Printed and bound in Great Britain by
Butler & Tanner Ltd, Frome and London

List of Illustrations

1. In the complex, the 22,000-ton multi-purpose bulk carrier, ship number 1431, nearing completion
2. Down hand on the deck at sunset
3. Wing tank section on a Kamag transporter in a pre-fabrication shed
4. Welding inside the bulbous bow
5. Inside a double bottom in the lube-oil sump under the engine
6. Burning a pipe tunnel
7. The morning of the launch
8. Peter Callaghan, the last yard convener on the River Wear
9. Welder entering a confined space on the shell
10. Erecting the bulbous bow
11. Welders (in cherry-pickers) and burners working on the bulbous bow
12. Positioning the propellor
13. Lifting the propellor boss
14. Preparing drag chains for the launch
15. Welding on the bulbous bow thirty minutes before the launch
16. One of the waxed ways prior to the launch

All photographs by Tom Pickard

Acknowledgements

I would like to thank the men of Austin and Pickersgill for their generous co-operation, their patience, solidarity, and humour, even though I was often the butt of that humour. But I am most particularly indebted to them for helping me keep the faith and strengthening my belief in free trade unionism as the most effective means of protecting our civil liberties even during this period of fearful reaction.

Additional thanks to Mick Dodds who tirelessly proofread the seventy hours of transcripts.

Thanks also to the Artists Agency, and to Northern Arts for a grant to cover the expenses of printing the photographs, and to my wife, Joanna Voit, who made the prints with a lot of dodging and burning from often thin negatives.

I am grateful to Sunderland Museum and Art Gallery where some of these photographs appeared in an exhibition held in 1987.

Thanks also to the editors of *Rolling Stock* where an extract from this book appeared.

Finally, thanks to Mike Elliott for being there when I needed an interpreter: the best stand-up comic in the business.

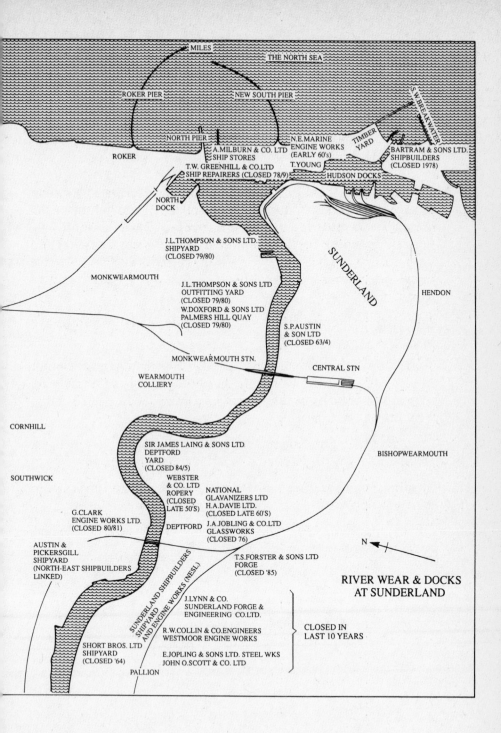

MILES

THE NORTH SEA

ROKER PIER

NEW SOUTH PIER

S.W.BREAKWATER

ROKER

NORTH PIER

A.MILBURN & CO. LTD
SHIP STORES

N.E.MARINE
ENGINE WORKS
(EARLY 60's)

TIMBER
YARD

BARTRAM & SONS LTD.
SHIPBUILDERS
(CLOSED 1978)

T.W.GREENHILL & CO.LTD
SHIP REPAIRERS (CLOSED 78/9)

T.YOUNG

HUDSON DOCKS

NORTH
DOCK

J.L.THOMPSON & SONS LTD.
SHIPYARD
(CLOSED 79/80)

SUNDERLAND

MONKWEARMOUTH

J.L.THOMPSON & SONS LTD
OUTFITTING YARD
(CLOSED 79/80)

W.DOXFORD & SONS LTD
PALMERS HILL QUAY
(CLOSED 79/80)

HENDON

S.P.AUSTIN
& SON LTD
(CLOSED 63/4)

MONKWEARMOUTH STN.

CENTRAL STN

WEARMOUTH
COLLIERY

CORNHILL

SIR JAMES LAING & SONS LTD.
DEPTFORD
YARD
(CLOSED 84/5)

BISHOPWEARMOUTH

SOUTHWICK

WEBSTER
& CO. LTD
ROPERY
(CLOSED
LATE 50'S)

NATIONAL
GLAVANIZERS LTD
H.A.DAVIE LTD.
(CLOSED LATE 60'S)

G.CLARK
ENGINE WORKS LTD.
(CLOSED 80/81)

DEPTFORD

J.A.JOBLING & CO.LTD
GLASSWORKS
(CLOSED 76)

N

AUSTIN &
PICKERSGILL
SHIPYARD
(NORTH-EAST SHIPBUILDERS
LINKED)

T.S.FORSTER & SONS LTD
FORGE
(CLOSED '85)

RIVER WEAR & DOCKS
AT SUNDERLAND

SUNDERLAND SHIPBUILDERS
SHIPYARD AND ENGINE WORKS (NESL)

J.LYNN & CO.
SUNDERLAND FORGE &
ENGINEERING CO.LTD.

R.W.COLLIN & CO.ENGINEERS
WESTMOOR ENGINE WORKS

CLOSED IN
LAST 10 YEARS

SHORT BROS. LTD
SHIPYARD
(CLOSED '64)

E.JOPLING & SONS LTD. STEEL WKS
JOHN O.SCOTT & CO. LTD

PALLION

INTRODUCTION

When I left school in 1960, a few months before my fifteenth birthday, I had my card marked as a welder in the shipyards. There was a slump on the Tyne at the time and I never did get a start on the river.

I left my native North-East more than twelve years ago and have since lived in London or abroad. I spent some time in Poland during the period which saw the rise of the Solidarity movement in the shipyards of the Baltic.

In January 1986 I was selected by the shop stewards of Austin and Pickersgill's shipyard for an Artists Agency placement as a writer in residence in their yard at Sunderland. I spent almost a year with the workers, taking photographs, tape-recording conversations and filming interviews.

I have decided to disguise the identities of the people in this book for two reasons. The first is that the recordings were often made in noisy circumstances and with a group of people, so in some cases it was difficult to be certain of who said what. The other reason is more serious. Although exposures of the Economic League in the *Observer* and elsewhere may reduce its effectiveness it will still continue to compile secret lists of active trade unionists. Even if the Economic League is dismantled there is no doubt that other such agencies exist and will continue to supply the need of employers to have their employees' ideologies match their own as a primary condition of employment. Because there is a very real danger of workers in this book being blacklisted for their thoughts, opinions and principles and because jobs in the North-East of England are so difficult to find, I have decided to identify none of the workers who spoke to me. Given the unexpected loyalty and dedication to craft and community – in the brutal circumstances and nature of the shipbuilding industry – I find the necessity for anonymity ironic and alarming.

A disturbing number of the men who speak on these pages have been forced to leave their industry through serious injuries and are

1

permanently crippled. Even though they are unlikely to work again I have felt it prudent not to identify them either.

Many of the interviews and conversations took place either at the men's places of work, or in their cabins during the morning and lunch breaks. The cabins are personalised places, often built by the men, with distinct identities where the intimate, humorous and sometimes cruel banter takes place. Even in the most desperate circumstances a laugh was never long in coming.

Austin and Pickersgill's shipyard is one of the most modern in Europe[1] and in 1986 it had a complete fitting-out quay with an incredible concentration of skills. They had recently won the Queen's Award for Industry, and, in 1986, there had been no serious strike for thirteen years.[2] When I arrived there they were fighting a rearguard action against casualisation with its consequent erosion of hard-won safety standards and working conditions. The industry was lurching from crisis to disaster and it was that predicament which ate away at the workforce, as much as the penny-by-penny battle with management.[3]

This is not a book of nostalgia. It bears testament to a struggle for survival, and resistance to the government's systematic attempt to break the back of the shipbuilding industry as well as the spirit (and sometimes health) of those who build the ships.

Austin and Pickersgill was an amalgamation of three separate companies: S. P. Austin, Wm. Pickersgill, and Bartram and Sons. The oldest firm in the company was S. P. Austin, founded in 1826 to build small vessels used in the transportation of coal to the South of England. In 1954 they amalgamated with Pickersgill's. The amalgamation with Bartram's came in 1968.

Bartram and Sons was unique on two counts: it launched ships directly into the sea, and it was remembered with affection by everyone I spoke to who had worked there.

In 1975, after a £30,000,000 investment in a ship factory, Austin and Pickersgill cornered the world market with its best-seller standard design freight, the SD14. By 1976 they were employing

1. There is a scale model on display at the Maritime Museum in Greenwich.

2. Sunderland, where ships have been built and skills developed over hundreds of years, was, at one time in its recent history, *the* largest shipbuilding town in the world.

3. Extracts from a secret report commissioned by British Shipbuilders: 'There are daily "Board meetings" over lunch when major company wide issues (e.g. *when to take on a workforce*) are discussed communally.'

3,000 people and by 1977 when the factory was complete they were building eighteen SD14s per year. They took fifty per cent of new British orders. In March 1982 the total workforce of Austin and Pickersgill was 2,850. In 1986 it stood at 1,192.

Towards the end of January 1986, when I first went into Austin and Pickersgill's, the yard convener generously allowed me to photocopy his diary from the previous year. It contains detailed accounts of meetings with management, shop stewards' meetings, and notes on the progress of the ships they were building. Sometimes it reads like the logbook for the last few days of the Alamo. It reveals the brinkmanship which prevails in British shipbuilding: management try to impose new practices and wage deals when the workforce thinks there are no orders on the books and the yard is in danger of closing. 'Management by fear' was a phrase I was to hear often. In response the workforce threaten strike action when a ship is due to be launched or moved to a tight schedule. The diary also notes events outside, such as the miners' strike. Monkwearmouth Colliery is situated a mile from the yard and is the only other major employer of labour in the area. The diary locates shipyard industrial relations in a particularly strident context.

15 January 1985
Resume the collections through a raffle for the miners.
The stewards report that it is more difficult to sell for the
miners' hardship fund than it was for the Christmas
appeal. The morale of the miners is very low. Another
1,300 went back today and coal is moved from
Wearmouth for the first time. They are being slowly
starved back to work after eleven months. How Kinnock
can say that nobody is starving in the British coalfields
is amazing and shows how out of touch he is with the
rank and file of the movement.

During my time there I was continually hearing complaints from most trades in the yard about the incursion of subcontractors into parts of the production process normally carried out by the permanent workforce. Amongst others I saw the blacksmith's shop closed down and the men made redundant. Skilled proud men looked with disbelief at the shoddy work coming into the yard from cowboy subcontractors. The ideological aim of the government

3

(through BS management) was to casualise the industry, and their justification was cost. But, as the blacksmiths will tell you, much of the outside work was being dumped by the skipful or having to be rectified by the few remaining outfitters in the yard. The costs must have trebled.

I won't forget a fifty-year-old plumber in a state of shock, standing in the former plumbers' shop a day after the roof had been torn off. He showed me how he had made elbow bends in piping, and how the subcontracted work that was coming in had joins every time the pipe changed direction. He also pointed out that each join was the possible source of a leak. But what's safety against cost?

Shortly after my residency was finished I was commissioned by the BBC to write a piece of TV faction to commemorate the fiftieth anniversary of the Jarrow March of 1936, (*Left Over People*)[1] I accepted on the condition that I could deal equally with the crisis in the present-day shipbuilding town of Sunderland. As the play was being written I kept getting messages from the head of the BBC department like, 'Tell Tom we're not getting management point of view here ...' While I was writing it, Norman Tebbit made his notorious attack on the BBC and its ace reporter Kate Adie. The morale at the BBC perceptibly sank. Rumours ran round the corridors like joggers on skateboards. The script was sent to the BBC solicitor who thought it OK but added, 'In the light of recent publicity I have not considered that the rights or wrongs or slant of the subject matter come within my brief ... Mrs Thatcher is obviously the main target for the criticism with passing insults to Neil Kinnock but I do not consider they are likely to sue ...' The play was a mixture of satire, music from Alan Price, slapstick comedy from Mike Elliott, archive footage, contemporary news footage of Thatcher, and some scenes set in a contemporary shipyard. The dialogue and certainly the arguments were very much taken, sometimes directly, from the tapes reproduced in this book. The production went ahead and exists on videotape, buried in the BBC's archives, along with the bollocks of its upper management.[2] There were some acrimonious arguments with the director over artistic interpretation. Before the producer could show it to his superiors he wanted changes in Jude Alderson's (of Sadista Sisters) marvellously funny impersonation of Thatcher. I was unhappy with

1. or *Left Over Play*, as it has become known.
2. I believe there is a pirated version of the rough edit in existence.

some other aspects of the production but thought it could be put right in the editing. Suddenly on-line editing time was withdrawn. A promised slot of November (when the marchers returned to Jarrow in 1936) was lost. The producer was writing to say, 'With the election coming, there will be no chance of showing before; and after the Election – it depends, I guess, on what happens.' What happened is history. Conservative Party pressure continued to silence dissent in the BBC and the secret police raided their Scottish offices over the Zircon affair. The government ran skilfully made TV advertisements offering shares, to those who could afford them, in public industries about to be privatised. The advertisements ran several times a night for months on end up to the election and were thinly disguised promos for Thatcherism. Earlier Norman Tebbit had described a subversive BBC as drip-feeding anti-Tory propaganda, like a Chinese water torture, to an unsuspecting public (something he was unable to substantiate when challenged). Like Thatcher's 'enemies within', it was a form of projection.

I found it disturbing, not just because of the work put in by everyone concerned, or because it was part of a much wider and systematic dismantling of our civil liberties, but because the voice of the shipyard worker, whose existence was threatened, was silenced. (Ironically I had avoided the use of a single 'fuck' in the play, so as not to threaten it.) The arguments weren't aired. At least not by the BBC. Fortunately Alan Fountain at Channel 4 came to the rescue and commissioned a documentary film (*We Make Ships*) where I was able to put the arguments expressed in this book forward.

The cruellest irony of all is that the skills of the Wearside shipbuilders are at a level unparalleled in their history and unmatched in the world. In recent years they have built some of the most sophisticated high-tech ships to have sailed the seas.

In December 1985, a month before my arrival, the yard had no orders. Then management leaked the information that there was the prospect of two orders from a German owner, Oldendorf. Before the orders were secured they tried to introduce a package of redundancies, new work-practices, and the use of toxic welding rods. The shop stewards refused and balloted the workforce who gave them overwhelming backing for strike action one week before Christmas. Brinkmanship. Gaffers chalked on walls, 'Xmas is coming, think of wife and bairns. Don't strike.' British Shipbuilders

5

in London tried to persuade Oldendorf to place his orders with another of its yards but he refused. He had had good service from A&P in the past and wanted his ships built there or nowhere in Britain. With a strike threatening, on Friday night Oldendorf called management with a deadline: he told them that he would sit by the telephone in his London hotel room until 11 a.m. the next day. Cars were sent to bring the union negotiating committee into the yard on Saturday morning. A compromise was reached and the orders were secured. At the beginning of 1986, one of the coldest winters in living memory, I began my residency in the yard and the keel for the first 22,000-ton multi-purpose bulk carrier, ship number 1431, was laid.

August 1988

JANUARY

20/1/86

Danny Morgan was assigned to me as my guide, the man
who would introduce me to people in the yard. He was
made the shop stewards' arts officer and I was his ward.

Danny was all argument. He liked to put a case clearly,
so there'd be no misunderstanding. His attitude
reminded me of a pal from my youth who, although in
no way as articulate as Danny, would spit a gob of
phlegm on the ground and say, 'Pick the bones out of
that.'
I began by asking him what effect unemployment was
having on the town.

Sunderland under threat

Danny: It has a tremendous effect. I mean, take the local labour
club [of which Danny was chairman]. It costs a tremendous amount
to run the club because of the rising rates, the rising rent, electricity,
gas charges, and the general overheads of the club which are astron-
omical. And, of course, at the other end of the scale, there isn't as
much money going about because of redundancies and closures in
the town. At one end the money is streaming out and at the other
it is not coming in and that has had a hell of an effect on some
clubs. It has caused closures of clubs, certainly cutbacks within
clubs. And again, it affects the people that you employ in the clubs.
You have to cut back on wages because you haven't got the money
coming through to be able to pay them. That's just part of the
social life. From the other angle you've got closures of shops
throughout the town because there just isn't enough trade going
about. People say that there is more money getting spent in the
sense that the goods are a lot dearer than they used to be. But
people are just going into a hell of a lot of debt to get them,

9

particularly round about Christmastime. And, if the truth was known, some of that debt is not getting paid back. You also have the effect of people living on the breadline and the council not getting the rents in as they should, the rates are not getting paid as they should. There are pressures all round the community and this has all been directly affected by closures and the run-down of companies. But shipbuilding, as I see it now, is under severe threat and the effect it would have on the town in general if either Sunderland Shipbuilders or Austin and Pickersgill closed has to be highlighted.

If you take it to the extreme and say the two shipyards, Sunderland Shipbuilders and ourselves, were to close, or one of the two were to close, then you have to look at the devastating effect it would have on the community in the town. If you ever walk round the town you'll see the massive amount of shops that have closed. Then you've got, like I've said, the clubs that have closed, the general run-down of the town. Naturally one of the biggest effects is people with the ability, money-wise, to be able to pay their way. For example, the council having masses of outstanding rent, masses of outstanding rates – the effect of that is that the council are put under more pressure by central government through rate-capping, having to up the rates, but at the same time as upping the rates they can't even collect rates in off last year. For example, they are putting the rates up this year and yet there are people closing businesses down. A lot of people have lost their houses. The miners' strike was a classic case; where lads who were on strike for a year, lads who were buying their own houses, lost them because the mortgage repayments couldn't be kept up. Now that, it might well be argued, was because of a strike, but we can also cite you examples of people who've tried to buy their houses and had to give it up as a bad job and have had to revert back to trying to get a council house because they couldn't afford to keep the payment up. So there are all these effects throughout the community.

You've only got to gan to Barclay Court, a housing estate next to a shipyard that has closed down, and I doubt very much if there is anybody in Barclay Court who is paying rent. They must all be subsidised by the council. I would say there must be very nearly forty per cent of them boarded up now, because they cannot let them. It's right outside Thompson's shipyard which is a perfect example of a shipyard closing down where a workforce lived right next to the shipyards...

Once I had unpacked, Danny took me round to one of the union offices on the site. I wanted to find out if the shipyard workers were as overpaid as they are reputed to be.

overtime – you sometimes feel a bit unclean

Pickard: Tell me about overtime.
Tony: We used to have overtime limits. The union district branch would send out a circular saying the overtime limit, thirty hours, has got to be strictly adhered to, and anybody who exceeded the thirty hours would be fined. And we did get some exceeding the thirty hours.
Pickard: The reason for that was what? To make the job last longer?
Tony: And try to force the company to start more people. The redundancy payment scheme, that's had an effect ... The first time anybody mentioned to us that there is gannin' to be a pay-off, the immediate reaction was to put a ban on overtime, or suggest work-sharing, to stop the lads getting finished. When the Redundancy Payment Act came in, they started to get money, and there is no way you are going to put a ban on overtime for a lad that's gonna get four or five hundred pounds and gannin' out of the door with two thousand or whatever. So then, it not only had the effect that there was no action when the redundancy money was paid, but also you had the reluctance to put the restrictions on overtime, or any restrictions on piece-work, when you knew that them lads which were on the dole had volunteered to sell their job. So you would say, 'Why should I restrict my earnings when he has selt his job and now he wants to be back in, do you want me to put a ban on overtime for him? No way.' That's the reaction you get now. Like I say, you sometimes feel a bit unclean going to negotiate overtime knowing full well that unemployment is what it is. Here you've got the two pressures on. It's the only way now you can earn money because the rate without overtime is not worth a wank.
Pickard: What is the rate without overtime? Take-home pay?
Tony: About ninety pound, that's without overtime. The pressure

11

is to get money into the packet any way you can, so that's why you negotiate overtime.

Pickard: What do you reckon people take home now with the overtime that you have negotiated?

Tony: What do you walk out with now with two half-shifts and a Sunday?

Jake: One hundred and thirty-two pound.

Danny: On a flat week it is about a hundred and four.

Tony: I'm out of date.

Danny: When you consider you pay twenty-odd pound a week rent. The rates are going up in April and the rent is going up in October, and personally I'll be paying about twenty-seven pound a week for a council house. Then I've got fucking dinner monies to pay when the kids gan to school. Then you've got your grub, bus fares, you've got fucking insurance ... It costs us more than eighty pounds just to keep our house going. And on a flat week you've got no fucking pocket-money at all. Some lads in the labouring sections that's only taking one wage into the house, I don't know how they live.

Pickard: How much do they get?

Dodds: Some take about fifty-two quid home. Single lads sweeping up.

Danny: There's lads claiming family income supplement. There was lads working in here prior to their redundancy – who took redundancy because of it – in the labouring section, actually claiming rent rebates. They couldn't work overtime, because if the overtime wasn't on for a long period of time, for like a couple of weeks, they used to take their rent rebate off them and by the time they got it instituted back in again they had lost out.

Pickard: And a lot of unemployed people are faced with the unpleasant choice of having to fiddle, turn to crime or avoid paying the rent and rates and face the bailiffs.

Dodds: The system encourages it.

Danny: There are lasses who used to work as a secondary wage to support their houses. Now, because their husbands are made unemployed, they cannot work, because the little amount that they are working for is took off the husbands' dole, and they've got to declare it, otherwise if they are caught they go to jail. Even lasses with jobs that are only a few hours a week, they cannot afford to work. At the club where there was four lasses working, some clever bastard shopped them and three of them got done. They were

12

working in a club for a contractor who was giving them a few hours a week and their husbands were claiming for them and they got fucking done. And that's one case in thousands in this town. It goes on all the time.

middle-class feminists

Tony: What annoys me most about middle-class people, even the feminists in the middle class, is that they think that our wives is some way like bloody slaves to us. And they think that we treat our women like fucking shite. And they come down and try to say how women should be liberated and all this fucking crap. It gets up my nose because we run our family unit the best way we can to survive together, and it's not a question of me not giving her fucking money or owt, you've got to and the majority of lads do. They've got to chip in to keep the house going. But, if they can get a little job on the side to supplement the income, then they do. But now it becomes more essential for that woman to work, because if our lass didn't work at the school dinners, I wouldn't have no pocket-money, no social life or nowt. I would be working day in and day out just to bloody well exist. And it is not a question of reversible roles: I could do it easy. People say, 'The man's got to be working, the man's got to be the breadwinner.' It's a load of crap to the majority of the lads. If our lass could come to me and say, 'Look, I've gotten a job for three hundred pound a week, but you would have to look after the bairns and the house,' I would do it immediately without thinking! I'd say, 'Aye, do it.' And also you see when the lads become unemployed and that situation is enforced upon them ... I can see the lads doing it in our street, ex-shipyard lads that have took their redundancy, they do all the housework, they do everything. And their lass is going out to work, so there is no problem. That's just being created by people who don't know us.

> At that point a young lad, who had had a steel wedge smack him in the face, came into the office. Tony introduced him to me.

13

Tony: Fucking hell, you don't come to work to get your face fucking smashed in. We've been pushing for years for compensation without having anybody's fault, just for actually working in the yard, and if you get injured you should get compensation. But not so. He's got to prove that there's some way that the company has been negligent, or the job, or somebody, has done something wrong. There's this morning: they are on about fucking bizzies, policemen, how dangerous their job is, fucking riots and all that, and how hard the fucking job is. There is more construction workers killed in a week than all policemen put to-fucking-gether. And yet they gan on about how dangerous the fucking job is and yet our people is dying every fucking day. The ships we build are fucking covered in friggin' blood, and blood on the coal, blood on every industry all the fucking time. Lads dying of working, of asbestosis and fucking bronchitis, and they get on about them cunts. Aye, fucking hell ... they are well compensated, they get well looked after, but we've got to gan through the full legal rigmarole. And all their parasites is on there, solicitors, QCs – if you gan to court – all getting a good living off our fucking backs, off our pain and suffering. They are the real fucking flies on the fucking shite.

Danny: You should see the fucking number of funerals we gan to, lads that is clapping out at young ages, not old fellahs. Young people, leaving families... We've had a campaign going for years for what's known as 'welder's lung', but we've never been able to get it classified as an industrial disease, because the medical profession, in the main, say that it is not caused through the job, only by contributory factors such as smoking. If the welding didn't have an effect why are we losing so many people at an early age before retirement? In the 1960s here, there was a spate of deaths of lads in their thirties and forties in the welding department... The welders were out on strike to get the paint removed from the ship, they put it down to that.

Tony: We started the main campaign about 1977 to try and get compensation. The lawyers have got the case now. We've had all sorts of surveys carried out by doctors, covering aspects of the welders' environment, and then medical examinations. Now the QCs take it to court, arguing that anybody with a bad chest, part

14

of the damage is due to his employment. We've got that, but you see what the opposition always bring in: 'Do they smoke?' Once you smoke you are knackered, because every time you say, 'His chest is bad through his work,' they say, 'Did he smoke? His health is damaged just through smoking.' And then, if you are a non-smoker, they say, 'Look at the area you live in, the incidence of cancer and bronchitis is far higher in the North-East than anywhere else. Because of the climate that you live in and the heavy industry you could possibly have not been a welder and not worked in a shipyard and suffer bronchitis, and suffer lung cancer.' And these are all the arguments they put to us. They tell you, 'It's your environment!' What they try to do now is say, 'All right, so much is to his environment, so much is to smoking, but there is some percentage there that is due to welding.'

Pickard: So what you are arguing for now is a percentage?

Tony: Aye, well, that's all they'll be able to argue for. But even the miners, and they recognise the 'black lung', they have a right old carry-on to claim it. And even when they do, when they die, they cut their lungs out and put them in jars and send them to fucking London to see if the fucking dependents can get any fucking money. Fucking great, eh?

Dodds: There's a miner lives next to me and it has taken them thirteen years to admit that he's got silicosis, and he can only walk about six yards and he's got to sit down.

Tony: They diagnosed Ned's asbestosis and they operated on him cutting out the part of the lung that was clogged up by asbestos and then said he was all right and he didn't have asbestos and so he couldn't have a claim. They cut it out. You get into situations like we've been in when a lad gets telt that he's got terminal cancer, and he knows, he's been telt. He's got to make decisions: Is redundancy on? Should he take his redundancy? How much would he get? How long would it last? Or should he wait until he just dies and he gets more money back from the insurance scheme for his family? At the same time he wants to gan and see his son in Australia, who he's never seen for twenty year, before he dies. We get into situations like that, talking to lads who start to look clinically at their last few months in life to decide what they are going to do. They are not very nice situations I can fucking tell you. But the system is like that, that's the way it is. That's the status quo. As society is today, we are at the bottom of the pile.

21/1/86

The next day I was introduced to Mack, from the Tyne.
Even though he had been working in Sunderland for
years, his Tyneside ancestry was something he found
difficult to live down. He was describing his membership
of a club, which caused immediate laughter:

freemasons

Mack: I was a club member for years.
Tony: Where's that?
Jake: Next door to the freemasons. Of course, that is very prominent
on the Tyne, the freemasons.
Mack: We haven't got them prominent through on the Wear, have
we?
Jake: Not as much as yours.
Mack: Get away and fuck off.
Jake: You are fucking noted for it, you cunts, King's men,[1] free-
masons.
Pickard: Have you got freemasons in the shipyard?
Jake: They've got shop stewards as masons, these cunts.
Tony: Three shop stewards that I know of.
Jake: I dropped out, I couldn't keep the payment up.
Tony: I went in there but they wouldn't serve me anyhow, soon as
they heard my twang they totally ignored us.
Jake: He's first, I'm behind him, and I says, 'What's he ganna do?'
He gets to the counter, wallet out, I says, 'He must of fucking won
something here, paying first.' Money out, next thing I know: 'Here,
fuck this, they're not ganna serve us, howay.' So he's last in. He
was braying on the bar with a sponge, trying to attract attention.
Tony: I got them in eventually.
Danny: You cunts.

1. Wearsiders' term for the allegedly traditionally loyalist Tynesiders.

16

Mack: We've got no maggots here, have we?

Jake: Not really.

Tony: Aye, but you've got more.

Mack: Get away and fuck off, man! No maggots!

Danny: Every demonstration we went on and every fucking rally we went to, he used to grab a hold of the same bloke, then we found out he was a freemason.

Mack: I didn't know that, he telt us that.

Pickard: How did you know he was a freemason?

Jake: Kissed him.

Tony: We got to know, we got telt off the lads on the Tyne that there was a certain movement within shop stewards' committees on the Tyne that were freemasons.

Brian: You can tell the way they walk as well.

Dodds: Like you.

Jake: Are you gannin' through to Durham tonight?

Tony: Aye, if the weather is all right, but it's forecast snow.

Jake: I said fucking *Durham*, man, not fucking Norway. (*To Pickard*) Can you let me know what days you are coming back so the company can get the insurance cover for you?

Pickard: Does that mean I can claim compensation if somebody drops a hammer on my head?

Danny: There's not much chance of that the times you're here.

Mack: There's every chance of it happening over the complex.

Danny: You missed your breakfast this morning so you'd be in time for the meeting, didn't you?

Pickard: I had a coffee.

Danny: We'd better put the meeting back. You should have seen our gaffer, he might have got you a pot of tea and a scone. He's good like that.

Jake: I hope you're not ganna start abusing the lad.

Danny: He has to be educated to the ways of the yard, it's no good being soft with him, otherwise he'll never learn, will he? He's got to get used to it.

Jake: Who's gonna learn him, you?

Danny: Well, I've got to try and do me best with him. He's got to be toughened up.

Pickard; It'll have to be a crash course cause I'm only here six months.

Danny: It won't take me that long.

how to resist compulsory redundancies

Danny: What happened was, round about early October, middle of October last year, the company came and said that they wanted compulsory redundancies. It meant, of course, that people would be shoved out the yard against their will, which we firmly stood against. I mean, there is, albeit a flimsy bill, a Blackpool agreement on no compulsory redundancy. What we did, in a matter of a week, we had a meeting and we set aside sections of that committee on to subcommittees to organise and campaign against the compulsory redundancies. For example, we set up a DHSS committee, and them lads on that committee would work in conjunction with people from the Citizens' Advice Bureau who would then give us advice on how our people could claim in a strike situation. We also set up a finance committee: now, that committee had letters printed to send out to all the various organisations calling on them for assistance in the strike situation. The chairman and the secretary were the press liaison officers and they would link up with each subcommittee who would be reporting in and we would arrange for a weekly mass meeting outside the gate. We had a picket committee...

Mack: And an occupation committee ... we were going to occupy the yard. In a responsible manner, not like you've seen in some situations, we were doing it to actually preserve the yard, to keep people out who would come in and do damage, if you like. We saw an occupation as a way of preserving the yard. And we got a hell of a lot of volunteers, so the interest was there. I mean we canvassed everybody in the yard and the response was great. Without that, we couldn't have done it.

Danny: You see we went through a couple of situations, we went through the one that Mack is talking about a couple of years ago, where we had no orders. Just prior to getting the Oldendorf orders we were actually out of work ... we had people on lay-off. It appeared that we weren't going to get any orders and the yard was going to be closed and that is when we set up those commitees. And at that time we were talking about occupation because we felt that by occupying the yard we could highlight ourselves in the situation we were in nationally as well as locally. And, as Mack says, we got a hell of a response, we got over three hundred people to volunteer to occupy the yard on a rota basis. We were saying, maybe do four hours at a time. We actually had lads saying they were prepared to do night-shift, occupying the yard during the night, so nobody was going to get in or out, on the basis of acting responsibly, maintaining the yard, making sure there was nowt getting damaged, and all organised to that extent. The second time, last year, because of some of the situations in Swan Hunter's, for example, with their occupation and how the pressure had been applied to them, we felt the occupation might of been under attack more quickly by the state.

Mack: There was no way we were going to break the law, as soon as they used the powers of the law on us that would have been it. We would have immediately come out of occupation. But by then we'd have hoped to have made our point, and gotten the national coverage that we sought.

Danny: So, what we decided on, basically, was more leaning towards pickets than occupation. And again we got a response of about three hundred that was prepared to picket. In all honesty I think there would have been a bigger response if it had of come off. There are a lot of lads who don't volunteer until it actually happens, but when you are into the thing you find that people come forward.

Mack: We were getting this response because we are a very open shop stewards' committee. There is nothing goes on in there that the workforce on the floor doesn't know about. Because we see that as our job. We are told by the chairman that it's our job. He keeps nothing from us and as soon as he's said it he'll say, 'That's your job, get out on the floor and make the lads aware.' That's how we get the response, because they are all up to date and well aware of what's going on. There is no danger about that.

that inter-trade union feeling

Danny: You've got to realise that in a shipyard we have changed a hell of a lot over the years. You'll find it out when you talk to the lads I introduced you to yesterday, who will tell you of the days of demarcation where the welding department was a department on its own and it had nowt to do with the platers and had nowt to do with the shipwrights. Over the years we have changed and we've kept together as a boilermakers' committee and then eventually we came together as a confed [confederation of trades unions]

19

committee, as you see today. You've still got that inter-trade union feeling. I mean, I am a boilermaker, my feelings are towards my people, which is only natural, but we were faced last year with the position where the outfitters were coming under severe attack. Now, by them coming under attack it put us under attack because we are part of that confed agreement and a deal on parity and everything that gans with it. So we had a hell of a job, because the outfitters had their meetings and they were mandated to take strike action, or industrial action of whatever nature, to stop the compulsory redundancies. But they would have been lost unless they got the support of the unions like ourselves and the General and Municipal Workers'. So the GMW and ourselves had the job of having to get out and convince our people that, by taking the action that we were asking them to do, it wasn't only protecting the outfitters at the time, it was also protecting us when the attack came to us.

Pickard: Was that easy?

Danny: It was very difficult. I think it was the hardest job I've had to do as a shop steward over all the years I've been involved, convincing people. Naturally, eight weeks before Christmas they're not very happy about going on strike. Not very happy going on strike for themselves, let alone for sombody else, as they see it, albeit that wasn't really the issue. But we had to convince our people of the attack that we were under. We went round for about a week, prior to the mass meeting, every shop steward in both the general workers' section and ourselves, talking to our own members and telling them what attacks we would come under. Eventually, by the time it got to the meeting we had convinced them to the extent that they voted three to one in favour of taking industrial action in support of the outfitters. So that is the kind of organisation we've got in the yard and that is the kind of open democracy that stems from the chairman of the shop stewards all the way down through the committee to the floor.

Mack: That's a hell of a unique situation. I doubt very much whether they could achieve that anywhere in British Shipbuilders.

Danny: They couldn't have done it in any other yard. What we are actually saying is that we are taking members from other unions, of other trades, outfitters, into our sections.

Pickard: Has that ever happened before?

Danny: No, never. It is the first time ever. First time in British Shipbuilders.

Mack: It's a one-off. That's not to say we wouldn't look at it again. We say that, as a committee. Our own union said that it's not possible on a permanent basis, you couldn't do it. Think of the situation: we've got boilermakers outside this yard that cannot get a job and we've got outfitters doing boilermakers' work.

Pickard: What's going to happen to the status quo after March?

Danny: By the middle of March we've got a launch. Now, the outfit sections, which is your joiners, painters, plumbers, electricians – all them outfit sections – their work will start to come on stream because naturally once the ship is launched *our* work diminishes on that ship and *their* work comes away. For example, joiners doing the cabin on the ship, plumbers putting in the pipework, the fitters putting in the engine and so on. Now, what will happen, as we see it, is, as their work comes on stream, the lads that are working from their section in ours will be moved back into their own sections. The problem then reverses itself because we are the first trades involved in the building of a ship, the steel trades, so as we start to run out of work theirs comes on stream. At the moment, you start the ship and the outfitters are waiting to work, so they have come in with us to have them gainfully employed and not paid off or laid off. But then, as the ship is launched, it reverses itself, we start to run out of work and they've got work. So the ideology of it would be that we, or some of our people, gan and work with them. But it's not as simple as that, because naturally if they take thirty-seven lads, that's working with us now, back into their sections, to build their sections up again, is there enough work for them to take the massive amount of steelworkers who will be running out of work in March or April of this year? Lads that work in the stockyard and the plate preparation areas are running out of work now because there is no more work to be done. They will come out of those areas to work with us but, as they come out to work with us in the progressing of the ship, then we'll gobble the work up a little bit more quickly and as it rolls on the position worsens. That's the kind of thing we are faced with.

Mack: If we had this continuity of work and following-on orders, that boat should be progressing, and as that boat gets launched a few steelworkers do go afloat with it, the rest come off and start on another one. And then the outfitters get on with their jobs. But that doesn't happen: everything is piling into the first boat, *1431*, it's got to go off. Everything is piling on there, and that's neglected, *1432*,

21

there's nothing been done there. So when *1431* goes off, where the hell are they going to go? There's nowhere for them to go.

Danny: So you are then going to be faced with a position where you are pushing like hell in one area to get the work through and another area standing waiting of it coming. We are not particularly bothered about the lay-off because lay-off at the moment is voluntary. The gaffer can come to me and say, 'I haven't got any work for you. Do you fancy having a week or a couple of weeks lay-off? Seventy-five per cent of your pay.' That's my choice, at the moment. But as the work runs out, and the position becomes worse, and the lay-off becomes even more critical, he cannot get the volunteers in the numbers that he wants, then what does he do? Does he try to make the lay-off compulsory? Now, once he tries that, the lay-off compulsion is the same as the pay-off compulsion, the compulsory redundancy or the compulsory lay-off which we'll not accept.

Mack: We have a mandate from the shop floor: 'No compulsory lay-offs and no compulsory redundancy.'

Pickard: Lay-off means you get seventy-five per cent of your basic pay?

Danny: I come back to what I was telling you earlier: we are in a situation at the moment where if we are not working overtime, we are working normal flat week thirty-nine hours, we can barely exist. Then they take twenty-five per cent of your wage away. All right you are laid off, you are not working, but you've still got to pay your way.

Mack: It's not so long ago, and Danny will tell you because he went through the exercise, on a flat week, about sixty per cent of this yard could claim Family Income Supplement, and that's tradesmen as well.

Danny: I did a little exercise, I decided I would apply for a rent rebate. At the time, I had a boy just left school, not working, and I had two daughters still at school. So I went down and seen the bloke at the rent office and telt him. I said, 'That's my wage, the wife is not working, the boy has just left school, blah blah blah.' He said, 'Here is a form, take it away and fill it in and send it back and we'll see how it gans.' I got fifty-nine pence a week. I did it for a reason to be able to hoy [throw] at these people. My argument was: if *I* am a skilled man getting top wages in the yard, and Picky's has got the top wages in the industry, what the bloody hell is everybody else getting?

Mack: It's horrendous when you think about it.

Danny: Since then, the boy has got a job. It's not a very good job, but it fetches a few quid a week. I didn't do it for myself, but it proved a point. If I can claim – and I am an average bloke with an average family living in an average council house – and I can earn an above-average wage in the industry, I can finish up claiming a supplement. Since then, the wages haven't advanced that much and I would say at that time we were getting £130, and now we are getting £158, so our wages in the last four or five years has gone up about twenty-eight to thirty pounds, and the purchasing power . . . My rent then was twenty-two quid and now it is twenty-seven quid, so there's five pound rent that's gone up in them four or five years. Out of the twenty-odd pounds, I've got tax and stamps and everything else, so the twenty-eight pounds becomes about twenty. I'm already paying a fiver more rent, I'm paying God knows how much more on groceries, I've got higher electrical charges, higher gas, dearer school meals, increase on bus fares. I could go on for ever. And again, in your social life: what was the price of a pint of beer then as to now, the price of a packet of fags as opposed to now, prescription charges? Last Friday night my wife took bad and I went in and she had two items on the prescription and it cost me four pounds out of my pocket-money to buy her two lots of tablets. So them's the kind of pressures we come under all the time. And if the shipyards go, we've only got one pit left in Sunderland, Monkwearmouth colliery. And that's all we've got. We've got three major concerns in the town: two shipyards and one pit.

Pickard: Are they the largest employers?

Danny: Without any question. We have one local engineering factory, Coles; we have this new company Sunderland Forge Services, we have local factories on the trading estate now laying people off. Everywhere you look, right through the town – and Sunderland is not very different to other towns in this area – all we've seen is either closure, or cutbacks in the industries. The male population of the east end of the town is something like fifty per cent unemployed. In Southwick it's a similar picture, and I would think now the male population in the whole town must be over twenty-five per cent unemployed. If that is the situation now, what would be the situation in six months' time or twelve months' time with the closure of these two yards? Or the closure of one? And that is the kind of situation that we are in.

23

Nissan

Mack: The mass media covers people starting up jobs, take Fine Fare in the town, they've opened a new shop and created two hundred and fifty jobs. They neglect to mention that they are part-time and probably women that will take them. You get what? The creation of five hundred jobs at Nissan, God knows what that is costing per job. If that money had of been put into shipbuildng, the existing industries here, it would have been a damn sight better.

Danny: I'd hate to think what that cost. The big con was that they publicised Nissan coming here as the birth of new industry in the area. They neglected to mention that the old industries have been decimated. Well, so be it, if the argument is that the old industries have got to go and the new industries have got to come, how the hell can we justify bringing the likes of Nissan which brings pressure to people down there in the Midlands working in the car industry, and up here create two hundred and fifty jobs at a phenomenal cost to the area?

Mack: The catchment area that it covers! People applying from Newcastle, Gateshead, Jarrow, Hebburn, Sunderland, Teeside, all over the place. Consett and out that way where steelworks have closed down and pits have closed down.

Danny: You pick the local rag up and it says, 'Marvellous achievement, congratulations to the Sunderland Borough Council ... to this one and that one.' We've actually created something like five hundred jobs in Washington from Nissan. And then you see stuck in a corner where Birtley factories close down with a loss of a thousand jobs. The Royal Ordinance Factory in Birtley is closed down with a two-and-a-half-thousand job loss. The shipyards have had further cutbacks where eight hundred jobs is gone here, or a thousand jobs. And this is going on all the time, but all this is in little corner pieces! Five hundred jobs created at God knows what cost!

Pickard: Is Sunderland Borough Council Tory or Labour or what?

Mack: Right-wing labour.

Militants and stewards

Danny: I have to tell you Mack and myself are members of the Labour Party. Our view of the Labour council in this town is not very good at all. Maybe it will get better.

Pickard: I saw a lot of press cuttings about Militants being expelled ...

Mack: They are jumping on the bandwagon up here. Silencing their critics.

Danny: One of the problems at the moment is the leadership of the party, nationally, with Kinnock's speech in the conference last year giving the impetus for the right wing in all areas up and down the country to attack. And none more so than in this town. You see I have always thought of the right wing of the party as people always looking for money and power, the left wing of the party as the socialist conscience of the party, looking for fairness and decency and a better deal for all. So these people have just come out from under the stones that they have been under for years and they have come and attacked us.

Mack: If you had said to me a couple of years ago that the right wing would be defending what Kinnock said, I would have laughed in your face because they hated him! Hated him!

Danny: I remember it clearly, at the meeting that we had at Sunderland that we mandated delegates to gan to conference and who to vote for. And the right wing voted in block against Kinnock, and it was the left wing that voted for Kinnock, not me, mind. And we were scorned in Sunderland by the so-called left wing for not going for Kinnock. And you look today, the very people who scorned him then, he's now their idol, and the very people that scorned us are now running all over the place getting accused of being Militants and getting expelled out of the party. That's the thing that has happened in the last couple of years.

Pickard: Fucking hell, I have fallen into a hotbed of Militants.

Mack: Without a doubt. He might be a fucking fifth columnist. Well, I wouldn't say they are very politically motivated in the yard, they realise that the only hope of survival is to elect a Labour government. Maybe I'm being unkind to most of them, but they know Maggie Thatcher is no good for shipbuilding, put it that way, and the Labour government is.

Danny: In this area in general, if you could gan round, and see kids throwing stuff at the lass on at the pantomime at the Empire because she was imitating Maggie Thatcher, that's the kind of hatred up here that you'll find for Thatcher. But that, as Mack says, is as far as it goes. They say, 'Well, why does the Labour Party fight amongst themselves? They are not doing themselves any good.' They don't understand the underlying feeling and the problems within the party. But I'll tell you straight, if I'd said to the lads yesterday that you were a Tory, and they thought I meant it, you wouldn't get a lot of co-operation.

Mack: We've had Bob Clay the MP at gate meetings. He's a fucking grafter that fellah, I'm not kidding, he's a workaholic. Considering that the MP before him never owned a house up here, he never lived in the area, he got the night sleeper back when he had to come up for constituency meetings. Clay lives in the area, his kids are educated in the area, and he'd come down here and do anything for this yard, he'd do anything for anybody. We've had him down for gate meetings and we cannot generate enough enthusiasm to get them there in numbers. They'll pass as they are coming in the gate and they'll have a bit of a crack and have a word with him but, if you organise a meeting here, they wouldn't stop and listen to him.

Danny: We've had him down on two or three occasions to talk about really serious situations; shipbuilding in general and the decline of shipbuilding, the support of the intervention fund money [an EEC subsidy] and so on. He's come down to explain all this and yet we haven't been able to turn very many people out because that's during the dinner hour, and I accept that some lads go home for dinner. But there are a hell of a lot of lads just sitting around the yard reading papers or listening to the wireless or playing cards or whatever they do during the dinner hour, and yet it is very difficult to get them to come up. Now, if Tony was calling a meeting during the dinner hour the whole fucking place would be packed. 'Oh aye,' they'd say, 'it's a meeting for us.' But they cannot relate that.

Mack: The way they look on it is, 'Oh well, the stewards are gannin' and they'll report back to us.' In that way we have probably spoilt them. Not so much me, but the long-term stewards. I mean, it carries on, and I've become part of it in the last four years. You get embroiled in that situation and you become embroiled in it anyway, and then you'll find the lads will say: 'The stewards will be there and they'll tell us.' Honest to God, it sounds daft, but we pamper them, we do everything for them. Fill forms in for them and everything. You saw that yesterday with the lad who had his face smashed in by the wedge. We do that for everybody.

Danny: I don't think there is a lad in this yard who would have an accident and go away and fill in the form himself.

Mack: He'll have an attempt maybe, but he'll bring it to us and we'll say, 'You cannot say this and you cannot say that.' We always tell them to put it down on a bit of scrap paper, then we'll sort it out and put it in.

Danny: I'll tell you what the stewards have become: they have become experts in all kinds of affairs, because they've had to do it. You know, for example, we've described industrial diseases now like white finger.[1] Now, lads come along and say, 'What's the latest on white finger?' And you have got to find out what's happening about white finger, or what's happening about asbestosis, or what's happening about claims in DHSS for the injuries, or what's happening on all kinds of things. We've got a crazy situation at the moment where a lad had an accident, and he puts an accident report form in to the union, the union passes it on to the solicitor, and on that form it's got to have the shop steward's name and address. And we get inundated every week with letters from the solicitor, saying, 'How did this accident happen, were you involved, etc ...' And we are filling these forms in all the time.

Mack: Not a week gans by without us being down at the solicitors. Actually gan there and talk to them apart from the forms we've filled in.

Danny: We've finished up doing seventy-five per cent of the work the solicitor is supposed to be doing, because we fill the forms out, we've got to fill forms out when we get them from them, we've got to gan down and see them, explain what happened ... and this gans on all the time.

Later I met a few of the general workers' shop stewards.

1. White finger: the blanching and numbing of the fingers caused by over-use of percussive tools.

Tommy: It's just that we have taken a hell of a blow with regards membership, we are down from nearly nine hundred and fifty to just about two hundred. The last round of redundancies we took a sixty per cent cut. We think, and we seem to get the impression time and time again, that although shipbuilding is probably dying as such, ancillary workers have borne the biggest brunt. We have took the biggest cutback in manpower all the way along the line. And the more and more the management gan to Japan and come back with these ideas – finding that there is no ancillary workers at all in Japanese shipyards. None at all. There is nowt in the scheme of things for the ancillary worker.

Pickard: What exactly do the ancillary workers do?

Tommy: There are the jobs where we are completely independent of the tradesmen, such as my department where we've got drivers who drive fork-lifts and side-rolls and Kamags [low wide-based trucks], and you've got the crane drivers who drive the cranes. We've got what you call the sailor gang ... they are the lads who went out on sea trials and do a lot of the ropes and launches and things like that. They are the independent people, they've been cut back a lot. The other people who work with the trades ... You've got platers' helpers, burners' labourers, some welders' labourers who sort of set the job up and do the – for want of a better word – menial tasks allied to the trades. But they have been cut back rather dramatically, as if to say, 'There's no place for you.'

> Tommy told me if I wanted to see some art I should look at the graffiti in the men's bait-huts.

the comedy of cock-ups

Tommy: The graffiti written all over the shed ... it's a real macho industry, and if anybody puts a foot wrong or does anything wrong they really torture him.

Bob: They make poems up about him...

Tommy: If anybody steps out of line and gets caught doing something silly, or something effeminate, they really get stuck into him. And it gans for months. One of our lads, he fell in the acid bath,

29

he was only about two inches in – he got a new pair of boots and trousers out of it – but of course the joking went on for weeks. He took some stick for it. That is a common occurrence in the shipyard, if anybody puts a foot wrong, they are into him.

Tommy: I've always thought there was a comedy to be made out of the cock-ups. Not that you would be allowed to do it, but some of the management cock-ups that we've seen ... it's unbelievable. These fellahs that's in control now, I don't think I am speaking out of turn, but the shop stewards have no confidence in them at all. I don't think the workforce has either. The whiz-kids who were fetched from Benton House,[1] they've been turfed in here too ... they haven't got a lot of shipyard experience, and BS policy now is: you don't get a manager's job unless you've got a degree. By God, they are pretty heavy on theory, but practical work they don't know a lot about it. We've been inundated with officebound people and they have been put into here, and they didn't know a lot about what they were doing. That's the way we feel: we haven't got lot of confidence in them.

Pickard: When Thatcher came in, did she change management? And did the Labour Party make appointments when it was nationalised?

Tommy: No, but we were in the process of getting rid of the managing director who was a radical old Tory. In fact, I think he stood as a Tory candidate, and he addressed the workforce, prior to nationalisation, with the sole intention of getting the whole workforce to be vehemently against nationalisation. The lads will probably be able to explain a bit better, but there were definitely moves afoot to get him the sack in 1979. Unfortunately we were defeated. But, following your argument through, although the Tories never sort of took control, it appears over the last few years that they have, and Graham Day [chairman, British Shipbuilders, 1983–86] is a bigger butcher than MacGregor. It might seem a daft thing to say, but possibly we might of had a better future under MacGregor, because Graham Day has slashed the industry to nowt. Nowt. And there has been a series of appointments by the government, and aye, at the back of it, they are probably all political appointments. And they all are Tories, and they will all carry Thatcher's policy out to the bitter end.

Pickard: I saw him on TV and he seemed an arrogant bastard.

1. Benton House: the Newcastle-based headquarters of British Shipbuilders. The national headquarters are in Knightsbridge, London SW1.

Bob: He was brought in to do a hatchet-job and that's it.

Tommy: I would like to think, and it may be wishful thinking, at the end of the day, and hoping that we get in next time, that these bastards get chased. Oh aye, that's what I'm after. That's my view of life here. They have put the thumbscrews on us and I want my party to get these bastards out, and I want people that is in the nationalised industries to make sure that they believe in national-isation. I don't want the sort of hypocritic effort of the last fellah who fought like hell against nationalisation, and at the end of the day kept his job and ran about with his Jag for three year before he got the push. How anybody that's got any character at all can fight as vehemently as he did against nationalisation, and when it comes in still has a job! That was wrong. As I say, my viewpoint is, when we get in, we chase these fellahs.

23/1/86

A bitterly cold morning and Mack took me across to the complex where a 22,000-ton multi-purpose cargo ship was being constructed. It was a very long ship. One side of the shed was completely exposed to the River Wear where it turns towards the sea. The shed is built on to the bend in the river to give the ship the widest berth when launched. The wind travels down from the snow-covered Weardale hills in a straight line and gathers speed all the way until it smacks into the ship on 'Picky's' stocks. Mack introduced me to a couple of welders who were sitting directly beneath the keel with their necks cricked back. The biting wind from the river was ripping into them as they sat rigid, bodies contorted to weld the seams above their heads. They sat like that all day, slowly burning sections of the ship's underbelly together.

Under the welder's masks, their faces were blue and weatherworn, with broken blood-vessels across their chapped cheeks. They were wearing protective clothing, a kind of thick chamois-leather like a medieval soldier's hood, and a leather apron and leather leggings over their boots. I thought it was meant to keep them warm, but it is supposed to stop their flesh or clothes burning when the fountains of molten metal shower on to them.

welders – it's purgatorial

Jim: I'll tell you, this last couple of weeks down here! We've just been saying we were trying to tell our wives and explain what it's like, they just don't understand. And Davy said to me, he said to his wife, 'Gan and sit in the back garden in a chair all day and then tell us what you feel like. Just sit there.' Isn't that right, Dave? They don't understand, you try to explain.

Jim: We cannot wait to get into a good bath and lie there.

Dave: It gets to a stage where, once you get in, you don't want to go out of a night. You know you are that cold from the day, you get in and get warm, get your tea, and you just settle on the chair and you cannot be bothered. You just don't want to go out.

Jim: That's the way you are sitting all day. Your arm is up and aching, and when the cold gets in you, dear me! What's it like, Mack? It's purgatorial, it is!

Pickard: I can imagine it with these winds.

Dave: If you'd been down here Thursday, oh dear! The screen was getting ripped off your head.

Pickard: Do you hold the screen by hand?

Brian: You can get hand-held screens but these ones fit on your head.

Pickard: Does that put a strain on your neck if there is a wind blowing?

Jim: It doesn't half, man, when it catches you.

Dave: You put more pressure on yourself by jamming the screen against the ship to stop it blowing off, so that is putting more pressure on your neck anyhow. And that is going to make it ache as well.

Pickard: Have you got no back support?

Dave: That's been made up myself: an old chair that's been hoyed out. We've just welded a bit bar to the bottom to try and make it a little bit easier for yourself. . .

Mack: . . . You dare not take your eyes off the arc, whereas if you are sitting in the shed and doing a bit downhand and you can talk to somebody . . . In this job you have to sit there in one position and just look at that all the time. At the end of the day your eyes are sore with eye strain.

Pickard: So what are they doing? Just joining the two bits of the ship together? Incredible sight.

Mack: As they progress the units the shipwrights fair them up, then they follow on. They weld on the inside first, then the arc air fellahs come on, back gouges, and these fellahs follow. That's the finished job. This unit should be turned over and then when it's done there it can be turned over and done in the downhand position. That would be a damned sight easier as far as we are concerned, but, 'Production needs,' as they say, production comes first so they get it out like, get it berthed and we'll do it when it's over there. This

33

is the result: the lads have got to stand and sit out here to do it. Bloody freezing cold, awkward work, terrible. It's years since we've had it the way we want it, we aren't lucky enough to turn and do it, so it's a terrible job when it gets out here. But you'll always have the join-ups, there is no way you can avoid it altogether. But *this* can be avoided, that could have been done; the join-ups always have to be done, you can't avoid them.

Pickard: Is that called a join-up as well?

Mack: Not really, that could have been done in the shed, that's work that should have been done over the shed, but it didn't get done because they wanted the unit out. The line manager over there says, 'I want this out of my area on to the next stage.' He's obviously got so many hours to do the job and he wants to clear his area before his hours expire.

Pickard: Are the managers on piece-work?

Mack: No, not really, but they are under pressure I would say to get the units out, they've got schedules to meet and launch days to meet, so it is all push, push, push. Usually it's the workforce that suffers through it, like. If they cannot get it finished it's not their fault and their gaffers say: 'Come on, get that gear off and get it out the shed,' and the lads know it's not finished. We have these problems all the time, we've got to gan back to them and say, 'You shouldn't be pushing this on, give the lads a chance to get it finished, its making it harder when it comes over here.' But some you win and some you lose.

A burner was working high above us on the shell and we stepped aside from the shower of molten metal which rained down. There was a cloud of fumes.

Pickard: We are downwind of it, aren't we?

Mack: It seems to be drifting over that way. It's very still this morning and it will just drift whatever way the slight breeze is.

Pickard: That means if there is no wind it will hang about?

Mack: It does...

Mack then took me on to the half-completed ship, through No. 1 hold where the scaffolding, erected to reach the seam beneath the decks, was very unstable and lurched at a disturbing angle. It should have been secured

34

to the bulkhead but wasn't. He pointed out the hole in the deck which the welders have to climb through to get beneath the engine bed and down into the lube-oil sump for the final welds. Everywhere that steel touches steel has to be welded. The ship has two skins (double bottoms) and the welders have to crawl between them along narrow seams, wearing bulky protective clothing and dragging their masks and tools. They also pull an extractor pipe after them. Their journey is through steel hatches and over steel ribs which stick up every few feet and scrape the spine. Once inside, they work in cramped conditions, usually alone, lying on their sides in a steel box sometimes no higher than eighteen inches high, breathing fumes all the while.

Almost every welder I spoke to dreaded working in the 'lube-oil' and they all, without exception, recalled at least one occasion when they had 'thrown a wobbler' in the double bottoms. One man told me that his mate had gone permanently mad after being kept on the same job all the time, moving from ship to ship, double bottom to double bottom. Another man described a claustrophobic attack when he became so swollen in panic that he couldn't get through the narrow hatch. If the light fails it is pitch-black, and the boom and screech from the burner and caulkers becomes terrifying. Shuddering echoes run through the cold steel which surrounds you and makes the very darkness itself shake.

Mack: When they first started that, the fire brigade was brought in to see if they could every get anybody out of the damn thing, in case owt happened. Imagine a bloke collapsing in there.

After lunch I met old Geordie Hill. He had been the yard convener (confed chairman) for many years. We talked about the problems for the joiners and the outfitters.

Hill: The thing is, the outfitters have always been a cost-intensive affair because there is not always outfitting work to do and they've got to find alternative work for them. They have always been a target for management. Douglas [first managing director after nationalisation] started it with the joiners. In the early seventies he was going to close the joiners' shop and buy the furniture in, but of course it wasn't up to the standards required. I hear these modules that they've put into SS [Sunderland Shipbuilders] ships, which have been manufactured elsewhere, when fitted are a little bit noisy. They are rattling! They must be a complete unit and they are not the normal quality work you get from an outfit department. They've now become the target for economy. They see them as being a means of making economies such as through subcontracting. We've seen subcontracting. In past years they reverted back to doing the work themseles, even at A&P. The plumbing used to be subcontracted and the company took it back over themselves, even the engine installation was took over by A&P as a better economic measure than a normal engineering company installing ships' engines. It's just these things have evolved each decade and each management thinks it's got a better idea than the last and I'm afraid all they are doing is trying what's been tried in the past. And a lot of it has failed. I think they just intend to build the hull here, that's all they intend to do, the rest is ganna be subcontracted. It is very, very obvious that they are trying again and again and again, constantly coming back at the shop stewards. They have meetings upon meetings with the men and get mandates on the information given, then the men is backing them, but they constantly come back at any weakness that they can find in any agreement. They're at it all the time. It's obvious that they only want a steel facility here. What the long-term plans are nobody knows. I don't think that they've even ever hinted that they wanted to privatise the place other than when they've been questioned and admitted that they've thought about it. Only they've never pronounced any overall plan about the yards.

Pickard: How much autonomy do they have, how much is centralised?

Hill: I think we've seen now that the people in charge have all the autonomy they need. They seem to have endless money to waste. We've never had any money for a long time and yet they're still going out buying new machinery that's as obsolete as the machinery that they're supposed to be dispensing with, so they must have a licence from government to continue to spend. Personally I think all they're doing is trying to get to a point where they produce a massive deficit in the company just to prove that nationalisation doesn't work, and they don't care how much money they spend to get there. They have a number of staff, what do we call them? Technicians, planners, quality control, the way they have expanded that is totally out of control. They will prove at any costs that shipbuilding doesn't work as a nationalised industry. I think Swan's is very significant of that,[1] and even Tyne Ship Repairers. You know recently when Tyne Ship Repairers was took over by a private consortium of management they suddenly had millions of pounds worth of work when they had none before.

Mack: Never been idle since.

Hill: We hear already about Swan's that the management have declared, according to the local press, they are not really interested in merchant shipbuilding, they've always built a high percentage of defence work, M.o.D. work, and that's what they are looking towards. As much as six hundred million pounds for M.o.D. work.

Mack: Another example of the Tyne: you know the Redheads' one, the workforce buy-out? The lads put their own money into the yard, well that was wound up. Now that's been taken over by another group and now all of a sudden they've got a load of work. So they are not even content to let the workforce have a go at it themselves with their own money, they want their own people in to make it pay.

Hill: Classic example of mismanagement on the Tyne at this moment, in my opinion, is Swan Hunter's strike. This management that has took over the yard, had them out on strike for seven weeks about the fact that they were not prepared to continue to keep the Hebburn Dock on a mothball basis. The management wanted to close it. Now, since the strike the management have booked two ferry contracts worth a million pound each, and they've put them in Hebburn Dock. I think that it personifies that the men had more idea of what was gannin' on than the management.

Mack: We've had too many examples of places being shut down

1. Swan Hunter's: Tyneside yard specialising in naval ships.

on a care-and-maintenance basis, I mean there is a yard – classic case – down the river on a care-and-maintenance and they just took the roof off so they don't have to pay rates, and once that's done the place is finished. It is never gan to open again. Classic case: naval yard, on the Tyne, care and maintenance, stripped now, there's bugger all there now. We've got no confidence at all when they talk about 'care and maintenance', it is another word for closure, finish. Never going to build anything there again. It's been proved time after time after time.

Pickard: Do you think this government has any idea, other than this fanatic ideology of market forces and free market and all that? It must be obvious to them that if the Koreans are cornering the market they'll up the price, so you if you have fucked your capacity for shipbuilding...

Hill: It is difficult to believe that they are that naive, but they do, they actually think that a competition between the Koreans and the Japanese, and us not having an industry, a marine industry anyway, or a commercial marine industry, means that our people is going to buy cheap ships. Anybody with an ounce of sense knows that is not going to happen, because once they have got that to themselves there is nowt to say that the Japanese, who are clever negotiators, won't form a consortium or cartel. To move a car factory [Nissan] into this area, that was clever negotiation, it will only attack *our* car industry. The same Japanese with Korea will make sure that they become a consortium between them. And then they'll put the prices up all right. Anyway our fleet has been destroyed by Europe, in my opinion, all the famous lines have wrapped up because of Europe. There was need to bring food, for example. We had first-class food supplies in Australia and New Zealand. They provided us with finer food then than what we get now despite the fact that it had to be shipped here. Well, all the old fleets have become redundant. Its unbelievable the number of famous fleets that's gone. Shipping has, commercially, become unnecessary in these people's minds. But, of course, that is in so-called peacetime. In wartime it would be wild if we lost the facility, the know-how. Well, no doubt if we are fighting China, the Koreans and Japanese will build us as many ships as we need, at the price.

Mack: That's where nationalisation fell short anyway. They nationalised the shipyards when what they should have done was take all the shipowners and nationalise all that as well. We still had no control over that, plus the fact you had the boards of directors of all the individual shipbuilding companies who didn't want nationalisation and when it came in they were still in charge. You had people in charge who didn't want nationalisation. Now, who are the ones that could make it not work? And they have done that. As he says, them we had here were totally against nationalisation but were still left in charge.

Hill: I was in London at the inauguration of BS when he stood up on his footstool and read a cablegram from the British Shipping Federation, stating the long-term association British shipyards had with British shipping companies, and they intend to continue them ties. It was a complete fabrication and a lie. Ever since that day the percentage of British tonnage built abroad just continued to increase year by year, it never stopped increasing abroad. It is just the same. The other fatal thing of course is they left the same management in charge of the shipyards that were totally against it. We had a classic example of it with some of them here, in this region, they hated nationalisation. Mind, they were very disappointed when they didn't get a position on BS board. But they still hated it. And them Tory MPs who used to come up here wining and dining themselves then gannin' back to Parliament and saying, 'They are lying about up there and they've got the shipyards on the rocks.' They didn't say anything about the Scotch on the rocks they'd been plugging down their necks when they were swanning around in the hospitality suites.

This site here where we are standing now was called the Shipbuilding Corporation and I served me apprenticeship here. It was formally Swan Hunter's shipyard. They moved away from here in the thirties. They then said that this site couldn't be used for shipbuilding because there was overcapacity. At the time when the world was crying out for ships we couldn't build them, or wouldn't build them for thirty-five years. And if you take it from 1947 to this re-opening in 1978, there is your timing. It so happened that in the former South Docks – Bartrams' shipyard – the lease was running

39

out, it had a couple of year to gan when they decided they were going to build this complex up here, the restriction was removed from this site. And that is how far these people can see ahead. But the people who decided to do that was an organisation called Wear Shipbuilders, that was a committee of representatives from senior management of the shipyards that existed at that time on the river. You've got a group of men in business can decide whether a site on a river-bank is utilised for any kind of industry. What kind of power is that? That's what's happened all through history: people make decisions about everybody else. People doesn't realise how much these decisions affect the community. The Corporation Yard [yard next to A & P] is a classic example: it closed down because these people knew it was a facility that might give them some competition. They have done that over the years. They used to do that before the war, they used to give each other deals and close sites down because there wasn't enough work to go round.

Pickard: National Shipbuilders Securities Limited.

Hill: That's them. But they've done that since 1918, shipbuilding in this country has been a contracting industry since after the First World War. They've never stopped contracting. They contracted in so far that they use contraction for productivity. The capacity at the time: the old Shipbuilders' and Repairers' Association put a booklet out that listed all the tonnages they'd built over the years, and they had only once built two million ton. All they ever wanted to build was a million ton, and all they ever did to maintain that million ton was to close shipyards, rationalise, contract the number of people but maintain what they call increased productivity with less men. And that is exactly what they are doing still. And it is just going to make the industry disappear. After the war the world was crying out for ships, we were one of the countries that had facilities to build ships, and they just didn't do it, they didn't expand. In my opinion it was totally political, and if you've got to use the word, a *capitalist* attitude, 'Why the hell do we want the Third World to develop except on our terms?' And their terms was: 'We'll maintain a strict-sized fleet, and when they get ships they'll be the ones we don't want, the old ones.' It's caused the present crisis. All the British ships and companies have selt their ships second-hand to the Far and Middle East or wherever and that is why there is no orders for ships. Because there is abundance of tonnage all over the world. That's not an inspiration, that's a fact.

scrap and build

Pickard: So are you saying the government should have given credit facilities to the Third World?

Hill: If they wanted to expand the industry and maintain it, aye. Scrap and build, you've heard that story many times. I've heard it all my life. Scrap-and-build had never been a runner in this country because shipowners were not interested in scrap-and-build. Shipowners in this country were only interested in selling their old ships to foreign buyers at a good price rather than scrap them. They wouldn't scrap a ship to get a new one when they could sell it abroad. They would accept help in building new ships but they wouldn't scrap them, no way. So they selt them in competition to themselves. I have seen ships that come in here, immediately after the war, that I would scrap – either bringing it in or taking it out. They have actually patched the shell up, holes in the shell, welded patches on in the South Dock where they've been carrying scrap into port. The ships themselves very often took a ten-thousand-ton load of scrap out and the ship was ganna be scrapped with the scrap ... Look what British shipping did with the Liberty ships,[1] and how they patched them up. They were prepared to spend years in the British Channel all the way down into Wales, repairing them, strapping the old Liberty ships up to get another twenty years out of them, rather than build new ships. They bought them cheap because America had that many lying about in port, they were buying them for a song and patching them up, and they got twenty year out of them. That's why the SD14 became popular,[2] because the Liberty ships were starting to fall apart. There were six hundred Liberty ships still at sea around the late sixties and they started to fall apart. That was the whole reason why the SD14 came about, was to replace that particular tonnage, but unfortunately the management in A & P, such as Kimber, thought they were going to build nowt else but SD14s till they replaced six hundred Liberty ships. And that just didn't happen. In fact the modern assembly line in the shed was specifically designed to carry SDs. When we

1. Liberty ships. Built by Henry Kaiser, all welded, prefabricated, mass-produced in the USA to replace ships sunk by enemy U-Boats during the Second World War. The original design was produced by the Sunderland Company, Newcastle-upon-Tyne, in 1879.

2. SD: standard design; the SD14, an A&P design for multipurpose dry cargo.

came to build bulk carriers they've got to take them off those conveyor lines and put them on to concrete on the ground because they cannot accommodate them. And our 'friends' talking about twenty-four SDs a year. Some of them said twenty-four, some of them said twenty-one: JH who's now in Harland and Wolf in Belfast, he 'would be satisfied with twenty-one'. When you ask yourself the question: in this facility, to build twenty or twenty-four ships in a year – where you build half here and it's transferred on to the other berth – you know you are talking about (we have nearly six weeks holiday a year) forty-six weeks for building twenty-four ships.

Hill: (*Laughing*) You'd have to build one every ten days. It's just ridiculous. When Henry Kaiser was building Liberty ships every day, he was on the west coast of America with about a hundred and fifty berths, and that is how he was building a ship a day.

Pickard: What do you think the capacity is here? How many ships a year?

Hill: I think about the first year we came up – it was 1978/9 – they proved it had a good potential. I believe there was ten ships launched out of the yard that year. I think six of the ten came out of here, the rest were launched outside the complex. It proved it's got potential, there is no doubt about that. But what am I doing standing here? Because there is no continuity, I have never seen the work flow so bad, it is totally disorganised. I have never known the organisation be so bad. I started catching at Picky's in 1940 when it was Will Pickersgill and Sons and they were all riveted ships and there was a war on, but by God they knew how to keep continuity going. And they knew in the forties and fifties, they knew throughout the sixties and up to the seventies. But since we've got this new organisation ... well, we've got the visual display units, we've got all the technicians and all the planners. They are planning our downfall, they are planning us into oblivion. We are certainly not working as we could work. And I am not talking about people killing themselves, I'm talking about doing a steady day's work every day. You are lucky here if you work three days on a week. They are building one thing at a time: look at the size of this. There is just no organisation. They have no idea.

42

Hill: What they are doing with this industry, what's left of it, is turning it from a labour-intensive industry to a cost-intensive industry, and once you get a cost-intensive industry then the labour content is not required. That's what automation is all about, that's why that factory [Nissan] has been built at Washington because there is tons of automation, robotics, in the place, probably more than they could get in Japan, but they are getting them here. Technology is going mad, but technology is forgetting about people. When I first got telt about technology I attended the Sunderland Technical College in 1960, they were talking about technology then. They were talking in terms of industrial relations, a consideration that people might never be out of work, so the technology should provide the capital to put these people in a life of leisure, to take the time up. But not with the people that are running this country, they are not going to do that. People have become surplus to requirement, they don't even need them for wars now.

the working class can kiss my arse

Hill: And Mack will tell you the number of men that have took staff jobs that were on a redundancy list because the place 'wasn't worth a fucking candle, we were getting nowt, it's down the bank, it's finished', and within a matter of weeks they took staff jobs. The excuse, for going on the voluntary redundancy list, when challenged by anybody: 'You're on the way out, at least I'll get my redundancy when we finish.' Now then, this surely shows the quality of management: nobody on the management side thought to ask them, 'Are you just taking this job so you'll get your redundancy?'
Mack: There was nobody applying for staff jobs told: 'You don't want to work here, your name's on the redundancy list!' The last three made up here from the welders were on the voluntary redundancy list.
Hill: We got a one, he was only a young fellah, a welder, and somebody warned him when he was younger about the dangers of welding and he read the notices on every welding packet, same as cigarette smoking, 'It is dangerous to inhale fumes from welding,' and he did the next best thing to it, he just stopped welding. He

43

never breathed them any more. He got a staff job and training. But before that he's got his name down, he's leaving, it's not worth a candle. There is a higher job in the technicians' department, he applies for it and gets it, and he's on a list, he wants to be out. The personnel are the people that do the interview in both instances of redundancy and enhancement, if you want to call it that. How the hell can anybody that's in possession of all these facts say, 'This fellah's on a redundancy list and he wants a staff job,' and they've never put the begging question? To me it proves what I've just said, they just want the place blew to hell, they just want it to fail and probably think they'll buy it for buttons, like Swan's has been bought for buttons. Five million pounds for about what?

Pickard: That's all they sold Swan's for?

Mack: They'd just done ten millions' worth of refurbishment on it. BS will pick up the tab for that.

Hill: The land is worth more than five million, never mind about what's standing on it.

> He suspected that the government would sell off Austin
> and Pickersgill, probably to management who would get
> it at a bargain price.

Hill: To write it off as a total loss-maker, they will claim its capital value no matter what they paid for it. The original conversion of this yard, this place where you are standing here, plus the extra work in the shed on the other side of the yard, it cost twenty-seven million quid, and that was only ended in 1978.

how to be a shop steward

Pickard: How do you get elected for shop steward?

Mack: What usually happens when we know we are going to the meeting, we have it in December every year, because there are all sorts of other business, we have a welders' meeting. The chairman will get us together, the six of us, and say, 'We are going to elections, are you all willing to stand again?' We just say aye, or no, or whatever, and in this case we all decided to stand again. We open the meeting and the first business is the election of stewards. The chairman will say, 'Nominations for anybody that wants to be

44

steward. The present stewards are all willing to stand again, are there any other nominations?' The avenue then is open for anybody to put forward anybody's name. And if we do get names we hold a ballot.

Pickard: So how did you become one? Did somebody put your name up?

Mack: You've got to get round a few friends and let them know you are interested otherwise, if nobody nominates you, you cannot stand. So you obviously make your feelings known, that you want to stand and somebody will nominate you and hopefully you get elected. As regards canvassing, I've never known any lads do that, not to my knowledge.

Pickard: Who elects the chairman? Shop stewards?

Mack: Well the boilermakers meet, we've got a boilermakers' joint shop stewards' committee, and the stewards elect a chairman and a vice-chairman and secretary. But usually in the inter-departmental stewards, when they are elected we have two from our department, two from the welding department, go on the joint negotiating committee. In the past what we've done, when we've had an election, the ones that take the two biggest votes, they go on the joint negotiating committee. That is not necessarily so, if we wanted a change to give somebody else a chance, but that's the way we've normally done it.

24/1/86

The next day I was visited by Bill Sharp, a young driller.
I asked him if he like working in the shipyard.

hey, I'm a sheet-metal worker

Sharp: The novelty wears off after so long. It gets a little tedious.
You get sick, you get put on shit jobs.

I started my apprenticeship in 1976 at Swan's. I was sixteen.
What I had done is, I had went to the Careers Office master who
came to the school at Shields. I dunno how he noticed, but he
noticed I was suitable for a sheet-metal worker, as a job. I didn't
know myself what a sheet-metal worker was, but he was saying,
looking at me qualifications and what I was expecting, 'You are a
sheet-metal worker.' And there was me, coming out and going to
me mam and dad, 'Hey, I'm a sheet-metal worker, it's amazing.'
So I applied for all these jobs all over the shop as a sheet-metal
worker, not thinking about anything other than a sheet-metal
worker. Thinking the careers master had put me in the right direction and found my vocation in life. And I went all over, I didn't get
a job as a sheet-metal worker. I got anything but. But I laughed.
Now when I think about it, I think, Christ, I must have been so
stupid. But they wield so much power them sort of people, and
young kids are very naïve, they are open to anything. I went to
Swan's for an interview as a sheet-metal worker. And they had
the interview, and I passed the interview, and there was another
interview (there was twenty-five of us chasing this job) and there's
me, daft arse, thinking, oh aye, put in for it. I could have probably
done something else like an electrician, or fitter or plumber or
plater. I didn't get the job, all I got offered was a driller or a caulker,
or something of that description. Well, it's like me saying to you,
'Do you want to be a driller?' Well, at the time – 1976/77 – it wasn't
as bad for jobs then. It was starting to get pretty bad; after that it

started getting worse for jobs. Me mate, who I knocked about with, he was already started as a driller, so I says, 'Oh, I'll try that.' Me father was an influence in one respect, he said, 'Take on the drilling job, because caulking is crap, and see what it's like.'

My father served his time at Shields in the repair yards, as a shipwright. Shields has been known for a long time as a merchant place. At seventeen my father went to sea, and he was at sea for twenty year. I can only remember me dad from when I was a kid, coming in with a white sack and putting it down and we were looking for the toys. But he left there and has been working at the NCB for a lot of years as a teemer.[1] He works on the waterfront. I didn't want the shipyards, I wanted the pit, or sea. I wanted to go to sea. Obviously you get influenced by your parents and I thought it sounded great, me dad going to these exotic countries and coming back sun-tanned. Plus like, me uncles were seamen as well. Me mam was always giving me the shit, 'I don't want you to go away, it's a crap life, it's only for a single lad and it's no life for me.'

they'll eventually phase us out

Sharp: I served me time as a caulker/burner/driller/riveter, because we were took on as *shipbuilders* which in effect they are doing now here. This phase-five agreement which they're getting thrashed out will no longer relate to trades.[2] We're like boilermakers in a sense. They'll eventually phase us out I would imagine and there's only twelve of us. I've been here four years and there's been fourteen men offered redundancy. I worked it out the other day, I was talking to a couple of lads and I says, 'Christ, there's nobody here, in this yard, from when I first started, and that's only four year ago. It's amazing.' And a couple of years before that there was two thousand two hundred men here. And I just stood back and we started working out who we could remember who was here: and there's fourteen blokes gone. Fourteen jobs up the Swanee. They got offered redundancy, but they had been here all their lives, and they were fucking brayed out, some of them. If they had carried on working here they would have gone out in a coffin. I think they

1. Teemers levelled coal in ships' holds.
2. British Shipbuilders' phase-five agreement was anti-demarcation and laid the groundwork for interchangeability of workers in shipyards.

would have. I mean, I served me time at Swan's, as I say, I worked with this bloke and he was a great driller, he was one of the best, fantastic, and he died of cancer of the throat. And we were working on the ship, a destroyer, and he started getting a sore throat and he couldn't talk. And he was a huge man he was, and he had been in the Navy for a lot of years. He kept himself really prim and proper. I mean, he could go into a bucket of shite and he'd come out looking like roses. We used to laugh about it. He left me loads of his gear. He got a sore throat, as I say, and he started coughing all the time and he couldn't get his breath, so they sent him to hospital, operated on him and he came out about two weeks later. I always remember this bloke, I hated him, called Geordie, and we were getting our bait, cause we used to get our bait round this fire, and he says, 'Oh here comes Tommy and I remember him the way he was,' right? Well I didn't know what he meant. As I say, he was a huge man, well, when he come round the corner and he was like a fucking skeleton. He'd had cancer of the throat, and he couldn't talk, he was like ... A man like that – he just wasted away. And the unions were saying to his wife, 'You want to get him autopsied, he'll have died with asbestosis' and all this, but she was saying, 'No, no, I'm not doing it.' They were up there trying to talk her into it, but she wouldn't. Years ago when them worked in the engine rooms they used to lag the pipes with asbestos and he used to work in there all the time, and they attribute his death to that. He was fifty-four. He just went like that. It's terrible. A lot of the blokes took their redundancy.

I served me time with two old guys: one was sixty-one and the other was sixty-two. They were characters in themselves. One had been a professional boxer. As a kid he was fucking hard as bell metal. He'd worked that hard he couldn't move one of his arms properly. But, as I say, a lot of these older blokes have given up their life for the younger lads to get what they get now. I don't take anything I get for granted, but there's a lot of people do. They tend to slag trade unionism off but the trade unions have done a hell of a lot. The conditions that some people had to work in have changed. I'll never know.

We used to sit round the fire at Swan's, we had to get our bait in the shed, we used to nick planks of wood and chop them up and make fires. The gaffer used to come along at ten past nine because he was a bastard, and boot the fire over, because he thought he was

48

great. We used to sit round with the old guys and they could talk the hind legs off you. It was great, man. But the things they experienced and the things they done and what they had to put up with, is totally different to what we do. I mean, during the war and everything, they seen some sights.

As I say, I worked at Swan's and I served me time at Hawthorn Lesley's [another Tyneside shipyard]. At Hebburn there is a pub called the Kelly, because the ship was renowned. Mountbatten was the captain of the ship and it got torpedoed when they went outside the waters. Now they brought it back, they brought it back into the dock. A few of the old-timers I worked with at Swan's worked in that yard at the time. I don't know if you've been in a destroyer, but they've got collision bulkheads. What they are is just an open space, like a room, nothing in it. It's for impact. Obviously it's for stress. So that it'll take the stress of the ship. This bloke was saying to us, he was saying, 'I had to go down to drill the watertight doors off and drop the doors because there was pockets of water all over.' They were, like, drilling these doors, and what they used to do, years ago, was drill the rivet-heads out, and bang the rivet-head back in and the plate used to come off. They were standing there, the two of them, and doing this job, and he banged the plate and the plate dropped. There was three sailors come floating out with the water. He says he shit himself. There was a fight to get up that access ladder, between him and this bloke. He said it was really scary. And I was saying, 'Eh, you lying cunt, you.' Well, obviously I didn't know what was going on. Now on all your doors on naval ships you get anti-dust mats, but then they were like clippy mats [coloured rug made from rags] like you used to make for your door. But this bloke says to me, 'I seen this clippy mat floating about the engine room, so I went down and I pulled it up and it was this bloke's head. His hair. Just his head floating about.'

The things they've had to put up with: piece-work. Piece-work was like slave labour. You got paid nothing for it. I worked there until 1982, and this bloke who died, Tommy, he had never spoke to another lad, BF, ever since piece-work had been on, because BF had apparently ripped him off of a couple of pound and they just didn't speak. You see it was all management manipulation. They used to force one man against another man, and the gaffers and managers used to cause animosity between people.

49

them and us

Sharp: Look at the foreman here, look at Picky's (as I say there's fourteen drillers gone from my department, I don't know how many men have gone from other departments), but it would be common sense if you were going to reduce the workforce to reduce the staff, but they don't. The staff's increased. They've taken I don't know how many redundancies in the welding department, but up until recently they've made two new foremen. How can they justify that? It's just crazy, it's nonsense. There's more chiefs than there is Indians in this place. You see them walking about; they create jobs, they create work. The management create situations where they ask for foremen and they don't need them. They've got all these big ideas.

Pickard: Do they always get the foreman from the shop floor?

Sharp: Some foremen start OK. Our foreman, in the drilling department, JF, he was a great bloke, a canny lad off the tools. You know, he was a great crack on, a bit of a lazy pig, but he was good. He got the gaffer's job and I used to take the piss out of him because I used to take me bait with him. I used to say, 'Hey man, Jimmy, you've changed now, they've twisted you round and they've manipulated you, you're one of them now.' And he said to me, 'I'm not, man, what happens is the men change you.' And I says, 'How's that, you were one of them yourself, do you not remember?' And he goes: 'They make us like we are.' And I just laughed and thought, fucking hell, give them a few pounds ... I don't know, there used to be a bloke here called Langly and he used to say to the foreman (some foremen used to give men lifts), 'I don't want to see you giving men lifts.' He used to try and drum it into them that they are somebody else, somebody special: and they're not. They're no different to me or you, just a person, a human.

serving your time

Pickard: So how does the apprenticeship system work? How old are you?

Sharp: Twenty-five. You get picked as an apprentice and you go through a training programme that lasts four years.

Pickard: How does it work on the shop floor? Do you get assigned to a couple of blokes or one bloke or what?

Sharp: Well, what you do in A&P, young lads can't get on the ship until they are eighteen. It started off when the lads got killed at Swan's on the *Glasgow*. There was a few young lads got killed there. And they had said, 'No young lads to go on the ships till they are eighteen.' So welders and platers will go with another plater, or two platers, a young lad would go on his own just doing downhand in the shed, easy jobs, till he got confidence in himself and they would start giving him bits of jobs here, there and everywhere. And once he starts working and gets proficient in his trade he would ... I would say the first two years is just general muck about, find out your capacity ...

Pickard: Were you not assigned a tradesman?

Sharp: Well, drilling is more of a manual job than anything else, you used to go with a man, a bloke who would teach you the job. There is no training school here, whereas there are training schools further over the yard, in the shed where apprentices go in and learn burning and all that. Say, for instance, the drillers, they would do six months burning and six months caulking, as part of their training...

Me personally, I served me time through the Tyne. I went with two old blokes and I sort of done the work but they were showing me the ropes. In Picky's you get sent with one or two men but you also work in the sheds for a few months where I'm working now... You eventually get moved on to the ship.

We knife out holes sometimes up to seven-inch. But through Swan's we used to put eighteen-inch. Swan Hunter's, as I say, is a different place, because they are different ships altogether. The drillers through Swan's have got a harder job because everything is knifed out, here it is burnt out if they want to put pipes through.

Pickard: What's the difference?

Sharp: Well, knifing: you've got a drill and you've got an extended arm which moves out over to increase the size of diameter of the hole you are going to knife out. So you have got a drill and a knifing blade that traces the hole out. It's not used very often here, but it does get done. Through Swan's it gets used a hell of a lot. It just depends on the makers. Some makers reckon that it's the temper of the steel and that it needs roughing up. We work normally up to two-inch on the ship, but the engine beds, they are about two and an eighth. You put bolts in, you tap loads of holes, you clear holes, drain holes.

Pickard: Is that done before it is assembled?

Sharp: Once you go on the ship ... All sorts of jobs are done on the ship, but if you can get them off the ship, before structures get put on, bulkheads and all that, you try to get them out the way. That's what they are practising now over there at the quay, they've got the accommodation up, they are trying to get as much work as they can before the wooden bulkheads go up.

Pickard: Are they building the furniture now?

Sharp: The joiners are.

Pickard: How soon after a ship is launched do the outfitters get on?

Sharp: The outfitting trades are on the ship now. What happens is, normally a marker-off or a charge hand from the joiner shop will go on to the ship and mark off where he wants welded brackets for all the wood to be fastened into. He marks off where the bulkheads for the cabins are going to be, they get them welded on and then they start putting the sheets in, because they are only like laminated sheets between cabins. They are only about an inch thick and they slide them in, doors and everything. They start with the engine room here, but at Swan's they start with the keel because they build on a slipway and they build it lengthways, like the engine room and the keel together, whereas through here they start laying the engine room first, and then they slide it over, in the complex, and they start building the boat up from there: all the holds. It is called a 'half-boat', they build half a boat, and half the boat is the engine room because it is launched from the after end on to the water...
All ships are, but at Swan's when you build on a stockyard you start laying a keel near the engine room first, and then you build up over. Down here they build the engine room up first so the outfitting trades are used. They get pipes in, they get parts of engines in, they get it really fastened out down there.

Pickard: Do you enjoy seeing a ship launched?

Sharp: Yes I do. I get a certain amount of pride, especially if you've given up a year of your work. Sometimes you sweat blood, or you give blood. It's not the most safe aspect in the shipyards. It's not the most safe job in the world. You can lose count the amount of times you get stuff in your eye. You cut your hands. You just get on with it. You've got to, you can't afford to be on the sick. You wouldn't. Through here they launch the ship then it goes round to the quay, so if you're not working on the ship you're probably not going to see it again. What happens is, they've got a procedure at A&P's that takes the ship round to the Tyne and the ship's finished at the Tyne. They're commissioned at the Tyne because they get them docked through there. All the launching plates what's on the front of the ship, they've got two stabilisers and they are chocked with wood and when it gets launched it is to stop it tilting. They do as much as they can on it and then about a month before it's going it gets taken through to the Tyne and it is docked in one of the dockyards and it is finished off there by A&P workers who go through on trip buses to work on it. So you might work on that ship ... what happened to me loads of times is that I might be the last driller off the ship because I live near there, at Shields, and it's easier for me to go there and leave there. But I wouldn't see the ship go away, I would probably leave and it would probably go about a week later. You don't get the same thrill here. When we used to work on the Tyne they used to top and tail a ship, put flags from stem to stern, and the hooters would go and everything, and you'd get a tear. You'd feel it's the last time you were ever going to see that ship. It's funny, it's emotional, especially when you think I've worked two years on that, up to your paps and everything. But you don't get that same thrill here. You see, this is a high production yard in a sense. It's gone down a hell of a lot since its heyday in the early seventies, but it is still geared up for high production and they just work! They were banging them off that quick, you know they weren't bothered I suppose, so they just get them out. Whereas through Swan's everything is done on cost and the best goes into them, and if they are not happy with them the supers on the ship will get it done again until you are happy. Whereas these ships here are built for one purpose and that is for quickness, so that once they are launched and in the water they have paid for themselves after about two trips.

I don't think they want us to have ships

Pickard: I asked your chairman whether he thought Thatcher was thick or whether she actually believed this ideology of free market forces that you can decimate your shipbuilding industry even though you are an island and can buy ships cheaper from Korea...

Sharp: It's like anything else, look at the maritime fleet in England, we are an island but there's just no ships, is there? I don't think they want us to have ships.

You see my idea is this: Japan *used* to be cheap. Now look at the Japanese car market. Now, do you think for one instance that they haven't got it all planned and pre-planned. Japanese motor bikes were very cheap years ago. Now they're not cheap, because there's no competition for them. And what the Koreans and the likes of the Japanese will do, is they'll get backed heavily by the government, they'll smash the shipbuilding industry in all the rival countries, the Western countries, and they'll say, 'Now, we are the only shipbuilding nations and you are going to start paying for your ships.' You've got no option, what can you do? You can't say, 'Well, I'll go round to Fred Bloggs's shipyard,' cause there's just nothing there. You'll be surprised what they do when the shipyards go bust, or if they close down. Everything goes, they don't leave a bean. I mean Cellend's [a small shipyard closed in 1982], everything was stripped, parts came here and went all over the place. It's a big con, man. Swan's' management got Swan's shipyard for nothing, five million pounds, or whatever they paid. It's incredible. You couldn't buy the land for that. I mean they are building destroyers, they'll know they are getting an order for a destroyer. I've worked on a destroyer through the Tyne, and it's an open cheque book. Because its M.o.D. work, and the tax payer is paying it, fuck expense. It's crazy man. No wonder they take so long to build. You've got to wait for clearance to drill a three-inch hole. It's fucking mental, man. The gaffer used to say, 'There's a job down there, I'll get it passed, I'll go and see somebody.' You could be there all day. Then he'd say, 'Oh, you can do it now.' You can't do anything on your own. Everything's got to be given the order, more or less.

I still think this place will go private. I think they're gearing themselves up to sell it, and they'll eventually get what they want. It's like Swan Hunter's, isn't it? You keep the workforce wondering all the time and then it goes through. They never tell you, the management are very shrewd, they never tell you what they've got in the pipeline. They keep the workforce guessing all the time, because of fear. Fear, it keeps you going, keeps you working, worried. You'll not put up a resistance. They manipulate you through the media. It's always in the newspaper that they are doing

54

great and they are taking on a hundred men, but anyone who is in the trade union, or a trade union shop steward, doesn't get started. A bloke took them to court because he's saying, 'I've been victimised, because I was chairman of the boilermakers' section. I've been unemployed for so long, and I tried to get a job and was telt to fuck off.' It was in the paper a couple of months ago. When I was gonna take the job on, and this is fucking stupid, this, but, when I was going to take the job of shop steward on, me mate says, 'You don't want to take the shop steward's job cause you go on a fucking computer.' [*He laughs.*] I says, 'Div I?' He says, 'Aye.' I says, 'Fucking hell, I didn't know that.'

If they could get what they wanted ... I mean in this yard you know yourself they only want boilermakers in this yard. My job's secure in a sense, because I'm a boilermaker, but I mean you cannot do anything if your national executive is not going to back you up. Or if they are going to fuck you about, or just like they don't care. You see this yard is a thorn in the side to BS because we are on a higher rate of pay than everybody else. I took the shop steward's job on, I didn't want to, because I thought I was a bit young, still do, I mean I've only been in it a year and I think I'm still green. Green as grass. I take an active interest in the yard, but obviously it restricts me to taking any interest outside of the yard because I don't come from the Sunderland area. You get a certain amount of hostility, which may be said as a joke, but I know a lot of true things are said in jest. When I first came I hated it. I used to get the piss taken: lads saying, 'Coming from the Tyne you shouldn't be in here.' And I used to say, 'There's lads working from the Wear on the Tyne.' I'd get back, 'Do they shite,' and all that. As I've said, and as I've always said, if there'd been drillers on the dole in Sunderland there's no way I would have gotten a start. And at the end of the day I would have still been at the Tyne now. I was working at Swan's and another lad, a driller, was saying there was a job at Picky's and 'It's fucking good money, loads of work,' and all that. Well I was sick of where I was working, it's a completely different environment at Swan's, it's hacky dirty, they've got no conditions. We've got a shower block round here, I get a shave every night, get a shower if I want, to go home. Leave me work gear here.

I go for a run outside of an afternoon, in the dinner hour, get showered. I go for a run around. There used to be about fifteen or twenty lads but they've all gone. There are a few Harriers, there is a lad that runs for England here, a joiner. He is working with the boilermakers at the minute, but he is an England 'B' international. He was in Spain the other week, Brian Uswash. He's only a little lad, but he's an England international. There are a few lads in Sunderland Harriers, and we go running. You see, you're swallowing all this shit and dirt, you want it off your chest. You hockle it up as you run around, you're hockling it all over. You spit a lot here, it's horrible the atmosphere.

the rot always starts at the top

Sharp: Don't get me wrong, we don't work like madmen, but if the job is there you do it, and it's like anywhere else, if the management can keep the job flowing... The rot always starts at the top ... if they can keep the work flowing, then the men will do it. It's obvious, that's what we are paid for, and that's what we'll do. You cannot just, on your own bat, take a job over or do a job. That's what they are trying to do on the float side, if there is anything stopping you get it done, burning or welding. Or if anybody asks you to do a job, do it, which we have done all the time. But there is no incentive at times, there is no incentive when you see the gaffers working Sunday afternoons and ducking about in the yards during the week. They just work the Sunday afternoon. They used to have job recorders, they used to call them counters, and they used to go round and sort the job out. Years ago when they used to be piece-workers and when everything was on piece-work they used to have ten job recorders who used to go round and work out the job and make sure what was going on and they paid you. So if you done a load of welding and you got paid a pound a foot and you did six foot you were on six pounds, you didn't get that, but that's an illustration how they worked it out. They went out years and years ago. When I came to this yard, I didn't know what they were, I said, 'Christ, there is no such thing at Swan's or any other yard' ... They just worked out the job you done and put your times into the yard, and they knew where you were working. They'd come up to you and say, 'Are you working in the engine room?' and I would tell them I'm in the accommodation. 'You're in the accommodation. Who is working in the engine room?' 'Davy.' 'Davy in the engine,

John?' 'Oh, he's on the deck.' There was always six drillers on the ship, two on the deck, two on the accommodation, and two in the engine room. So they would work out man hours and all this crap. It was a load of shite. The gaffer knows where you are working... They have gotten rid of the job recorders, and the foremen were telt that they would have to do the job recorders' job, like write your job down on your board. And they said no, but they were in on Sunday to work it out.

Pickard: The tank rats, the labourers, which tanks do they clean out?

Sharp: Any tank ... you've got the double bottom running from one end of the ship to the other, and what happens is, it has to be cleaned out, because contractors go down and spray-paint it black. Like painting the Tyne Bridge, you work from one end to the other and by the time you get to one end you may as well start again because it is the same again. It is just a continuous cycle. What they do is, as the ship nears completion they go down and clean everything up, and the painters go down and paint it. But they are working in the tanks all the time, sweeping up and cleaning, pumping all the water out. They get like a miner's hat and gan down sweeping up. Their job, Christ! And they get paid buttons.

accidents

Dodds: But, like I say, we made great strides in the last few years, especially in the safety rules. You're talking about men getting killed every week in shipyards. It's a high-risk job, there's no question about it. I've seen quite a few gan in my time. When I was an apprentice, I mean at Short's, as regards staging, it was pretty good because it was a very old-fashioned yard and they still used the riveters there, and the riveting squads obviously would bring all the equipment, and they had to have a platform so the staging was always pretty good. But you gan to other places ... I mean, even here when we first come here in 1978! The staging is not that good here now, but then! I've never seen staging like it. It was terrifying.

Pickard: I was on some the other day and I was fucking shitting myself. It was leaning at an angle and wasn't secured.

Dodds: Aye. We had a lot of battles when we first came up, in fact

I had the factory inspector in every other week about the staging. He's been himself, obviously, a few times since and we've got a pile of letters there where the factory inspector himself is complaining about staging.

Catwalk: She's cut back on the factory inspectors.

Dodds: Oh, aye, she's sacked quite a few of them.

Brian: In the ten year that I was over there, in the old yard, I think there was a dozen fucking people killed in the yard. It was fucking horrible.

Dodds: They divvin' care.

Catwalk: What happened to him that got caught between the cranes, down at Bartram's?

Dodds: Big Macky. I hadn't been down there very long and there was an accident on the ship. It was ten to nine, the men were just coming away for their baits. It was one of the New Zealand ships, refrigerated boats; it had three decks in, and the sea had washed the shores away and two shell panels come out, three decks fell down. And all the men, they were just leaving, the bloody whole lot came down; engine room, all that came in, the lot. It all collapsed.

Brian: We done that every day down the docks. That was one of your jobs every day. 'Mend them shores.' The sea used to come in and wash the sand away from underneath the fucking shores. The shell would fall out, fucking pull it in with cranes or wires and pulleys. 'Mend your shores.' They were fastened at the peak with a couple of wires inside the shell, pulling in, and the shores on the outside. The wires used to stretch. The shores took the main weight, and the tide used to come in and undermine the sand under the wedges and the fucking things would gan. The next day you'd come in and pull the fucking lot in again. It used to gan on day after day.

Catwalk: It was them what went on strike, wasn't it?

Pickard: About the sections?

Brian: Once they are welded in they're all right because the weight is off the shores. They tie each other up, sort of thing. The steel section will use shores.

Dodds: I was on a one where, again, it had been washed away from the port side; I was on the staging and I felt it start to gan out. And the staging was collapsing as I was jumping down. Me and the welder, Davy Baxter, we were jumping down to get under the rudder pintle and we just got there and the whole lot of the staging just come out.

58

Brian: You're building on sand.

industrial relations

Dodds: I've never know them to be very good in this industry. Like I say, we were telling you the other week about Melenby, I mean it's a terrible thing to say about a bloke's death, like, but you can only tell the truth, he says, 'This is me final offer,' and he died that night.

Pickard: He was the previous managing director?

Dodds: Yes, down at Bartram's. That was the one who kept that health report secret for five years.

Pickard: It's hard to believe the vindictive fucking pettiness.

Dodds: Like I say, when you were on piece-work you had to pay. You got a percentage knocked off your wages for the compressed air, for *their* tools, for using *their* machines.

Pickard: You're joking.

Dodds: I'm not kidding. There was a percentage took off; you had your piece-work rates and we used to lose, I think it was eighteen per cent for the compressed air and then another three per cent for your tools.

Brian: They often doctored the piece-work prices when, for instance, shipwrights were on the wood deck: you had stubs every three foot and it was all bored by hand. Then they give them a drilling machine, and they knocked the fucking price down for them to use the drilling machine. Riveters had to pay for the use of compressed air. Them sort of things happened. We're not talking that fucking long ago...

Dodds: No, I'm talking about sixteen, seventeen year ago. In our particular yard that was another way the foreman used to get at you as well, when you were on piece-work. You used to get counted up every day, or sometimes twice a day, and the counter would gan and tell the foreman that you had gone like the clappers and got two good days in, you've got three days' pay nearly. Then he would come and send you on to another job where you couldn't make the pay. It used to flatten you. That was another way of getting at you. You'd gan like the clappers for three days then he'd give you a job on ordinary time, gan on a test or something like that, or gan grinding.

Pickard: But you've got it better organised now?

59

Sharp: Years ago, it used to be blue eyes [favourites], didn't it? You used to get all the fucking overtime in the world. Up until the last six year the drillers didn't used to work overtime. Apparently they didn't, that was the foreman's idea. But on 'A' Bay there was a bloke called Jimmy and him and his mate used to work every fucking Saturday. And *they* didn't work overtime. He's a gaffer now.

Dodds: Ripyard Cuddling [Jack Davitt, ex-Swan Hunter's worker], one of his books is about the 'royals'. They say that they were the mainstay of shipbuilding. The 'royals' were the people who were in the yard all the time when we got paid off. They'd get all the overtime and the cushy jobs. To me they were just a load of fucking shitbags.

Brian: Freemasons.

Dodds: Aye, that's right. As long as they were all right they couldn't give a fuck about anybody else.

Pickard: So they wouldn't be union activists?

Dodds: Would they fuck! In some cases I've seen them been shop stewards, but not now, there was no way you could get any reaction out of them. In fact, in the apprentices' strike we had one lad in the caulking department and he didn't come out with us. As far as we were concerned he was a scab and we sent him to Coventry. After we got back to work, at the time before the new rates come through, we used to get an extra fifty pence, or ten shilling, on top of your money, and the gaffer knocked it off us. We went and seen this scab and had a look at his pay check and his was OK, so we went and seen the shop steward and didn't get a great lot of satisfaction out of him. So we went back to the gaffer and we telt him we wouldn't be working any more until we got our new rates. We went on strike, me and Hazard, again. The shop steward says, 'Send the fuckers home!'

Pickard: Well, thank God we've had the revolution and everything is all right now then.

Dodds: Not really. It used to be twenty-five per cent for the machine we used to use. It was minus eighteen per cent for the compressed air and then the machine itself I think was three per cent. And then these fuckers used to put it down as a tax loss. They had all the machines marked, and even just before we moved up here the compressed air was on the dock. All the machines were in a trench under the floor, and they were all marked with a number and they

60

were getting *depreciation* on the machinery, yet they were fucking charging us for the bastards. And you were talking about machines forty and fifty year old.

I wonder how much Short's used to charge for the horse? In 1963 they still had a horse and cart in Short's shipyard. It stood on a welding cable once in the wet and got a shock. You should have seen it gan! It would have won the fucking Derby.

Brian: Fucking ironic, isn't it? They're ganna buy a cover in to cover the unit to protect the paint. The men's worked over there for weeks on end in all that fucking weather.

Pete: Half-past one.

Dodds: It's not man, its only twenty-seven minutes past.

Pete: Do you wonder why people call you rivet-head?

the Labour Party

Danny: We've gotten new members in, young people, and we've progressed where the left wing in the constituency was in the majority ... And the right wing were in the minority ... It came to re-selection, because the MP is retiring at the next general election, so the seat was up for grabs. We got Chris Mullins to stand. Now, as I say, up to that time the left wing were in the predominance, we had the strength at that time. That's 1985. Albert Booth, who is supposedly a left-winger, an ex-minister, wasn't ganna stand in Sunderland, but then suddenly decided he was. Our union, the General and Municipal, were phoning delegates up, like Micky, myself, and other lads out of the boilermakers, telling them who to vote for: 'We expect you to take cognisance of the view of the union, and we are saying that we are pushing Booth.' They had telt Booth to stand in Sunderland South and he would get the votes. But he didn't get the votes – well, he got the right-wing vote – and the left-wing vote went to Mullins and Mullins won the seat. And we are now suffering for that, because the right wing has gone off on a tangent and they've built the strength up so it is now predominantly the right wing that's got the strength in the constituency, because they've flooded the place with delegates. And they're not stopping at saying that we were wrong to get Mullins, or even supporting Mullins, but they're now going on a witch-hunt. They are now talking about expelling people out of the Sunderland South Labour Party, and it all stems back to the re-selection meeting last year when Mullins was selected and Kinnock's speech at conference about Militants. And it's not a case of saying I'm a Militant, or he's a Militant, or Joe Bloggs is a Militant, it's if you read the paper – *Militant* – or if you are connected, or if they don't like you, now. It's not a case of being a member of the Militant.
Dodds: What also happens as well, over the last few years, we've

been attacking G—, he was our MP, and showing him up for what he was. I don't mean attacking him by shouting and bawling, but exposing him for what he was. And he's seen the build-up and the way the votes is gannin' and he knew he wouldn't survive the re-selection, there was no question about that. And he handed his resignation in then, saying that he wouldn't stand. If it hadn't been for attacks from us, he would have gone on to seventy-odd or eighty-odd years old, like they normally do. But the thing is now, you can gan and win an argument. In my ward itself, they are all right-wing, the councillors and that, there's only two or three of us who gets into them, and I can gan and wipe the floor with them: not shouting and bawling, just flatten their arguments, flatten their policies, show them up for what they are. But it makes no difference: comes the vote, they've got all their friends and their pals in. This is what they wanted with the re-selection, they wanted everybody in the party to have a vote, that was all the people in the wards. Now that would have been unfair on the likes of Chris Mullins and any candidate who couldn't get round all the wards, whereas G— is the sitting MP, he's got it anyway.

Pickard: Presumably that was just a tactic to defeat your moves.

Danny: You see the argument that Micky is saying is exactly the same argument that we have about Parliament. Take the ship-building debate as an example. Two of our lads went down to the House of Commons with Bob Clay, MP. In that debate never at any time was there any more than six or seven conservative MPs in the house, while the full strength of the Labour MPs were attacking the Tories on the shipbuilding industry, and I mean they absolutely wiped the floor with the Tories, but the divisional bells rang and they all came out of the bars and into the lobbies and the debate was just absolutely defeated. So what we say is, you win the debate but you lose the vote, so where is the democracy in the House of Commons? As far as we are concerned we cannot see any chance of getting real democracy through that system. It's like somebody quoted the other day: if we win an election (the Labour Party) the Tories only lend us it, only lend us the place, because it is theirs, it's their system. And if people honestly believe that we can get democracy through Parliament they are living in Cloud-cuckoo-land. I cannot ever see it being achieved.

Micky: When Edward Baluka was here a few years ago, down at Bartram's yard, he asked us how we seen the road to a social government, that's all he would talk about with us, socialism, and he was on about the bureaucracy over there in Poland.

Pickard: How does the trade union operate in relation to the Labour Party?

Danny: We have certain boilermaker branches that's affiliated to the Labour Party, and we as delegates, from our branches, as individual members, we gan along as members of our union. Now the constituency is made up of trade union delegates and ward delegates, and you've got this clash a lot of the time between them. I always find that the lad who is a trade union delegate is far and away more advanced in the problems than the ward delegate. In fact I would go as far as to say that a lot of them despise trade unionism and attack it a lot of the time. You get attitudes like, if you make a comment on something, 'You trade unionists are all the same.'

Pickard: It's not too popular at the moment, trade unionism. I was at a conference and Marghanita Laski told me that 'trade unionism has outlived its usefulness'. Of course, she couldn't tell me what it should be replaced with.

Danny: Nearly all the lads in here are married men with families. Now some of us is fortunate enough to have a wife in work, and a lot of the other lads are not so fortunate and the wife isn't working. And you can see the difference in their styles. Then you've got some of them like Brian. Brian is fortunate to have his lads in employment. Other lads' families have got no employment through no fault of their own, so it even comes down to, amongst us, we've got different incomes, depending on your circumstance. And some lads: the likes of the labouring man who has only the one income going into the house, I just don't know how he lives. We barely survive, and we're only surviving on a week-to-week basis. All right Brian might be able to afford a little bit more than me because he's got a little bit more going into the house, but not much. And yet these other people, the middle classes, no problems at all. They turn round and say, 'We'll vote Labour, but we don't really want to change the system, cause the system is pretty good to us, and we don't know what you are cribbing about.'

We say that politics is involved in every aspect of your job, every aspect of your life. Now at times there are lads in the yard cannot understand that until it directly affects them.

Eddy: And there was that film on with Clint Eastwood, right. So I'm watching it, and he gans to take this tart to the airport, and they're walking through the airport – it was only about five minutes since the film had started – and she says, 'You know, we never fucked, did we?' That's what I'm trying to say, they're good films but they have that in.

Chris: That's life though, isn't it?

Eddy: Aye, it's life, but what would you do? You're sitting there with your missus at your shoulder. Because a lot of women don't like it.

Jimmy: What time was this film on?

Eddy: The particular film I'm talking about was eight o'clock at night on Channel 4. I mean they could have scrubbed 'fuck' out and put 'sex' in.

Pickard: One of the reasons I don't swear in front of me three-year-old is because me missus says, 'Divvin' swear in front of the bairn.' The reason is partly hypocritical because I know if he gans to the school or the playgroup and says fuck off or something like that, he's ganna get ostracised, so you cannot. But as a writer – I suppose you could say, 'This film might offend so if you are going to be offended don't watch it,' that's fair enough – but I don't believe in censorship because you have to have freedom to write... Otherwise you are fucking about with reality. If I wrote a play about the shipyard, could I write it, honestly and accurately, without using the word 'fuck'? I couldn't.

Eddy: We know that.

Pickard: Well it's like you are suddenly censoring reality, and what else have you fucking got?

Rick: You've got to be careful. We were watching *Watership Down* over Christmas, the cartoon, and the fucking seagull turned round to the rabbit and told it to piss off. I turned to our lass and said, 'Did the seagull say that?' (*Laughter*)

Chris: And the bairn said, 'Sure he did.'

Eddy: A week gone Sunday, 'Spitting Image', at the end, it showed a news-flash, and he come on and says, 'Bernard Manning has just farted.' Well every cunt fell about laughing. And when everybody finished laughing I says, 'It's awful that.'

Chris: But you watch 'Spitting Image' and you expect it, right?

Eddy: I like a laugh.

Chris: 'Spitting Image' has got to be obscene at some time, but you still watch it.

Eddy: I know I do ... but, as you say, for seventeen- and nineteen-year-olds, fair enough, but there are things that come on and there could be other words used. But it wouldn't have the effect, like he's saying, I know that! I'm fucking not daft, and censorship is fucking crap, because when we were young, when you went to films, to be fair, you went to see Brigitte Bardot, and the best bits was fucking cut out, as far as we were concerned.

Tommy: We used to sneak in under somebody's coat.

Eddy: They showed you the difference a few years ago, on television. A Polish film, where they wheel in a corpse, it was a young tart that had been murdered...

Chris: He's married to a Pole, you know...

Eddy: I'm not saying owt about the Poles, it was a Polish film. It showed you the English version where they were wheeling the corpse in; when they pulled the cover off, the camera was at the point where you are just seeing across her belly button, but when you seen the Polish version, when it was released in Poland, you see the full view. But that was censorship, that's all I'm saying, it showed you the difference.

Pickard: That's when it gets dangerous, when somebody makes a decision on your behalf.

Eddy: We know that, they are making decisions every day down in Parliament about us, I mean they are ganna tax us on fucking rates now. They're ganna change all that sort of thing, we know that... But when have you had enough? When do you say enough is enough.

Chris: Get the kettle.

Eddy: When I was young, swearing wasn't in. Even when I went drinking with me father, this is no kidding, and a bloke from where he worked come along, and I mean I was drinking with him, and the bloke says 'fucking hell' and me father says to me, 'You get out of the way.' But that was his way. If I was with our boy now and you started to swear I wouldn't chase him away, I'd just let him fucking stand. I'm not saying your boy hasn't got the right to swear, because he has.

66

Bill, a crane driver, looks in the hut.

Bill: Have you got any spare choccie biccies, or what?
Eddy: No. You've got to be in the syndicate before you can get a chocolate biscuit.
Pickard: The brotherhood, the lodge.
Chris: You've got to be in the lodge, Bill, sorry.
Bill: Well I've got a funny handshake.
Silence
Bill: There's no answer to that, is there?
Rick: Did you read about them police starting a freemason's lodge?
Chris: The police freemasons at Scotland Yard?

the Church

Chris: That's what we were touching on before, about the inner cities and what the Church is doing. What the Church should be saying is how much land and property they own in the inner cities. They own some land, and they've got some money, but they never give any of it away.
Eddy: No, they never give any of it away. I'm a catholic, a practising catholic, but they haven't done enough for what is happening in the country today. They haven't done enough. No doubt about that. It was only the cricketer, Shepherd, he was open about it, but they are only verbals, there was nowt.
Pickard: The Tories went mad when some of the bishops started.
Chris: That's right.
Eddy: One of them just said that there's Trotskyites in the church, didn't he?
Chris: It was that idiot what's-his-name.
Eddy: He was fucking caught three-in-the-bed, or something, wasn't he?
Chris: Aye, it was one of the secretaries.
Eddy: What you touched on about people being on the dole: luckily, meself, I've only been on the dole twice. My lad – he's on the dole. It's crap. He wants a job.
Chris: But what's more obscene: that, or somebody saying 'fuck' on the telly?
Eddy: Oh, I get Tom's point. That's what he does all day, you know,

waits in all day for me coming in so he can have a bit chat.

Chris: It's a wearing-down process, man.

Eddy: He's praying for the summer so he can get down to the beach, or something like that, so he can kick a ball around. This weather, it's terrible. Where I live you've got people, I'm not begrudging it, but you've got people with four workers in the house. The estate I live in: it's mother and father, son and daughter, that's the average, and you've got people there who've got four wage-earners going in, and you've other houses where there is only one wage-earner and four fucking people... But, I believe, when you gan shopping and you are looking in shop windows you should be able to gan and get that fucking article. You should be able to gan and get it, because the best part of the fucking articles you've contributed to or your father has. Talking about tax-wise, you've contributed...

Rick: With fucking blood and sweat.

Eddy: We don't get what we fucking put into it, man, we don't get that back.

Pickard: All you make is your bus-fare back and forwards to work, isn't it?

Chris: I'll tell you what, when you write a book, if you ever want any war stories or owt like that, Eddy is your boy.

Rick: Or if you ever want to know anything about sharks.

Eddy: King Farouk. Queen Fareda.

Chris: I don't know which way you want to read into this, but he was the *camp* plumber in Egypt.

Pickard: For the elbow bends?

Chris: Aye, all the war stories, he's your man.

Pickard: Which war was that?

Chris: He's seen some wars down here.

Eddy: National Service.

[*Ronnie starts to whistle quietly to himself in the corner.*]

Chris: You obviously know that Ronnie is a retired singer? A choirboy.

Ronnie: Oh aye, me, without a doubt. (*He starts to hum.*) You're going back forty year ago.

Eddy: In these three offices there's some fucking talent, like.

Pickard: Some comedians.

Eddy: We've got a bloke here who beat fucking Sebastian Coe, running.

Pickard: Oh, I heard about him.

Chris: Who?

Jack: The Rabbit.

Chris: Especially if he sees his mate in a fight.

Rick: Eh?

Eddy: His theme song is 'Run, rabbit, run, rabbit, run.'

Rick: So would you if there was fucking twenty of the cunts.

Chris: Aye, but you left your fucking mate getting bashed up!

Rick: They were black and white bastards.[1] (*To Pickard*) No offence, Tom.

Pickard: Oh, I'm red and white,[2] when I'm over here.

Eddy: He's the type of bloke, who, if you were under fire, would volunteer to gan for the ammunition but he wouldn't come back.

Chris: We wanted a meeting once up at Roker Park.[3] It shows you how they look after the community, we wanted a mass meeting – cause we had a two-thousand membership – and we went to the company and they wanted £5,000 for a meeting cause they wanted us to sponsor a fucking game.

[*Dicky comes in for his tea break.*]

Jimmy: Amongst all shop stewards you have a village idiot.

Ronnie: You know when you got bleeped yesterday?

Dicky: Yes.

Ronnie: Where did you go when you went out?

Dicky: I went to Reaker's office.

Ronnie: There's been fucking hell on.

Dicky: I don't blame him.

Eddy: How's that?

Chris: Tell him! We've just been on about the bloke.

Dicky: The procedure was...

Eddy: Aye, but here! The foreman hasn't been able to fucking bleep you, has he?

Dicky: No.

Eddy: Right then. She could cause fucking delays.

Dicky: Since I've had this it's worked perfectly.

Eddy: Aye.

Dicky: There's been no complaints in the past. But when he started making his mouth gan...

Eddy: But you know that, your number tells you, doesn't it? When

---

1. Newcastle United Football Club supporters.
2. Sunderland Football Club colours.
3. Sunderland FC ground.

it bleeps the number comes on for where you've got to gan to. So what I'm saying is, you know if it's the fucking ambulance room.

Dicky: That's right. The first one was at the ambulance room. I went down to the lot ... She says, 'You'll have to come back for the gentleman.'

Rick gets stick

Chris: Rick had an accident and they took him to the hospital, and the nurse came out and said to the lad who was waiting, 'You might as well get yourself a cup of coffee because as soon as Rick seen the needle he fainted.'

Rick: Load of fucking shite.

Chris: He's got three stitches in his brow and the nurse said they would take them out and these two lads had to take him round there.

Eddy: We took him in to get them out...

Rick: You fucking bastard...

Eddy: ... and the nurse was taking them out...

Kevin: Your knuckles were white.

Eddy: ... and one stitch dropped down her front and I'm looking for it. And when we came out he said, 'She's hardly got owt on under that pinny...'

Pickard: There's not a stitch on her.

Eddy: While the wound was open he was trying to get his krugerrand in before it was stitched up.

Chris: Don't say anything about his krugerrand on the tape. And that's how he's got the scar on his brow that he tried to claim for.

Dicky: That lad who broke his tooth the other night, is there any dental treatment that he can charge?

Eddy: No. We tried that before.

Chris: A pipe come back and knocked the lad's teeth out, but we couldn't claim.

Pickard: But it happened at work.

Eddy: I forgot what their argument was, but we can't claim.

Eddy: Billy says to Joe the Duck – Joe the Duck was heating rivets – he says, 'Twenty to twelve, 'eat them two pies up for me, will you.' Joe ate them and Billy went mad.

70

Rick: Four letters, in the crossword ... sorry, three letters, part of the ear. Lug. I'm not kidding you, lug.

Rick: When the new MD came, he come in and spoke to us as though we were schoolkids, he made a speech. He turned round to Tony and says, 'Well, what do you want to say about that, then?' And Tony just laughed. He said, 'Well, we've had lion-tamers here before.'

Chris: Tony, he's got a fucking good vocabulary. When he finished he said: 'Any comments?' And Tony said, 'We've had these lion-tamers, the big blokes with the big boots on, coming in here.'

Eddy: You know the personnel director used to say to us, 'Don't upset him, he's a bad bugger.' And Tony would say, 'Fuck off, fuck him.' But *they* were shitting themselves.

three-point turn in a hearse

Dicky: Did I ever tell you about the time I went to the wrong house for a funeral? We all pulled up at the door to get the people. We were about five minutes early like, so we had a bit fag and a bit natter. After a while the undertaker said 'Come on we'll mak a start.' So he gans to the door and knocks. No answer. He knocks again: still no answer. So he looks in the window and this woman next door came out and says 'You've come to the wrong hoos, he's getting buried from his son's.' That was on the other side of town. We dived in the cars and there was a mad dash with everybody doing a three-point turn at once. The driver of the hearse was stopped for speeding.

Pickard: When did you do that?

Dicky: I used to do it all the time when I was on nightshift.

Chris: When he looks at you he's measuring you up.

Eddy: Keep fucking moving.

Dicky: The first page we look at in the *Echo* is the deaths, so I can work out the permutations.

Eddy: He knows his measurements. Tell him how the undertaker uses less wood.

Dicky: Pulls the feet back. Just lie in bed tonight, just forget about it and relax, and you'll find your feet are pointing away from you.

Rick: Marvellous, like.

71

Dicky: That's why they put shoes on the body. They gain two inches on the shortness of the coffin.

Eddy: When the lid gans on there's a gap; they screw it and the fucking bloke's nose get's squashed. They'd have a job with Barry Manilow.

Ronnie: Cut a hole in the top.

Dicky: We did a bloke with no legs once. We had to pack the bottom of the coffin. I'm not kidding, he'd just slide down wouldn't he? Otherwise it would have meant getting this funny-shaped coffin to stick his little body in. He'd had a war accident and they were off below the knees, so there was nowt like, just empty. When you tipped the coffin up he just slipped, and you couldn't get a coffin that sort of shape anyway. So we just got a normal coffin and packed the bottom, to keep him up the top end of the cupboard.

Eddy: His wife would have been saying, 'My, he's grown.'

Chris: What did you use?

Dicky: Egg boxes.

Pickard: Was he getting buried or hatched?

FEBRUARY

10/2/86

soaps

Dodds: There were times when we were going on the knock, canvassing, and you knew for a fact that you couldn't gan between
half-past seven and eight o'clock on a Monday or Wednesday, and
times that blend in with the soaps, 'Crossroads'. It's a fact, they
just wouldn't listen to you, 'I'm sorry,' bang, door shut. You went
back at a different time when they weren't watching 'Coronation
Street', 'Crossroads', or 'Emmerdale Farm' or whatever, they would
stand and listen to you. It was frightening.
Pickard: We should make *Nineteen Eighty-Four* into a soap.
Dodds: I was telling you there was seventy per cent and we've gotten
it back to about forty per cent. Seventy per cent not on electoral
roll. Only thirty per cent eligible to vote, seventy per cent hadn't
bothered to fill the fucking forms in, till we got that back up to
forty per cent. It's been going on for a long time if you think about
it. During the record boom-time in the fifties and sixties, people
started getting tellies and fitted carpets and things like that and just
didn't want to know. They handed it over to other people, and
again I think it is the fault of the working class, somebody that can
talk proper, that can write proper: 'They'll look after you.' I'm
talking about the intelligentsia. We've got numerous doctors, solicitors, barristers, representing us, but they've never done nowt for
me and my kind. We've always had the impression that they know
better.

> Later, over the tea break, Chris continued with his
> character assassination of Rick.

75

Chris: You see, he wants people to help him put up a fight for the blacksmiths' shop. What people want to realise is, when he gets into fights outside of the industry what does he do? Leaves his mate getting bashed up, jumps over counters and phones the police and his poor fucking mate is left in the gutter, fucked. Right, Mick? That's what he telt us.

Rick: I didn't say he was left in the gutter, fucked.

Geordie: Left in the gutter and all. There was about ten of the bastards kicking shit out of him.

Rick: I was doing the right thing, I was calling for the cops.

Chris: Aye, but what I'm getting at is, how can he fight for the blacksmiths' shop...

Rick: There wasn't ten of them when I went for the coppers, man...

Chris: ...and he leaves his mate with ten of them kicking fuck out of him?

George: That's without the lasses, mind.

Rick: Soon as I left them, they realised, 'Now is our chance, he's went to the phone so let's fuck off.'

Chris: Aye, but what did you do when you went for the phone? Geordie was getting kicked to fuck.

Geordie: Why they were kicking me to fuck was because I had two of them. You see I pulled the two that were keeping me in the car while he was getting a kicking, because he got a bit of a kicking. I kicked me way out of the car, right. And the two kids who I had over the car... they all looked round and I had a hold of these two boys. So I just went down. And I went down on the deck and their fucking heads cracked off the decks. And I just went into a ball because I couldn't do much. And they all come for me.

Chris: Aye, and this time you were where?

Rick: I had about twenty on top of me. That's right! And he come over and they all dispersed, and when they went like that, they just split like that, I was away down into the Chinky's over the counter to phone the police. And while I was doing that they fucking jumped him again.

Chris: The Chinky says, 'No need to phone we will give you orders straight away.'

Eddy: 'Nine-nine-nine, quick.' And the Chinky says, 'With chips or wice?'

76

Geordie: I was in the middle of the road, outside the shops in Thorny Close and this lad pulled up in a car, a white car, and he got out of the car and ran over and he was going to start kicking into these kids and give me a hand. So I said, 'Hey mate, I'd fuck off if I was you, there's too many of them.' So he fucked off, the twat.

Chris: 'Me mate's somewhere.'

Eddy: How did you get them fucking words out?

Geordie: Well, you see, they turned around to see what he was doing.

Chris: Right, when you phoned the coppers, all right they took five or ten minutes to get there, did you come back out of the shop?

Rick: Why, aye, I come back out the shop.

Chris: And what did you say – 'I phoned for the coppers'?

Eddy: He thought he'd help the Chinky and serve a few portions of chips.

Geordie: This all happened in about three minutes.

Chris: This is what I'm trying to get at: this bloke, is there fight in him? He's not one of these lads that runs away from a battle?

Geordie: One of them was a local thief, a burglar, and he was about eighteen.

Ronnie: Did you floor any of them?

Geordie: The two I got a hold of by the back of the hair were about sixteen or seventeen. They were shouting for their mates. I was going to bang their heads together and gan in where he was getting a kicking but, by the time I had gotten a hold of the back of their heads and started to walk forward and looked round, they were coming for me. That's where he got his chance to get away.

Ronnie: How did it start?

Geordie: One of them fell down in front of a bus...

Rick: We were driving along the road and instead of getting out of the way ... they were kicking the bus in front of us...

Geordie: I drove straight on and they had to jump out the way. I didn't think they would come over, like. Well, there was only about three of them at that time.

Ronnie: Did they catch up to the car?

Geordie: Well, we only went about twenty yards further on.

Rick: We only went for a fucking Chinky. We didn't get one, like. Well, I did.

Chris: The best part was when they went back home and he was telling me you were obviously cut to fucking ribbons and shirt hanging off you and Rick walks in the house...

Geordie: There was me kicked to fuck, me gold chain missing, me shirt ripped off at the collar, and jumper ripped to fuck.

Chris: And Rick walks in with a chicken chow mein and not a mark on him...

Geordie: ...and I never felt a thing until the next morning. I had a right skinful.

Chris: Another time he ran into somebody's house. You don't know that one do you?

Rick: Again, outnumbered.

Eddy: Imagine the family sitting and watching the television and a strange bloke comes straight into the sitting room.

Rick: There was thirty or forty lads ... OK, twenty.

Tommy: Any advance on twenty?

Rick: Twenty, you know, roughly. I mean, I didn't stand and fucking count the cunts. There was only four of us. So anyway we gets off the bus, these little young'uns giving it that, you know, Newcastle supporters through there like, black and white bastards, and we just ignored them, you know, daft little kids. The next thing we know they must have went round the community centre and tells all their mates and all their mates comes out and after us. So we just started to leg it up the street. Obviously the fittest survive, otherwise you have to be a canny runner. We didn't realise that one of the lads at the back just fucking went fucking over and had got the biggest kicking. We didn't know he was down. We kept on running and another lad dived off another way, and me and my mate, this lad following me, kept on running and went straight into this house: through the back door, through the kitchen and into the sitting room and here is the fucking people sitting watching the telly. Well, the reaction on their faces!

Geordie: Did he not tell you the rest of the story about the police?

Chris: You see Rick is always getting the fight ready...

Eddy: There is one thing about him, he is always getting mugged though, you've got to admit it.

Chris: As I say, if he had the old bottle there would be nowt stopping him.

I'd been reading an article/manifesto in the *Guardian* by the playwright Howard Barker and Tony Dunne, then photocopied a few and left them on the table. It led to a discussion.

art and class

Tony: Well it's arguing ... which way we are gannin', possibly in art. What we look for in art is all a reflection of Thatcher's monetarism really, isn't it? Anything you pay for is all right. You enjoy a thing more because you paid for it, and you've got to be seen to pay for it, and the people that's doing it are well paid and all part of your structure. They are élitist in their own field, watched by élitists and so that makes you feel comfortable in your situation knowing full well you've got a pocket full of money to pay for that kind of entertainment, and that's why it is good. And you cannot understand the thick-headed bastards at the bottom who don't understand it and nor do they want to, and you just dismiss them as the rest of the fucking crap. People, artists, are losing their way in the fucking philistine situation where it's just entertainment for entertainment's sake. All the capitalists do is self-feeding, it's self-feeding for the selves. They've got that much money, they've got that much leisure, they don't know what to friggin' do with themselves, and so they invent things, situations, entertainments, goods, whatever, to sustain their fucking will or need to fucking be seen to be succeeding, successful and enjoying life. And really they are fucking not, but they dinna fucking know it. They are conning them-fucking-selves that they are enjoying life by enjoying that sort of fucking entertainment you are talking about. Edward Heath and them – even he said, when they put the fucking charges on the fucking museums, 'My mother always said to me that you only enjoy something when you are paying for it, and if you get it for nowt then it is not worth fucking having.' And that's basically what it's about.

Pickard: But he is also saying, 'The Marxists in the Labour party still haven't advanced (in terms of the arts) beyond William Morris, a rich communist whose utopia is peopled with dull weavers and upright sanitary inspectors with no wit, no passion and very little sex. It reads just like the autobiography of Roy Hattersley.'

Tony: I would disagree violently with that. As a socialist I don't, and nor does any socialist I know, see everything as clear black and white as everybody being regimented and everybody being in their happy little homes. I know society doesn't work like that. There's got to be a place for culture, for leisure time, and in a Marxist socialist society there's got to be more so. We're going to spend more time on leisure. I find that a majority of socialists find the expression of their fulfilment, of why they live, of why they're here, is to help somebody, to help somebody less fortunate than yourself and that's which way you feed yourself, feed your ego, by helping, by pulling together and by all surviving together.

Pickard: There's a place for pleasure though, isn't there? And for self-enrichment, which is art.

Tony: Naturally. People will say 'art', and our people, our class, doesn't realise what they are talking about and don't have a lot to do with art. But I'll tell you one thing they do do, they know how to manufacture things, and, what I say is the greatest intelligence, the greatest intelligence of making something original, or making something with your hands. And you've only got to look round some of the allotments that working-class lads build up and see how much they've put into them, how much of their lives they've put into them, and how brilliant is the way they organise them. They get fulfilment out of growing flowers, leek shows, you know, fulfilment out of making things, or even drawing. Because that's the only way they can motivate their desire. It's a lie, everybody knows it's a lie, that people don't want to work. People do want to work, they do want to do something that they enjoy doing. There are all different aspects: the likes of Geordie in his workman's club, he gets fulfilment by making that club run well. All right there's some ego in it and he can say, 'I'm chairman of that club and it's making money.' All right, there's nowt wrong with that, as long as the members are getting the benefit. Brian likes to run a fucking football team and likes to help the young boys come through. All sorts of things like that. There's nowt wrong with that, it's part of what you do with your leisure time.

Pickard: I'm not saying that there's no working-class culture. In some ways they are also part-time activities, they have to be if you are a working man, but art should be professional. You describe two things there: one is a kind of activity like building an allotment, or running a garden, pigeons, clubs, etc., but you also referred to drawing. But with drawing there are specific techniques employed – as in shipbuilding, as there are in all art forms – that can be developed. As you know, there have been some revolutions in the arts. Skills can be developed to a fine point. My argument would be that you've got to make all the tools of art available and accessible to working-class people so that they can become full-time artists should their commitment be deep enough and their skills, talent and luck take them that far.

Tony: That was one of the arguments that we put up when we accepted you as a placement writer, because we said, 'OK, we might have a lad in the yard who's got a latent talent for writing, or drawing, or photography, but you need somebody to be able to show him how to do it to the best of his ability.' Some of the lads, they just do it themselves, and they're good. Drawing, for example at school, you get an arts teacher who's probably not even skilled in art himself, but he'll maybe show you the basics. But you don't get to know the best ways to use shades, or the best ways to use colours, what colours complement each other and what don't, whether it's best in black and white, whether it's best in colour; all them techniques, like you say, as we learnt all the techniques of welding, or building a ship, there are techniques also employed to be an artist or a writer. That's part of what you are supposed to be doing in here; if we've got any lads who've put pen to paper, but find it extremely difficult; they need help to do that. But at the end, when they've done it and they read it in print, it must be a hell of a fulfilment for themselves.

Pickard: The real pleasure has to come in the making, though.

Tony: Also, what we are saying, in every aspect of life we are denied access to certain areas: areas I've just covered. To rule your own life, to fulfil your own abilities to the extreme – I don't care what you are, whether you are the best fucking dustbin man in the world, as long as you are given the opportunity to be just that – and that's what's being denied. There's four million that can't get nowhere. Not even allowed to get on the fucking starting-blocks, all the potential is fucking gone. So there's other lads with abilities that's not even tapped, they might be the best artists, best song-writers, writing lyrics just like that, poetry just like that, just rolls off the top – don't have to think about it – but nobody is even helping, encouraging, or cultivating them to do just that. And a society that

81

is a caring society and a socialist society allows people to just do that: self-fulfilment.

Pickard: But we should be doing that, now. You know your argument of not having so many slavery 'how we got shit kicked out of us' wimpy songs, shouldn't we assume that we are in Paradise now, as it were? At least if we are not building Jerusalem in England's bright and pleasant land . . . Shouldn't we be taking the things now and demanding things even though we are still in the middle of a war, a class war, we should start actually taking some of the fruits of victory which we want when we fucking get there, and start fucking having them now, wherever we can?

Tony: Fair enough comment: start writing some songs and we'll listen to them.

Pickard: Is that a commission? I think you should put a resolution to your union that you have a permanent . . .

Tony: Writer! And a singer!

Pickard: In every yard! Singer, artist, photographer . . .

Tony: Like Robin Hood had, he had his own fucking . . .

Paul: Minstrels.

Tony: What did they call them?

Paul: Minstrels.

Tony: I know that, I mean his name, Robin Hood's minstrels. Alan Adair, was it?

Pickard: That's what the upper class has. In a sense it should be built in as a right to every fucking working institution like this. You should have, as well as your fucking medical officers and so on, and your union, shop stewards, you should have an artist available to fucking help bring on any fucking talent and to give advice and direction to fucking anybody in the yard whos's got that and also to research the history and document the place. That's what the unions should be fighting for as well, I reckon.

Tony: Then the constraints of the system start to come up on you. Who decides who gets it? Not only decides who gets it: if you want extra-curricular activities outside, who decides who is going to go there? How do you decide? Because straight away they would be saying, 'Look at him, he's just looking for an easy way out of shipbuilding, because it is a dirty stinking job and he's getting himself in and he's away.'

Pickard: I suppose what you do then, if it's not just a junket, and a free ride for somebody – and I say everybody is entitled to that

82

anyway – is you would know that certain people had been to regular meetings and they've obviously been developing their particular talent.

Tony: One of the good things about Marx is he's easy to understand. It's easy what he is saying, and even Trotsky and them get mixed up on the theory and you divvint know what they are fucking talking about. You hear different aspects of what Trotsky is saying on Marx, and Lenin even, but you gan back and read basic Marxism and it is simple and easy and I can understand what he's talking about. I need a dictionary to read this article.

Pickard: The bloke who wrote this article teaches in a polytechnic and the bloke who wrote the aphorisms is a playwright.

Tony: I've never read that one.

Pickard: Well this one is full of short pithy things like 'a carnival is not a revolution: after the removal of the masks you are precisely who you were before', 'ideology is the outcome of pain' . . . Some of them are quite interesting and not bad.

Mack: Who were they aiming at when they were writing that kind of stuff?

Pickard: Well, I think he was aiming this one at the intellectual left.

Mack: It worries me when you start talking like that: 'the intellectual left'.

Pickard: Well, there is an intellectual left.

Mack: I know but that worries me, because they have got nothing in common with what I've got . . . Maybe their aims are the same as mine, I don't know, but they don't come across that way, mind. They always come across to me: 'We'll tell you what it's about, we can educate you; what you've learnt at school is a load of shite because you've been taught by . . . we'll tell you what it's about.' I'm afraid they lose me off.

Pickard: Obviously there has to be a dialogue.

Mack: Half the time they lose me off, talking over your head, and I think they do it deliberate as well.

Pickard: It still doesn't get over the point . . . Mind you, the medium is the message, you could say, but you still can't get away from the issue that he makes some interesting points. Some of them are aimed at Kinnock! He's arguing against populism in art forms . . .

Mack: What do you mean by populism? Popular reforms and things like that?

Pickard: No. He's talking about, in terms of art, things like

83

'Coronation Street' ... something addressed to a broad mass of people ... without ...

Mack: To the masses and it's the wrong message?

Pickard: ... ideology. I think *message* is the business of individual artists. I think they are also talking about the form.

Mack: I got that, when I read it, which I agree with. Because people tend to forget because they are watching 'Eastenders' and 'Coronation Street' ... they think, well, things aren't so bad, it's not that bad. Because their brains are just addled. As far as that gans it's like their lifestyles as well ... But there is no message at all. There is no hope in it. I suppose that is what they are trying to say but it is the way they do it that gets me. But there the difficulty lies. The shop stewards we know round here, we chat with the workforce round here to get the message across. Now, if I went out spouting that stuff in the article I wouldn't be a shop steward five minutes. They'd say, 'Fuck off, you daft cunt.' If you want to put the message across you've got to get down to basics.

Pickard: What if you are putting the same message across in terms of 'Coronation Street'?

Mack: I don't put it across in that way.

Pickard: How do you put it across?

Mack: I put it across exactly the way I said: 'Coronation Street', 'Eastenders', the dribble that comes on the telly, the programmes that are imported from America. 'This is what success means, "Dynasty" and "Dallas", this can be your lifestyle,' if you like, for the people over here living in drudgery. It's just escapism!

Pickard: So how would you see art – the function of art – in that case? If art can be said to have a function ... what is the function of the artist now?

Mack: I don't know because I am not into the arts ... and I don't see life through rose-coloured glasses, I see as it actually is and that is fucking raking your arse down here at seven o'clock in the morning. And that is life, and your only escape from that is your weekend off, or your nights off where you can go for a pint ... What they do with that time, I don't know ... I couldn't fill that void for them. I've got me own ideas. I'm active, if you like, in the Labour Party and the trade union movement. That's not relaxation at all, that's a fight all the time. There is no relaxation. All you do for relaxation is go out and have a few pints. The people I am drinking with, they are exactly the same as me, you tend not to get

84

away from it at all, you are talking about it all the time: the Labour Party, work, the political situation. You cannot get away from it at all: the drudgery comes in. I assume everybody else is like that. The lads in here, when they get away from here they just want to forget about this fucking place and have a few pints at night and their game of bingo or whatever. That's how low we have sunk. You cannot activate them to think otherwise. Whether they are sickened and cannot see the end of it, I don't know. Who would have thought six years ago, or seven years ago, when she first come in, that there would be four million unemployed now, and nobody's done fuck all about it! I would have thought there would have been a revolution. Four million unemployed! What do you do? Nobody is doing nowt! They've battered us and battered us all the time and there is no response.

Pickard: He is putting the same point that you are: he is aiming part of it at Kinnock, and on the other hand artists engaged in theatre and other art forms...

Mack: Our ward meeting tomorrow night, it's very trendy, what we would call 'the flaccid left', very trendy...

Paul: Middle-class.

Pickard: Don't we need allies in the middle-class?

Mack: A few years ago before the boundary changes it was a very industrial-based ward and we have lost that. They changed the ward boundaries and we've lost that. It's gone from bad to worse. And they admit they are middle-class, they don't profess to be nowt else and they just bore the arse off me, and that is my own kind, supposedly.

Pickard: I think we need allies right across the class spectrum.

Mack: I've heard that argument before. Everybody can make a case for themselves of how they should be getting more money, I know that. Schoolteachers and all. But when I've said to these advice workers, at the end of the day if it comes down to it they are only friendly with the Labour Group in this town because the Labour Group funds them. Whoever was funding them they would be spouting their fucking politics. And I have always said, at the end of the day, 'If it comes down to it, if you lost that job, your fifteen-to-nineteen grand a year or whatever, to ally yourself to the working class you would lose that.' They fucking don't want to know. 'Don't talk like that: that's revolution that, lad.' They don't want to know.

Pickard: How do they ally themselves to the working class? By being more articulate and putting the case across more forcibly, or being more active or what?

Mack: Well they align themselves with the working class by standing alongside them if you like instead of talking down to them.

Pickard: On picket lines?

Mack: Anywhere, anything...

Pickard: OK, but you have the lumpen proletariat who are the uninformed, apathetic, couldn't give a fuck.

Mark: Which is the majority here...

> Later that day I spoke to Jake. British Shipbuilders had just announced the formation of a new company, North East Shipbuilders Ltd (NESL), which would entail the amalgamation of Smith's Docks on the Tees, Sunderland Shipbuilders on the south bank of the Wear, and Austin and Pickersgill's. I asked Jake how he thought it would affect the workforce.

North East Shipbuilders Ltd (NESL)

Jake: We heard rumours and half-expected it. The boss met us on Thursday morning at half-past eight and apparently while he was meeting us the other two companies were also meeting their representatives and putting forward the same statement. What it means to us is ... well, in BS accounts last year they had us down as closed and the Oldendorf ships saved us because he would only have them built at A&P, so that gave us a breathing space. Even inside that they then tried to stick us with a two-year wage freeze, and that was obviously trying to bring us close together with the other two yards that are mentioned in there. They failed on that so now they come in with this plan and what they'll do is just starve us of work, close us and then, if some of us get started back it will be on twenty pound a week less than we are actually getting now. So the immediate impact is going to come on the staff union: as I have said they are not going to keep the three departments going at three different yards when you've got one consortium. You are going to centralise it.

Pickard: Was this given to you the same time as it was given to the press?

Jake: Yes. There was a D-notice on it until twelve o'clock, I think, as a press statement. At the same time as we got a visit at half-past ten, Day was informing the press at Benton House with a similar statement.

Pickard: There was no consultation with the workforce in these regions about the reorganisation whatsoever?

Jake: They wouldn't even dream of doing that. It's an executive decision that has been took, as they see it, in the long-term best interests of the corporation, I suppose. You notice that P— becomes the new managing director, overall. What he said was that he couldn't really be specific on what was going to happen because until they set up this new review body, which obviously will consist of the new board I think, then it is difficult, as he put it, to answer any question. I don't believe for one minute he doesn't know who is going to be on that board.

Pickard: So a lot of directors will go?

Jake: Oh aye. Then again, they've got three boards. We've got six directors now and how many have they got at Sunderland Shipbuilders? Nine? Then you've got Smith's. So obviously you are only going to need one board for the three subsidiaries as long as they last.

Pickard: What was your immediate reaction to the bulletin?

Jake: Not one of surprise because we realised something like this was on the cards. The proximity of Austin and Pickersgill and Sunderland Shipbuilders makes it easy to do that, and I suppose at the end of the day it would have been silly if they hadn't done it.

Pickard: And they are maintaining the difference in the wages on either side of the river?

Jake: They say that each will maintain its identity and conditions of employment. But, having said that, on the work-load: if we don't get any more orders then we've got an under-utilisation of labour again, and obviously if that carries on, come the end of the year, there will be nobody in the yard. That will be it, finished.

Pickard: What is this phrase 'utilisation of labour'?

Jake: It just means people that have got a job and people that haven't. What he's saying there is: by the spring of 1986 he'll have a surplus of three hundred and ten direct employees. So there will be three hundred and ten who will not be gainfully employed by that time, and then seven hundred and fifty by the end of November, which in effect would be only steelworkers and ancillaries that work with them.

Pickard: Does this have any clause in it for moving people from one side of the river to another, if there is work over there?

Jake: It doesn't say that, but that is obviously the idea of it.

Pickard: Do they get the same kind of order over there? Do they build the same kind of ships?

Jake: They can do but at the present time they are on with the two Stena [oil-related support] vessels, which are very sophisticated vessels, and they are just starting with a big crane barge.

Pickard: Could they be built on either side of the river?

Jake: Oh yes. Smith Docks is actually building SD15s – our design, which brought in containerisation – and they are building them at the Smith Docks yard.

Pickard: With them centralising regionally, any orders that might come to Austin and Pickersgill because of its reputation – like the orders from Oldendorf – could they shove them to one of the other yards where the wages are lower?

Jake: They could. Obviously that would be the first step for trying to get a parity deal on wages, through just starving us of work. So, if you have no work in the yard, with the best will in the world, it's hard to mount any kind of fight. And you don't get much public sympathy, if any, because they say, 'Oh well, there is no work, so what?' But inside of it all it seems as though now they have come down more or less to the core numbers and they are willing to keep the merchant sector ticking over. There is only four big yards left, there is them three on that paper [A&P, Sunderland Shipbuilders, Smith's Docks], and there is Govan on the Clyde. Then you've got Ailsa Ferguson which is a small yard, and Appledore which is about the same size. So, inside that consortium now, it means that if there was parity of wages I have no doubt they would just pull people about willy-nilly where they needed them. That's the stumbling-block at the present time, and that's what they've done it for.

Pickard: The guys who come up here from Appledore are on lower wages, are they?

Jake: No. You see Appledore is different in the sense that there is a national transfer agreement throughout BS, and that lays down what people get who transfer from a parent yard to a different yard. Now they actually get less than our wage, it's only one hundred and forty-five a week, but inside an agreement like this ... now, where the national transfer agreement would gan, I would believe it would disappear, because what they are saying is there are three separate yards but it is a new company, NESL, so they will probably change the contract of employment that you don't work for Austin and Pickersgill but that you work for NESL and therefore wherever we need to utilise the labour inside that consortium, that's where you'll gan. Obviously it won't be as straightforward and simple as that, but that's the aim of it I believe.

Pickard: From their point of view that's what they are obviously aiming for?

Jake: Well it would be beneficial to them because it would casualise the labour market again to a certain extent.

Pickard: Will NESL be a private company?

Jake: No, it's still under BS, but because of the close proximity of the three yards they've just brought them together.

Pickard: So what's your reaction as a confed? How are you dealing with it?

Jake: Well, the reaction is pretty much what I've already said, we feel that they have brought it in possibly as a back-door method to close Austin and Pickersgill or certainly to level down the wages. They are not going to give the other two subsidiaries a twenty pound a week increase, so the obvious way to do it is to reduce our wages. And the only thing that would change the thinking was if we got orders immediately and that doesn't seem likely. But even that wouldn't take the problem away completely because we are talking about steelwork orders. So if it is only steelwork then we have got a problem again come November with the outfitters.

Pickard: Did you say the other yard in Middlesbrough can build the same kind of ships? Is it the same size yard?

Jake: It's not as big. It's a little bit smaller yard and they are building SDs now.

Pickard: Can you remind me how you've got a difference of twenty quid in your wage packets from people in the other yards?

Jake: It gans back to 1969. No, that was the boilermakers' agreement, wasn't it?

Tony: The way the differential started to increase was because of bonus earnings. We consolidated bonus earnings on the understanding that there would be no allowances. So then we got the bonus earnings consolidated at a wage with a permanent lump in there.

89

Pickard: What kind of allowances? The allowances that fluctuated depending on conditions?

Tony: That's right. So we don't have any allowances. They used to be: confined space allowance, paint allowances, dirty money, on the beach, on the sleck, on moving to dirtier yards.

Pickard: So everybody across the board in the yard gets all this money that others would get working in those conditions? So it is more sensible to build it into the wage packet?

Tony: We thought it was.

Pickard: Why didn't the union take it up nationally as a policy they could apply across the board?

Tony: Because there was that much disunity and differences in different yards amongst the differentials that there was no way that certain groups would give their traditional allowances up. It wasn't just allowances, it was a parity agreement that covered everything, and a lot of yards will just not do it that way. The groups within the yards will not allow that to happen.

Kenny: They think they are better off and they see their allowances threatened.

Pickard: So you were able to achieve some kind of solidarity across the board with benefits stretching to everybody.

Tony: The last big dispute we had was 1973/74 and we were out for two months, the boilermakers were on strike about the ability to earn the same as the outfit trades who then widened the differential between us. They were getting more than us. So it come to a head with a dispute. They were laid off. And we got promised that, on the understanding that it was during the first miners' strike, and where we had a negotiated position prior to the miners' strike, as soon as the miners went on strike, because of all the problems it would cause in industry then, and did cause, that the management were just prepared to leave us. Because it meant they couldn't continue: the steel would be cut off, the power would be cut off, so it made no difference us being on strike really, so we had to come back and negotiate a deal, which we did, on the understanding that we would achieve eventual parity with outfit trades. And that was achieved in April, and if you remember the Labour government was elected in February or March and there was a period of free collective bargaining in which we – the boilermakers – got an increase of twelve pound. Well, the experience of that dispute ... the increase started to push us up to the outfitters although not

90

totally in parity with them, it didn't come until about 1974, because we were again threatening industrial action. That drove the other trades more towards us and towards a common understanding, and we started to have meetings among ourselves, because we realised what we were doing was just riving lumps off each other. And so when that understanding came about, that's when the agreement on overtime and parity of earnings for everybody and a joint bonus scheme came in. And the first joint bonus scheme was about 1974/75, and when we had that joint bonus scheme, the way they bought the other trades out was they gave them a compensatory payment where they were earning more than us, they guaranteed them a parity situation and bought the bonuses out. And that's how we came to be all on the one agreement. And, ever after that, it just followed on, we just kept in line with one another.

The first one was a skilled trades agreement, that's us and the outfitters, then about a year later, maybe two years later, the general workers came into the scheme of things. That would be about 1976/77 and since then we've all been together.

Pickard: Do you think that could be a model for the rest of the industry? Or are there disadvantages in it now in the way you operate it?

Tony: I think it was on the correct path. There's no doubt about it, it's the right way to gan. And it has kept us together more than I would say any other yard, although we have suffered the same as any other yard. At least we have kept the organisation intact, and all we can say is we have usually been the last to succumb to certain proposals that BS have had on the board. We have been pushed and pushed along the line into certain situations that we've accepted, but the organisation is still there, plus the fact that they haven't gotten a hell of a lot. You know we've still got parity of overtime agreement which they've tried to break down. And we've still got tight control of the organisation in the yard and the subcontractors and the likes of that, that's one of the benefits of sticking together.

Pickard: Wouldn't it be in your interests to try and spread this agreement abroad to other yards?

Tony: I always say that ours might be a great blueprint, but at the same time I cannot base our blueprint on another yard. It doesn't work like that, it's evolving systems, and agreements just evolve over a period of time and I couldn't gan to Swan's and say, 'Look, that's our parity of overtime, you should work it like that,' because there would be all hell let loose. The outfitters in Swan's would see that as an erosion of their standard of living and they just wouldn't have it. It would just sow disruption. It's a gradual process.

Pickard: Has anybody from other yards shown any interest?

Tony: Oh aye, they all show interest in how we operate the overtime in particular, because it is always a problem for them. They are always squealing; one set's squealing about the other getting more overtime.

Pickard: Does that mean with the parity of overtime here that there is equal overtime for all the trades in the yards and that everybody who works in the yard is guaranteed so many weeks overtime over a period?

Tony: Aye. You see, it's not necessary for certain people to work overtime in certain situations because there is no work for them. When you have a full volume of work there are six and seven, eight ships a year. You build a programme on forty-seven hours a week, seven hours of them being overtime, so then it is always necessary for people who work overtime to have a parity overtime situation. When the order book starts to decline you haven't got that luxury of a throughput of a mass of work in all areas where they require overtime. So, what I have done recently is to say that initially the boilermakers, the steelworkers, will work overtime but the outfitters will not be required to work overtime, and then at the end of the programme the boilermakers will stop working and the outfitters will start to work overtime so you've got a balance. They've just done that the other week...

Pickard: Summarising: with the lack or orders, does it mean that at some time though there is overtime built in to protect wages when there's not the work there to do?

Tony: The outfit's not working any overtime January, early February, and they start to come on in the third week in February; they start to work two half-shifts and a Sunday, where we've been working earlier. And at the other end of the programme in August/September they are working and we are not. All that programme means that the capability of the steelworkers is one thousand seven hundred and fifteen pound and eight pence, the outfit one thousand seven hundred and ten pounds nineteen pence and the night shift one thousand seven hundred and thirteen pound sixty-nine pence, so you can see it is equal. Regarding built-in overtime: the company build in the overtime, the levels of overtime cover what their labour

92

requirements are – and haven't got because they've made that many people redundant in the first place – and cover absenteeism. If the absenteeism runs at ten per cent then you can guarantee that the overtime levels are running at ten per cent. Overtime is a cheaper form of labour than employing a bloke; you don't have to pay stamps for him, you don't have to pay machinery costs, or all his equipment and that, so you just let a bloke work overtime and it is cheap labour. Unfortunately we have come to such a stage that the wages is that poor that really you've got no option but to work overtime. Without overtime you couldn't survive. Once we used to have a greater control over the levels of overtime. We would reduce the levels of overtime to try to force the company to start labour, but, with the situation as it's went, the majority of the unemployed volunteering for redundancy, it would be difficult to argue with the lads that they should restrict their earning capacity to get lads, who had already sold their jobs, back in the yard. That just wouldn't happen.

Pickard: So all the redundancies you've had so far have been voluntary?

Tony: Aye.

Pickard: The argument doesn't extend to the people from other yards who might have been made redundant compulsorily?

Tony: They haven't been in shipbuilding. In engineering they have been.

wages

Tony: Last year me gross pay was £7,523. I did better in 1983 than I did in 1984. The general wages throughout the northern regions have declined against the standard of living. They still continue to say that wages have gone up as fast as inflation and they keep on saying it: our wages haven't; the manuals at the bottom, their wages haven't. The broad spectrum of other people's wages have gone up; we know that particularly in the middle-class areas their wages has went up; lawyers, doctors, dentists, all their wages have went up massively. The national average. But we are saying the actual manual workers' has went down; our position as shipbuilders: in the manual workers' wages' league we used to be round about second; now we are round about twenty-third.

93

George: If we were in the football divisions we would have been relegated.

Tony: The depression has took a toll on the wages. And it's also a reason why a lot of lads leave the industry, not that they are ganna get a better-paid job anywhere else because there is none. Or very few and far between. All right they might obtain employment on the rigs, on the oil rigs of the North Sea, or travel to Saudi Arabia, but they are only short gaps to fill in. There is no long-term prospects for employment, none whatsoever.

George: But even when they are on the rigs they are so many weeks on and so many weeks off without pay. If you take that average across the time when they get shore leave, the wages are still low.

Tony: What is happening now in the rig industry in particular is that, because market forces are prevailing and more and more people are unemployed, there is a wider range to pick from. And where a rig worker eighteen months ago would be getting five and six pound an hour, maybe working two weeks on and two weeks off, on full pay; now that's been reduced to about four pound an hour and two weeks on and two weeks off without pay. There are that many people who have flooded the labour market that are prepared to take anything, as long as it is some kind of job. And that starts to undercut, like everything else, the supply and demand of labour. You've got a glut of it. It's cheap. The trouble with us – in the good times, instead of screwing the arse off them, we don't.

George: There used to be about three joiners working to one cabin, or one berth as we would call it. And their wages at the time used to be about forty or sixty per cent lower than ours, but at the end of the week they might be getting more than us because of the actual overtime they were working. They were playing the Cole Porter tune 'Night and Day', and they wouldn't stand up and fight: overtime was their king, as long as the overtime was there they didn't bother about the basic earning. They might be working three half-shifts and all day Saturday and half-day Sunday where we weren't. We were still strictly individual piece-workers, we got paid by our own output.

Tony: If they are short of labour why didn't they take their people back and let us stand and fight and say that you've got to start people off the dole, and they've got to start on the same terms and conditions of employment as what I'm on. Instead, they are not covered by pensions, they are not covered by health and safety regulations, no overalls, boots, they are not covered by the Employment Protection Act.[1] It is casual labour and the dangers are that you are building in another group of people that will work with their heads in a bucket of shite, because they've been on the stones maybe since 1978 when the first redundancies were and now they've got a job back. Are they going to shout about conditions? Are they going to complain to the foreman? Are they going to complain to the manager? They start to undercut and undermine the wages and conditions, they try to get kept on.

Jack: I was talking to one of the shop stewards who took a look at the job vacancies at SS and they are only for five weeks apparently. Bloggs got a letter to get down there for an interview.

Pickard: So obviously there is no way you'll allow that to happen here ... but if the orders are reduced it's obvious from their point of view ... they'll put the order in the other yards. If the government says, 'OK, we'll keep a merchant shipbuilding capacity, but the reality of the market-place means we've got to rationalise a little bit and we'll keep something in the North-East, Middlesbrough and SS is what we can afford to keep' ... what do you say then?

Tony: We are knackered. What do you do? There is very little you can do about it when they start to say, 'OK, there is work over there, they've got work, you can either take your redundancy or gan over there on their conditions.'

Pickard: Which is why they include in here: 'each maintains his identity and conditions of employment.' It's not to protect you, it is to undermine you, to keep the other wages down?

Tony: That's right.

Jack: Plus the threat of the Redundancy Payment Act finishing. People who have got long-term service in are worried about that, there are one or two left.

1. The Employment Protection Act was introduced by the Labour government in 1964 to protect workers' lives and livelihoods in industries prone to casualisation.

95

Pickard: What is the effect of that?

Tony: It ends in 1986.

Jack: It's like a bloke leaving here under that threat, as Tony says, a bloke here, the likes of me for example with the full hog in, and I stop here in this yard and it runs out of work: he says, 'Right, you get your lot,' not forgetting behind your mind is the Redundancy Payment Act finishing, and you go over there.

Pickard: So when the Redundancy Payment Act comes to an end you don't get redundancy?

Tony: You get the state one but the major part of your redundancy pay is made up of BS's one which comes to an end at the end of the year. If you see that document there you'll see every yard's order book just about comes to an end at the end of the year. And that dovetails in with the end of the redundancy scheme. It is the easy way of closing the industry down if you want to, because how would I be able to mount a campaign if they are offering redundancy money and transfer? 'You can gan over there or get your lot.' It's as simple as that. Now if I say, 'No, we are gannin' to stop here and occupy the yard and fuck the fucking redundancy scheme and fuck that job over there.' So on two flanks I'm outflanked, and the lads would just dive out, they'd grab for the fucking money. They would even do what they've just done to the printers. 'So, all reet, you take industrial action you have severed your fucking contract, you get no redundancy, you get fucking fuck-all, so you can please your fucking self what you do.'

Jack: You are goosed. It doesn't matter what you do, you're goosed. You've got big decisions to make, what do you do, like? If we gan over there, rather than take your lot, how long are we ganna be employed for? What work have they got? It's short-term again.

Tony: We would have to see if there is any work, and it is very debatable whether there is any work there, or whether they can sustain the merchant sector.

Pickard: But they could create the work.

Tony: But the problem is the work is not there. We cannot look at ourselves in isolation and say, 'There is always orders there if they want them.' Aye, but at a certain subsidy which the government is not prepared to pay, and as everybody's order books stands now ... ours finish in November, and theirs is finished with the crane barge that they've got.

Jack: It's like the fucking Grand National, the hurdles is getting

96

bigger and bigger, you just cannot get over them. There is brick walls on all fucking flanks.

Tony: If they don't get you one way they're getting you a-fucking-other.

Pickard: It's economic fascism.

Jack: Of course it is. Putting the three yards together has fucking nailed us. It's the only way to get rid of the differential of twenty pound. We are a thorn in BS's side, and when you tell the lads out there on the shopfloor some of them don't believe it. They believe it, but they don't want to know, especially the young lads. They are shitting themselves, aren't they?

Pickard: Wouldn't you have more clout if you were all on the same wage with similar union structure as you have here?

Jack: They are already saying they want the same money as us.

Tony: It's about time they took action to get the same money as us.

Pickard: Do they know that?

Tony: They are saying it but they are doing nowt about it. They'd far rather we were pulled down as them come up to us, because they haven't got to do fuck all about it.

Pickard: It seems to me that as long as you are isolated you are fucked. You cannot speak with a regional voice and they are just going to play you off one against the other anyway.

Tony: That's what they are ganna do, but there is no way I can go to the meeting and say, 'Right lads you've got to take twenty quid a week less.'

Ronnie: You wouldn't get out of the fucking hall!

Tony: 'And the good news is that it's backdated.'

Jack: We'd be fucking dredging. There was a lad here put a cartoon up of a dredger dragging bodies out of the river, mortgages, holidays. Classic. It was a fucking topper . . .

Tony: We've got twenty-six of theirs over here and he is gettting short-term contracts in over there. Every time we want labour they just push them over here and start short-term contracts over there on a lower rate. You fucker.

Mack: Our long-term prospects are fucking zero. It's down there in writing what's going to happen, we must secure an order by the spring otherwise three hundred and ten are surplus in September rising to seven hundred and fifty in November. In other words virtually the complete workforce: the prospects are fucking zero. And that's all the steelworkers and ancillaries.

97

Jack: We are just gobbling up the work.

Pickard: Why don't you stop the overtime?

Mack: You are in a situation where you need the overtime to meet the delivery dates. It's a catch twenty-two situation. If you don't meet your delivery dates you won't get any more orders, so if you put restrictive practices on they'll not put orders in the yard.

Ronnie: If you don't meet your delivery dates you get no orders anyway. Even if some come available you wouldn't get them if you've got a reputation of not getting your orders out on time.

Jack: That's why Oldendorf came here.

Mack: If you put restrictive practices on and orders become available, do you think they are ganna place an order here? BS? They are ganna say, 'Fuck them, we'll put the order where the good lads are.'

Ronnie: Our local directors have to go out and get the orders because I have no doubt that if BS get them, get a BS contract, it would not come here.

Jack: That happened last year with Oldendorf. This yard was virtually fucking closed.

Ronnie: We would have closed if it had not been for them. Graham Day turned round and said to Oldendorf: 'Look, we've got problems at Austin and Pickersgill with the trade unions, so how about signing a BS contract, we place your orders somewhere else and guarantee the delivery, quality, etc.' Oldendorf said, 'Fuck off. You either build them at Picky's or I'm fucking catching a plane tonight and I'm getting them built abroad. Austin and Pickersgill build them or nobody builds them in this country.' That's the only way we got the orders, otherwise we would have been closed months ago.

Jack: Because he had ships built here before; and he says, 'That's it, I want them built at Picky's.' Otherwise this yard would have been shut last year. End of story.

Pickard: Well what's going to happen now with NESL?

Jack: They'll not be coming here, they'll not be fed into here. Tony asked P— that the other week. Tony says to him, 'If you are going to be managing director of the new shipbuilding consortium,' which he is now, he's ganna be based over at Pallion, 'any ships that comes up here, are you ganna feed them into here?' and he says, 'Aye.' What a fucking big liar. Do you think BS will fucking let him?

They'll say, 'Get away and piss off, they are gannin' over there [SS],' they'll not come here because of the twenty-pound differential.

say no to redundo

Chris: This bastard who's took over, this bloke who is going to be the personnel relations director, he's a right bastard, he's the type of bloke that says, 'Hey you, do that!' When we had a problem with our electricians, when seventeen of them wanted to stop in, he said, 'No way, they are going.' He sickened them that much that the lads did go. But what they are saying regarding the thirty-seven outfitters is: 'We'll just pay you off and we'll just tell our national officials.' But the only thing that is going to come out of that, that we can maybe look into, is now that the outfitting work is progressing on the vessel, there is more outfitting work, which is the plumbing side that we belong to, me and Eddy. We've got a lot of plumbing work and we could be looking for fitters to come into our areas. But having said that, we'll not absorb all of them.

With this new board taking over, if they want to take us on, they've got the cards. But at any time we are ready. The ridiculous part of it was, me and Eddy being in the plumber section, he wanted to contract some of the plumbing work out of the hydraulics. Well he contracted some out and he never telt us, he wanted to contract the hydraulics out which is a canny size job, the hydraulics and that, and what we says, is – we got it back, it's our work in a sense – is for the outfitters to come into our areas to work; such as blacksmiths, joiners, or more so fitters than anybody else. So all we are waiting for is March, what happens in March.

Pickard: Do you still have a mandate?

Chris: The mandate is: *if there is any compulsory redundancies or compulsory lay-offs we will walk out*. But having said that, we would obviously take another ballot, I think. When you are talking about a six to one majority five weeks before Christmas, it's a bloody good vote. And a secret ballot: it's not a show of hands.

Pickard: Are you obliged to hold another one?

Chris: By law within two months. If you don't take action on a ballot within two months, then you have to take another one. That's why when the plumbers and the electricians had a dispute regarding the transferring of work out – and they wanted electricians to

99

transfer to Sunderland Forge Services but on twenty pounds a week less – we voted to take industrial action, leading right up to strike action. Bearing in mind what the law says about it if you break your contract of employment. And what the company says is: 'Oh, we'll have a cooling-off period of two months.' They must have thought we were bloody daft, the cooling-off period was because the vote was knackered after two months, that's all it was for. They says they would extend the electricians to October, and that's all it was. So we'll have to take another ballot which would be nearer Christmas. So it is all tactics on their part. The main thing is that we stuck together. That's the big thing, as you'll probably find in the yard, that the solidarity in the yard is unbelievable.

Pickard: I was just saying to Tony this morning that, as you've got this structure, unless you can iron your differences with the other yards you are fucked.

Chris: But we are never going to. Soon as we ask the other yards to have a bit talk to us, they say, 'You fuckers is on twenty pound a week more than us. Are you ganna support us in a fight for more pay?'

Pickard: If they got themselves together over there to strike to get on a parity with you, would this yard come out in sympathy?

Chris: In my own opinion I think it would be very hard to get the yard to support them getting a twenty-pound-a-week rise. I think that would be very difficult.

Eddy: They once asked us if we would stand still while other people get rises and catch up with us. We said, 'No. By all means give them a rise but we want a rise as well.'

Chris: How are we going to get solidarity? That is the leading question. Just take the boilermakers: they had a regional conference last week and there was six of them and six general and municipal workers, and there was a motion put to the floor that they would not take any short-term contracts on. And SS, to a man, voted that there would not be any short-term contracts. Now they have started blokes over there on five-week contracts in the boilermakers' section. So how do we get, even if you forget about the twenty pound, the solidarity? Because you know in the back of your mind you wouldn't be able to trust them.

Pickard: Presumably it's because they've got no leadership?

Chris: That's right. You can respect Tony for his leadership: and he tells us sometimes what we've got to do, and if we disagree with

100

him he'll accept it but, you know, he's there and he's the leading figure. Across the river they haven't got it. How we would get solidarity, I do not know.

Pickard: Do you think that is the main issue, dealing with this new management?

Chris: The main issue is the issue of closing Austin and Pickersgill. To close Austin and Pickersgill, then you would maybe open Austin and Pickersgill to come back on his terms, which would be maybe the terms of SS. And in a way he could do that quite easily with the outfitting section. The joinery is going to be done over SS, they are being *regionalised*. But the joiners that's left here are just going to install the stuff here instead of building it. So, come November, we've only got a barge – and bear in mind that on a barge the most you are talking about is six outfitters working on it, probably plumbers – and they could contract the work out. What he could possibly do then is come to the existing outfitters and say, 'OK lads, the only work that I can offer you is at SS.' Now, you say to yourself, 'I'm not going over there, twenty pound a week less,' and the first shot that comes off the floor is only a natural one: 'Is there any chance of me getting my redundancy?' So what happens then is outfitters going and asking for their redundancies, and getting them rather than be transferred over the river with twenty pound a week less. He could be rid of all the outfitters in one go because if we are only talking about one or two ships a year, outfitting-wise you are only talking about us being in the yard, productively, about thirteen weeks a year. And the name of the game is to bring subcontracting into the outfitting section by saying, 'By the way I want six plumbers for three weeks,' because he's getting rid of us and that will be the tactic for getting rid of us. And it could be with the boilermaker lads as well, or they can go over the river on twenty pound a week less. And the first cry, and it's a natural cry, is: 'Give us me redundancy.'

Eddy: You've got the three yards and you've all got the same facilities. I bet we don't get a facility.

Chris: Tony thinks that the shot-blasting and plate preparation will be taken away from here.

Billy: I think Chris has hit the nail on the head: the only way they can run this company is to close this place and get the money down so they just rotate all the men.

Chris: Five weeks will tell. We'll see what happens in five weeks,

101

when the thirty-seven come up for redundancy. It has to be reviewed in March.

Pickard: So what are your tactics?

Chris: We will just have to play it by ear. They might come to Tony and say, 'Can I keep the thirty-seven outfitters in your section another few months.' But we know that Tony is under tremendous pressure from his union outside these walls. He was telling me that he goes round for different branches for elections to go to conferences – and it is just natural – you've got unemployed people there saying, 'Hey, Tony, you've got outfitters doing my work.' How can he answer that? But that's the commitment of this yard. Years ago that would never have been thought of, outfitters going into a boilermakers' section, but just to keep the unity of the yard and if Tony says in March, 'Look, that was the loan period, the outfitters' work is coming on now,' as outfitters we've got to try and absorb them.

Pickard: So what that means, by absorbing them, is breaking down demarcation. Does that happen in any other yards?

Chris: Under phase five it has done. Under phase five it says if there is any work surpluses that outfitters will go with outfitters, but there hasn't been any cross-section of outfitters and boilermakers.

Billy: But even having said that we never went this far as we've gone under phase five. I'm working with the platers and I'm doing the platers' work. I'm tacking, burning, plating, all kinds, doing the lot. And there is nowt being said; nobody says anything to you.

Harry: There was an occasion over at SS where they were in a similar position to this, and they would get a surplus, of maybe joiners, so he sent them out on the shop floor somewhere. When they went on the shop floor as joiners, they would be working with platers, but they didn't handle the gear. And some of these lads was more or less just picking a brush up and assisting in the menial tasks, or he might even try to pick the chart line up to assist the plater mark the plate off, and the plater would say, 'No, no, you don't do that.' So they didn't take us in fully, where here we work together and help each other.

Chris: The only thing that I would like to look forward to, and hope and pray, that sometime we could do the same for the boilermakers, bring them into our section if they were running down. Possibly later on in the year where he says three hundred and ten, at that particular time as outfitters we should be going hell for leather, and

102

we maybe could absorb some of the boilermakers in our section which we will do.

Billy: I would welcome them wholeheartedly for what they have done for our lads, but isn't there a situation with the boilermakers where they've got men here who want to be out? There is a volunteer situation, isn't there?

Chris: In the boilermaker section there is a volunteer situation but at the same time he'll not get rid of them lads because he'll not want to cause an imbalance. In one section there is, maybe, out of a section of forty, thirty-nine of them want to be away. So there is an imbalance there.

Rick: He could still look at that, come April, because them three hundred and ten is not just going to snap up in September from June. You are going to have people standing about with no work because the work is run out in April.

Pickard: Is there a possibility that the thirty-seven might be transferred to the other yards?

Chris: That could well be. You see, the name of the game is from the company's angle, 'I've got to sicken these thirty-seven,' and more so the fitters than anybody, because the fitters, the average age in the fitting department is thirty-six. Now, only two fitters have moved for redundancy within a year and he's got to break the fitters, he's got to break the fitters, because there is too many of them and he wants them out. Last week he asked for voluntary lay-offs in the outfitting sections, then he gets twenty joiners, he gets fifteen plumbers, and I think there was four painters and one fitter. I can honestly say if they had twenty fitters he would have had them out on that Monday morning by ten o'clock. Because he turned round and said, 'Just one fitter?' We tried to get it through to them as well as the blacksmiths. The average age of the blacksmiths is twenty-six, and there are some blacksmiths gone. The fitting department, at this particular time of the redundancy, they only lost about two. Not one of them is budging. So they know for a fact, fitting work, there is nowt out there. None of them is ganna get a job at Nissan, they are not ganna get a job at Nissan and there is nowt else out there. The lads are not moving. We'll just have to wait and see. But again they could come along and say, 'Hey look, lads, there is some work down Smith's Docks, or SS. You can either have your lot or transfer with a cut in pay.' The lads will just say, 'Give us me lot, I'm away.' If anything, that will do it. And not

103

only in the outfitting section but in any section, I should think. Once you are talking about twenty pound a week drop in wages, that's it.

A lot of lads are also worrying about the redundancy scheme finishing this year and that could put panic in people's mind. Lads are saying, 'Should I get out now in case they do away with the scheme?' Blokes who take nineteen thousand pound out or whatever, 'Should I get out now and do away with it or will things get better?' It's a terrible gamble. That's the worry.

Pickard: Is it possible for the company to do a Murdoch?

Chris: That's the scaring point. You see, if we got into a November situation where we have no work and we went on strike and he just telt his foreman, 'Tell them that if they go out on strike their contract of employment is broke, they get no redundancy.' You see lads is lads, and if they can take twenty thousand pound, if they are in that age-group, they can say, 'There is no way I'm gannin' on strike.' And that is why, as Eddy is always saying, we cannot get the upper hand of these people, it's going to be a long time before we get the upper hand of them. And I don't think we ever will unless we've got ten or twenty ships to do and that's the time. It's all in the hands of the gods. Maybe some of us should attend spiritualist meetings.

Eddy: Get on to the other side and see if they've got any orders.

13/2/86

boilermaker's meeting: an order

Tony: It is just a short report back first of all from this morning's meeting with P— when he met the Yard Negotiating Committee and all the representatives of the staff unions. You are all possibly aware of the press statement they put out: what they are saying is that we have won an order for a non-propelled barge for Geoffrey Knight Offshore. The dimensions of the barge are four hundred foot by a hundred and twenty foot compared to the three hundred by hundred foot of previous barges. She is some two thousand tons heavier and she will weigh about four thousand tons which is the equivalent of about one and a half SD14s. There is a press statement which you can get copies of to distribute to members in the yard. Because of the dimensions of the barge it should be built on the outside berth. That would mean the saw mill will have to be demolished. He said there are tenders out for that and, as BS tell him what he has to do, there will be three tenders out and one will be submitted for acceptance. So that's it on the order front. It gives us a breathing-space, it takes the steelworkers through to December, probably in line with the outfitters, so we are going to finish the programme together. Unless, like I said, hopefully we get ships. So, all in all, he is only doing the job he gets paid for, he gets paid to get us work, we do our part of the bargain, and he's done a little bit of his. He was his normal arrogant self, full of himself. Couldn't wait to tell us, it must have been choking him, because I believe they have had this order in the bag prior to amalgamation of the named North East Shipbuilding Company. He did get praise off one of the staff representatives, who thanked the board and greatly appreciated what he had done for us. But he is only doing his job: he should be getting us work as well, for the money he is getting.

Tony: On the other side we've got an issue to discuss: where we've got an agreement with the company, any contractor who works alongside us works the overtime that we are working in that area. We've always done this, it's always been controlled, and we've got a written undertaking from the company, late last year, that re-inforced the agreement. He is now coming and saying that Sunderland Forge Services, because we have stopped the work last Sunday on the half-shift and this week's half-shifts, they are not very happy and their managing director's supposedly said that the prevention of them working overtime or being restricted to our overtime levels would not allow them to finish the contract. So the company is saying that he would then say that he couldn't finish the contract because of reasons beyond his control. And that is rubbish. I am saying that that contract is in with the Oldendorf ships and we are quite unaware of any clause in the Oldendorf contract that says that he can invoke a paragraph that you cannot get your job done because of things beyond your control. That is just rubbish. We have probed that situation during the negotiations for the Oldendorf and afterwards when we negotiated the bonus system. So basically what he is looking for is unrestricted overtime for all contractors, it doesn't matter what overtime we work, if they need or require to finish their contract they can work what overtime they want. Well, I am saying there is no way they are going to do that. First of all, they are taking our work, then they are getting our rate, and they want to bring them in here and work half-shifts all day Saturday and all day Sunday, twelve-hour shifts, what you like. I am saying no way are we going to accept that. Now I know we could have just went and said, there is no way we are accepting it and blew out, and we'll control the plant. I know there are moves and statements made by their management that he work what overtime was required, and that A&P shop stewards weren't going to tell them what overtime they work. And BS personnel manager saying, 'That committee will not dictate anybody's overtime.' I am going to tell him that *that* committee will dictate anybody's overtime that works at A&P. There is no way they're going to come in. If they want it that way then we'll stop the bloody lot. There is no way... Why should our outfitters not be working any overtime

106

now and them working in the same areas? That's bad enough, but to accept them coming in and just giving them *carte blanche* on overtime working, it's just not thinkable. I want an endorsement from that statement in line with our policy, and that you tell the members what he's asking for. I don't care if we stop all overtime and it shuts the yard. Because I am no way accepting people doing our work which we are *forced* to give to them, and they are coming and getting our rate! That's galling! And they want to work more on top. They've got the facility, I say, to work shift-work if they want it: we've got an agreement on shift-working, so he can put shift-working on. But no they'll not. They want to work twelve-hour shifts. Anyway, that's what I'm moving, that we tell him he's got no chance with that one. And that's what I'll be going back to tell him this afternoon, if need be I'll call a mass meeting tomorrow morning. I want to know. If he says he is going to bring them in whether we like it or not, there'll be no plant, there'll be nowt switched on. I can either do it that way at a mass meeting, or we'll just pull the plug off and tell the lads on Friday that there is no overtime on. We'll decide later how far it gans. The important job you have to do at the moment is get out on the floor and tell them what he wants and what he's settled to do: bring them in without us saying OK, where we have written agreement. I don't know where the national agreement stands when there is limits on overtime for normal production purposes. I know our percentage is running about ten per cent, but that is steel. But what he is asking for is way and beyond the national agreement. He is party to the national agreement just as well as I am, and I'll tell him that this afternoon. Any questions?

TG: The contractor that is still in the tanks, does this involve them when you say all contractors coming in . . . ?

Tony: What I am saying is that we control the contractors' overtime, unless we come to an understanding on which way they work which is agreeable to ourselves, then that will be the prevailing situation. But if, like in this situation, like Sunderland Forge Services, there is no way we can accept that. If they come to some arrangement with the painters and red-leaders that is all right and we cannot see nowt wrong with it, OK, but it's not for him to ask just to bring them in when he wants them to come in.

HW: A point to bear in mind, the saw mill when it is demolished, it's asbestos.

107

Tony: Hopefully, they will get the correct people in to do it. We'll get more detail, where you are going to go to, which shop you are going to go to, whether it's the blacksmiths' or the joiners' [*laughter*]. I don't know where you are going to have to go, but they might have to build a new quarantine area for you, being shipwrights.

HW: I'm more concerned about me fridge and me microwave oven in there.

14/2/86

Rick took me over to the blacksmiths' shop. There wasn't
a lot going on and the place had obviously seen busier
days. There was a large hand-painted poster stuck on the
wall. It said WE WILL NEVER SURRENDER and was peeling
off at the top corner. Rick later told me the foreman had
put it there. Most of the men were young. I asked him
to tell me the names of the tools I could see around us,
and, as he did so, it was obvious that he took a great
pride in his work.

the blacksmith's mate's barnet

Rick: The majority of tools are pipe-clip tools, you've got different
swages [tools for bending cold metal] for high plates. These are all
swages. You get different pipe-clip swages, grain feeders, high
plates, deck high plates, taper tools to get a tape. Different jigs for
pulling pipes round and shaping pipes, and shaping balls should I
say. You heat your metal up, put in, pour it out. There's all sorts
of different shapes you can formulate. That's a kettle. Sometimes
the gaffer used to switch the boiler off in the afternoon so you used
to pour water in that and put it over the top of the fire and boil the
water in that for our tea, cause the gaffer would switch the boiler
off. He was a cunt. We used to have two hammers, that one, they
scrapped it, leaving us with one hammer. Now that one, the head
snapped off, sheared off, and instead of getting it repaired properly
they fucking just bodged the cunt up like that. We've always had
problems with ventilation in here but obviously as the shop numbers
went down there was less fires so the problem wasn't as bad. But
the management then, a bloke called H— decided he would insulate
the roof, insulate the lot. You know that grey horrible stuff that's
outside, well that's all insulation, now we claim to be the only
blacksmiths' shop in the world that's fucking insulated. You see

the windows that are black there and clear here? Well they were ganna do the whole lot but we stopped them. They were gonna blank the whole lot off. They've already blacked off the windows, cutting out the natural light that we used to use. We used to switch the lights off and use natural light. Now with them doing this, with them not being prepared to clean the fucking windows, they've had to buy these lights in. Now these take fifteen minutes to heat up. You can imagine how much juice it's costing to run them. Plus they need changing all the time. We argue: if you cleaned your fucking windows, cleaned them, and cleaned that shite off, you could revert back to having your natural light, which is better for you – you don't know what damage they are doing to your eyes over twenty, thirty years in here – revert back to natural light and also you are saving on your power. It's obvious. But they'll not have it. They take no notice of you, they justify it by whatever means.

Pickard: Money?

Rick: Well, they haven't got an argument with money because it's common sense, isn't it? If you've got no lights burning you're saving money. But we're only daft, thick-headed blacksmiths, we don't know owt about economics. Nowt to do with us. The management decide.

Pickard: What are you doing now?

Rick: We've had to give away all our work cause they were gonna close the whole yard down unless we agreed certain things in the yard: that was painters working with red-leaders, welders accepting low-hydrogen rods, and us, as blacksmiths, accepting that all our work is contracted out. So all the work we do, now, another blacksmith does outside. Fucking cowboys. Now they give us what they send in, we install on the ship, and if there is owt to be rectified (obviously not everything that is sent in is ganna fit) we put the job right. And up to now every fucking thing's been wrong. We've sent pallet-loads of fucking clips back, pipe-clips back, handrails, loads of jobs. We've only touched on it cause all the work hasn't come through from them yet cause we're still waiting for stuff. It's far below our standard. Our quality, we're not exaggerating, is fucking far superior. I mean, really, if they had said to us, 'Well, to do the job quicker and cheaper you do it like that, don't do it as good,' we could have done it: we could have turned out a shabby job, no problem. We have the right to do our own plant work, repairing crane rails, job rails, owt, all plant work. Anything to do with the

110

plant, we manufacture that and look after that. We still do all the tools as well, caulking tools, hammers, mauls. The original idea was to shut the blacksmiths' shop altogether. Our foreman is a right cunt. We had a vote of no confidence in him. For instance, he told the management it would be cheaper to buy the ladders in, which we produce. It's a big part of our work in here, you can imagine all the ladders that gan in a ship; we used to make the lot, put all the rungs in, manufacture it. He turned round and told the company it would be cheaper to buy it in. He's sent jobs out of the shop and over the shed to be done on the big press instead of us doing them in the hammer. That's the sort of thing he's been getting up to, so we had a meeting about it and we had a vote of no confidence in him.

That's part of our shop next door ... When we were booming in the seventies, they converted this shop, it used to be a store, an engine-fitting store, and they give it to us because of the size of our department and the work we get through. The jobs that were coming here was unbelievable. We'd do a hell of a lot of work for everybody in the yard, so they give us this department, but as you can see there is very little getting done. Pipe racks there, and the bar racks, the bars were laid out on them racks down there. Bars from inch and a quarter up to 6BR, six by five eight. All sorts of sizes, all flat bar, twenty-foot long. That used to be packed. Them racks used to be packed, chocker. You can see where they've bent, where some of them have bent. We had to put stiffeners on the bottom ones because that's where the heavy bars gan, and they were bending with the fucking sheer weight of the gear that was in. We used to gan through a lot of stuff. All the ladders were marked off, we used to put them on the welding blocks down there, and weld them all down there. These lads used to burn out jobs for us, and for all parts of the yard, with the profile burners. That guillotine there is about a fucking hundred year old. It's better than the one they've brought in, as regards being handy. That runs continuous when you switch it on, just runs and runs and runs, and the blades gan continuously up and down like that. *James Berry and Sons, Glasgow*. It's ancient that. But what a bloody good machine it's been; I mean you can cut bar on there. We've had three-quarter rounds: I even seen an inch-round cut on there. Cut owt, man. This one here, the new one, you can hear the fucking noise! But it has got the benefit of having different sizes in there, for your different sizes and shaped bars. And

111

there is a punching machine on the back which just punches holes straight through.

Pickard: It's noisy. The proverbial bag of hammers.

Rick: Fucking sure it is. Disgraceful. We tried to get it done, seen to, but they've had to put it back and it's no different. And they wonder why you put in for fucking deafness claims in the shipyards. I'll run the other one for you.

Pickard: Does it go up and down like that all the time?

Rick: Aye.

Pickard: So you've just got to slip it in when you want it?

Rick: Aye. Nowt better; slip it in when you want it. Once we had a bloke who wore a fucking wig, a brand new fucking wig, Willy Jordan, he was a labourer. So what happens is, you get a great twenty-foot long bar, and the labourer stands at the end of it, and the blacksmith, the tradesman, stands at the front and feeds it through, cuts it off where he's marked it. Well this lad, fucking Willy, was standing at the back with his wig on. Now, when you've a geet long bar, a thick bar, and you cut it on this machine you've got a kick back. So that, when you're standing, it shakes the bar so you're fucking jumping. By the time he got from fucking there to there he jumped all the way along and the fucking wig was well askew. It was a fucking scream. It was a brand new one and all, never had it on.

24/2/86

purge the poets

Tony: You've got to suffer to be a good poet, haven't ya?

Pickard: Well I've done a lot of suffering since I came here.

Tony: Where? When? You've only been around fucking five minutes, man. You've enjoyed your fucking life. Have you enjoyed life up to now? You've had a varying fucking life, all fucking sorts of jobs. Lived all over the fucking shop, so you've enjoyed yourself. So you haven't really suffered. So you should be fucking purged, shouldn't you! You should be fucking lashed! If you want to hear some real poetry listen to that group from the fifties, early sixties, the Settlers...

Pickard: I thought you took them for an acid stomach.

Tony: ... Some of the lyrics. They were real toppers:

I love the sea

I love the navy

I like my biscuit dipped in gravy.

Pickard: So that's the kind of poetry you like.

Danny: I've just spoke to Albert Beamish, he says Chic Williams been down and put a claim in for an accident.

Tony: He's had more fucking accident claims since he come here than owt else.

Pete: He's accident-prone.

Danny: No matter where he went, somebody dropped something on his fucking head. Fucking ex-soldier.

Tony: If it wasn't dropping on his head it was flying up and hitting him in the face.

Danny: We were working in the forepeak and somebody dropped a jackhandle or some-fucking-thing on him. Loads of blokes have hit him on the fucking head, lad. Down he went. I was working with him in the shed, on nightshift down the dock and there was a girder they wanted to back-weld and flange. They wanted to weld it and then turn it. They got it so far, he says, 'Keep hold of it and

I'll turn mine round to pull it the rest of the way.' Sure enough up it comes and hit him reet in the fucking throat. Whoop you fucker! I though he was dead that night. I thought he was a gonner. It hit him right in the Adam's Apple. Split heads! Crushed fingers! Drop something on his foot...

Pickard: What's your nickname?

Danny: The Gremlin. The Gremlin from the Kremlin. The Tasmanian Devil. I've got lots of nicknames. You know what your nickname is? *Daft-arse.*

Pete: Has Danny been good to you?

Pickard: He's done quite a good job. He's really made my life worthwhile here.

Danny: This has been one of the finest jobs of his life.

Pickard: It's one of the only jobs of my life.

Pete: He's in the top ten of the poets.

Danny: There's only fucking nine of them.

Tony: He was born too late. He should have been about fucking 1870, something like that. He'd be more appreciated then; he'd be one of the fucking lads, wouldn't you?

Pete: Can you play any musical instrument?

Danny: He's not a really literary person, him. Not really.

Pete: Just a working-class lad, man.

Danny: I mean, his spelling is atrocious. I just do it in about five minutes. I write songs in five minutes.

Pickard: Give us a rendering.

Danny: You want a song? I'll give you my latest: *A fireplace is a fireplace is a fireplace.* It didn't take me fucking long to write that.

Pickard: The Gertrude Stein of the River Wear.

Tony: *Couldn't give a fuck, drunk.*

Danny: You would have loved Tommy at the Labour Club.

Pickard: First and last poet to read at Sunderland Labour Club.

Danny: The miners used to gan in there regular until he did his bit.

Pickard: Now nobody goes there.

Danny: Thanks to you.

Pickard: I heard it was due to mismanagement.

Brian: I enjoyed myself.

Pete: It's only you that's saying it was a load of crap, everybody else enjoyed themselves.

Danny: I didn't say it was a load of crap, I just said that he was a load of crap.

Pickard: How could you tell? You were pissed as a rat all neet.

Brian: Yes he was.

Pickard: When we come in, you were fucking stotting all over the place.

Danny: What a useless cunt he is, lad. You fucker. I've met some fucking useless cunts but that daft cunt takes the biscuits.

Pete: He's more fucking useless than you are.

Pickard: I'll tell you what, Danny, I learnt it all from you, because when I came in here you were my fucking guide and mentor.

Danny: I tried my best with you.

Pickard: Obviously I'm a failure.

Danny: Miserable.

Brian: When you gan back, Tom, what's ganna happen to her like?

Pickard: Who?

Brian: The tart you've got here at Cullercoats.

Pickard: I haven't got one in Cullercoats.

Tony: When I'm in charge I'll shoot the bastard fornicating twats.

Pickard: You sound like the Reverend Ian Paisley.

Tony: Good old Puritan comes out. The Calvinist. Fuck you cunts. I'd have you on the fucking fire, yeez bastards, burn you.

Pete: Unless you give him the lass's address and telephone number.

Dodds: He's as pure as the driven snow.

Tony And Catwalk, what are you doing going round inviting people to the old men's fucking tea? Who the fucking hell do you think you are?

Catwalk: It was Joycey who first mentioned it.

Tony: He said it was you.

Danny: Did he invite you?

Catwalk: Was it me or Joyce?

Pickard: I can't remember who it was.

Ronnie: He's terrified of fucking Joyce.

Pickard: I don't want to be fucking hung upside-down by the heels like Ronnie was.

Tony: Whose is this paper? 'Measurements of the Royal Family: Queen Mother five-foot-two, Queen five-foot-four, Prince Philip five-foot eleven, Princess Margaret five-foot-one, Princess Diana five-foot-ten.' Lugs is 'five-foot-fucking-nine', he's no five-foot-nine.

Danny: His lugs are.

Tony: 'Prince Andrew six foot, Princess Anne five-foot-six, Prince Edward six foot.'

Brian: The Queen Mother is lovely.

Tony: Scrounging off the country, the bastard.

Brian: Fine pair of tits for an eighty-six-year-old.

Tony: They've hardly been used; wet-nursed all her fucking bairns. Never seen the cunts.

Brian: I'd like to give her one. She's got all her own teeth.

Catwalk: Who's been on the phone to you, Tom?

Pickard: I make no comments, me.

Tony: You know who it is, everybody does.

Brian: Play the tape and see if you can identify the voice.

Pickard: There's a subtle bloke.

Brian: Sherlock Holmes.

> **Voice on tape:** Hello Mr Pickard, are you fine?
> **Pickard:** Yes.
> **Tape:** I know you are fine. You looked very well with your friend, walking round the yard.
> **Pickard:** Fuck off.

Pickard: It could be you. Several people have said that Chris Reagan has got a good mimic voice. Speak Chinese.

Chris: It'll be the same people that was farting about Wednesday when Tony was away.

Tony: That's Joyce I reckon. What were they doing on Wednesday when I was away, the bastards?

Chris: The assistant chairman should be telling you. Oh no, he was away.

Tony: Where were you on Wednesday when the fucking phone calls were going on, Danny?

Danny: I wasn't here.

Ronnie: I was away.

Chris: It was atrocious what was going on in here. It was like a fucking kindergarten. Is that right?

Pickard: No comment.

Tony: Here, we'd better not give you too much information. If there's a crackdown on the trade unions and they get a hold of you and say, 'What were you doing at Austin and Pickersgill's?' you'll just spill the lot on us, won't you? They've only got to fucking strip you naked and fucking hang you by the balls and you'll just fucking capitulate straight away, won't you? In fact, they wouldn't get that far, just shine a fucking torch in your fucking eyes: 'Who were the subversives in the committee?' and you would just reel all the fucking names off, wouldn't you?

Pickard: No, no, I'd stick it out.

Danny: They'd have to shoot the cunt to keep him quiet.

25/2/86

Peter Gibson, a welder, came to see me today. He has written a history of his community, Southwick, and has published it at his own expense.

the Ginger Gissy gets a scone

Gibson: When I've been interviewed by journalists I've had to be careful what I'm saying. Sometimes you forget that they are writing everything down you are saying, and sometimes I get carried away with myself. Anyway, I thought it was just a by-the-way question and he said, 'By the way, how do your workmates accept your writing?'

I just said to him, 'Well, on nightshift I was just known as Catherine Cookson, and on dayshift I became Enid Blyton.' You know, shipyard humour. I was taking the piss. So he writes this down and it is in the *Journal* a couple of days later, 'His workmates have nicknamed him Enid Blyton.' So when I gan to the club I get, 'Is it Mr Blyton now? Or Enid Blyton or what?' I'm saying it happened a few years ago when I first started on the work. There was some embarrassment. I had the mickey taken in the yard since I've been doing the work so I've hardened myself to it.

I've worked in the yard for twenty years and just accept it, but I cannot understand it. I cannot understand why they want to get some lads right on the bottom. There was one lad here he was on valium. He wasn't a full shilling, so they should have left him alone. But he was on valium because of the tormentors. There was half a dozen of them. It's a big joke, you see. They would tell him lies. The six of them would tell him lies and, as far as he was concerned, it was the truth. And this is the main thing in shipyard humour: they tell somebody a lie and if you are daft and believe it they take the water out of you. Anyway, I'm talking about going five or six year ago, and this welder I'm walking about he's taken his

118

redundancy, as I said he wasn't a full shilling as far as the shipyard workers were concerned. It got that bad he appealed to the shop stewards and these half-a-dozen men were pulled into the shop stewards' office and warned about it. To me it's crude when they run a man down so he's that bad, it doesn't matter who he is, if he's crackers or what. He's on valium and that, and when they find out he's on valium they even torment him more, and I just cannot grasp it. Instead of leaving the lad alone. I'll tell you one situation what they did with him. A welder, he was known as the Ginger Gissy, he was about six foot. He was threatening this lad they were taking the water out of, Trotter. This was the lie: the Ginger Gissy was threatening Trotter, 'I'm ganna get you back!' Trotter was taking it all in, believed him, and the others were saying, 'If you see the Ginger Gissy, he's going to kill you.' And he's taking it all in and believing it. It was all a joke to them. I think there was five or six of them. They would say to Trotter, 'Are you frightened of the Ginger Gissy?' He'd say 'No, I'm not frightened of him.' They'd say, 'Should I tell him that?' This is the way it was going on. They were just tormenting him.

I've been working on nightshift and sometimes, when you're tired during the night, things are totally out of proportion. So this one night the Ginger Gissy gets hold of Trotter, 'I'm going to break your neck.' Anyway it gets sorted out. The Ginger Gissy is just taking the water out of him, but this lad is taking it serious. So they went and took it a stage further and the lie got bigger. Harry Jobs got a plaster and stuck it over his own nose. So he gans into the store where we are getting our bait. Trotter is sitting there: 'Look what Ginger Gissy done to us, he's stuck the nuts on us. You'll be next. Look what he's done to me.' Well, at that moment the Ginger Gissy is outside and walks in, a great big ginger bloke, and the lad's legs went weak and he just went out. He more or less ran out. 'Cannot stand any more of this.' And that was all funny to them. Anyway they were called into the shop stewards' office to leave him alone. Well, I walked down with Trotter into the showers, and I told him, 'They're just kidding you.' He says, 'I'm on valium.' As I say, he wasn't the full shilling. He says, 'You know what valium are?' I says, 'Oh, aye, they're tablets for your nerves.' He says, 'Well I'm on them.' It was an appeal. He was telling everybody that he was on them, because he wanted it to get back to them hoping they would leave him alone. But how ruthless they are; they kept at him.

So anyway they were pulled into the shop stewards' office and warned about it. I seen some shop stewards sniggering about it, as though it were a big joke, but other shop stewards took the serious side of it and told them, 'You've got to leave him alone.' These shop stewards said to them, a group of six of them there was, 'Who is this Hoy?' What they'd been doing as well was, as he'd been walking along, they'd been shouting 'Hoy' and when he's been turning around they've been up and away. And this was what was happening all over the shed. So they were grinding him all handles, and always they were getting at him. So when they found out about the warning from the shop stewards, it came out and didn't stop, 'Hoy.' It became more intense, they were tormenting him further: it was 'Hoy, Hoy' all over the yard. And he was cracking up. He was the sort of lad who was proud of his work, he'd get a wire brush and ... we weld and that, but you don't usually get a wire brush to shine your welding up, and he used to shine his welding up and stand back and admire it. He was proud of his work where they were cynical and taking the water out of him. One day, one of them would come up and spit on the welding. That's just nowt. I've had it done to me: you take no notice, that sort of thing is nowt in the shipyard, that. It's just nothing. So, anyway, when he gets away, another welder puts a rod in his pliers – in his electra-roller, the correct term is – and sparks his welding. He ran the rod all over his welding so there was spark-marks all over. When he came back after his bait he saw it all, well!

Here's another story: not only were the five or six lads I've mentioned there taking the water out of Trotter, they were taking the water out of each other and all. For example, the Ginger Gissy and Taffy were taking the water out of Bushy. Bushy was a bloke of about eighteen stone, and over six foot, big strong bloke, like. So anyway, this is what happened between the two of them: this is another story going back five or six year ago when they were on nightshift. The Ginger Gissy and Bly are taking the water out of Bushy, so to get his own back Bushy offered the Ginger Gissy a scone. Well, as I say, he was well-named the Ginger Gissy, he could swill the beer down and would eat anything. The Ginger Pig. He was blooming animal. He's ruthless, you cannot talk to them sensible. For example, they knew I was doing local history, so he says: 'Oh, I'm interested.' So I'm telling him what's going on, and he says, 'Oh, I've got a few photographs copied at the museum.'

1. In the complex, the 22,000-ton multi-purpose bulk carrier, ship number 1431, nearing completion

2. Down hand on the deck at sunset

3. Wing tank section on a Kamag transporter in a pre-fabrication shed

4. Welding inside the bulbous bow

5. Inside a double bottom in the lube-oil sump under the engine

6. Burning a pipe tunnel

7. The morning of the launch

8. Peter Callaghan, the last yard convener on the River Wear

All he's doing is taking the piss out of me. And I'm, like, believing him, and he's just telling me lies. And it's not genuine. That's why I can say I accept it. Twenty years working in the shipyard, I can accept it, but it's not genuine patter because you don't know who is telling you lies and who's not. So you've got to check, if somebody says something. It's weird you know, if somebody says something you don't take any notice, and you don't take it for gospel until it's established as fact, because they just tell lies and if you believe it you are a daft cunt. It's crazy. Anyway, to get back to that story about Bly and the Ginger Gissy taking the water out of Bushy: to get his own back, Bushy offered the Ginger Pig a scone. The Ginger Pig, he accepted it. He eats it, and Bushy watches him eating it and says, 'I blew me nose in there.' He blew his nose in, green ins and black ins, you get loads of black stuff up your nose in welding, and he blew it on to his scone and gave it to the Ginger Gissy and watched him eat it. The Ginger Gissy was sitting there like and he realised he'd fell for it. It's savage.

28/2/86

confed meeting: cowboys up the bank

A letter from the shop stewards' committee of Ferguson
Ailsa:
To all interested parties in shipbuilding.
Dear Colleague, the market situation for shipbuilding is
looking very grim and that is reflected worldwide where
the intake of orders is falling off drastically over the past
few years. Other countries' governments have supported
their shipbuilding industry by subsidies or by home
owners having to build their ships in domestic yards,
resulting in export orders falling off in the UK. British
shipbuilders have presented the state of the industry
report to all yard committees outlining the orders
confirmed for the next financial year. Needless to say the
outlook is bleak and this will result in redundancies and
the possibility of yard closures and lay-offs. This problem
is not only with BS in the nationalised sector but also in
the private sector. Now the time has come for the UK
government to support its own shipbuilding industry by
advising home owners to build British and make it
compulsory the same as other nations. We would ask all
shop stewards' committees in the shipbuilding industry
to support the suggestion and get your MP involved and
also your union and any other interested parties. Now
is the time to say enough is enough and not let the British
shipbuilding industry go down the drain as we have seen
with other industries ...

Tony: The company again proposed that we should accept temporary contract labour and they were arguing that because of the
under-utilisation of the outfit workers. He is arguing that the hours
are not flowing correctly because he has under-utilised in the

modular quayside area and that the accommodation unit is behind so stopping the full utilisation of outfit workers. To get round the problem, because he cannot take them from the steel shops, he cannot take them from the complex and he needs the labour to push that work on, he wants nine welders and six shipwrights on a short-term contract for five to six weeks. You know full well that even as the yard committee we rejected this approach on temporary employment. All unions had a policy in every aspect where short-term contracts should be severely reviewed and if possible, bearing in mind the industry, should be resisted. It was not the working practices for lads to be starting work for five or six weeks to be finished. And, in fact, in shipbuilding it is an attempt to take the industry back to the nature of casual labour, without a doubt. It is coming across quite clearly now that there are only two yards left in BS merchant sector that do not accept any contracts: that's ourselves and Govan. So from the start off I ask what the change was, why now? Even when on two or three occasions it had been rebuffed, not only by the boilermakers but by the yard committee. He said, 'Well, things have changed because SS have now got short-term contract labour. And in the North-East we are the only yard that does not accept short-term contracts.' So that goes back to my previous point: when other yards start to do things that we might resist, then it starts to affect us. We want to try and argue with the other yards that they should not be doing things that are going to affect the whole of the grouping because people will be saying to him: 'Look they've got it in SS, you get it in there!' And that is quite clearly what's happening now. We are being affected by the decisions of other subsidiaries. Not only that, we are being used to a certain extent because we have accepted transfers from a yard that supposedly had labour surpluses when they were transferred here. Them labour surpluses have immediately been filled up by short-term contract labour. So actually our policy has been undermined by them, and our position. So I might as well tell you that is why the boilermakers had a meeting this morning to clear our lines. It appears he could be coming on strong, we've naturally got to take our own decision because it is steelworkers that are going to resist any attempt at short-term contracts in this yard. And we expect the full support of the rest of the committee, because he was saying yesterday that if he goes back and says he can't resolve the problem PM is going to say, 'Start them, never mind the unions,

123

you start them people in there temporary! So we could be in a situation where we could be running into conflict. I have told him that if he wants to raise it further, first of all he raises it with the boilermakers' monitoring committee and then he puts it into procedure and let it go from there, like we always do at the joint negotiating committee. It is this committee's policy that we don't care what other people are doing, or if other people have selt their jobs or selt their birthright or whatever, and gan back to the way we were in the sixties. Not only in the sixties, they are going back rapidly to the thirties. That's where they are going. We were arguing as boilermakers that he's got scope there, our core numbers can be identified as possibly sixteen under strength and then you put on top of that early retirement through ill-health, and then you put on top of that natural wastage whether being sacked or whether being left to join the police force or the army (we know we've had some) and there is ample scope in there to start people on a permanent basis. And that's what we said, 'You make your plan labour force up to its number, you telt us what it would be and that is how you get round the problem of your labour.' And he said that BS, PM in particular, said that 'no way will we start permanent people because there will be other subsidiaries later in the year will have a surplus of labour and we if we want them can get them. In no way is the corporation going to start permanent people.' So it means if you are losing people through natural wastage eventually your core numbers get smaller and smaller and then you are utilising your labour force on two aspects: one the aspect of transfer from other subsidiaries, and two, the aspect of temporary labour. And that is the way it will run plus the third aspect of subcontracting. So your core labour force will dwindle and will be subsidised by the three aspects of running the company.

The only job you've got to do now, like I've told the boilermakers, is get out on the floor and tell them what these fellahs is trying to do: the casualisation of the industry. They can rationalise themselves up their own backsides because they can close Smith's Dock and they can close A&P and then close Govan so there's only one yard left and that will go down the drain. It is only a matter of time, because it will become that insignificant that it won't really matter, and nobody will do no shouting or nowt. By Christ we are down to ten thousand people from forty-seven thousand, it is going to be a hard battle to get them to realise that we are going to have to keep the merchant sector. The only thing that is going for us really is the Thatcher administration industrial policy is in such tatters and rags that every turn, whether it be British Leyland, or whether it be Westland, at every turn she is getting obstacles and her government is now becoming that unpopular we can only hope that if our MPs and our trade union leaders do the same job and raise the question in the House and draw the attention to the possibility of no merchant sector then they might just turn, they might just turn away from it. In fact that's our only chance, because all our leaders, the Labour Party and the trade union movement seem to be saying to me is, 'Hold on, two years time we'll get a Labour government back and everything will be all right.' But unfortunately we are in a situation where we haven't got two years, we haven't got time, we've got to take them on now. We've got to do something about it now, and people have to help us and give the leadership that they are put in the position to give. So we'll just have to wait and see how the whole situation develops knowing full well that it's just another one, just another battle. I think last week, the week before last, was the quietest week we've ever had, but there again they gan away, they gan away and they start thinking about something else to come back with. They mustn't be able to sleep at night.

Jack: I think it might be a time now to put out a bulletin, chairman, because we've got a lot of young people in the yard who have never experienced casual labour, like some of us. And I certainly don't want to return to them times. If they think because they've got a big mortgage and they keep their heads down it will gan away, by God they are on a hiding to nowt.

Tony: You're right we should get a bulletin out. A lot of the young 'uns, the majority of our lads now, I would say, are about thirty-five, the average in the yard, and some of them has never worked in the yard prior to 1969 when we did work on a casual basis. So we have to educate them. But we have to do that job also as well as putting a bulletin out, the stewards have got to do the job of educating or re-educating some of our people who have forgotten about it, or want to forget about it, or don't see it as a problem. I think a lot of people would like to have lackeys in, because what gans on when you've got a load of temps in, everybody just says, 'Do that job? Oh, get a temp, he'll do it, he'll work with his head in a bucket of crap.' That's the way it gans and slowly but surely that sort of situation undermines you, and it undermines the whole

125

trade union organisation. In fact there was a lad telling me in some of the rig yards in Scotland, they have two hundred permanent people and four hundred temps, and the temps don't go to any union meetings, the temps don't make any decisions, they are not allowed to gan to the meetings. The temps are just blew out every now and then, they are just blew out. And they get all the crap, they get no conditions that other people have, they are not even allowed to gan in the same canteens. They have got better conditions, they live off the backs of the temps. And that is the situation. Now, all right, it might gan on for a bit, but eventually it blows up.

Eddy: Chairman, these temps, best part of them, has put themselves in that position by taking their redundancy. I agree with Jack, these fellahs over there should be educated, because they need educating.

Tony: That's the other aspect of temps: it causes a hell of a problem. And I have explained before, the reason why it hasn't caused them a problem is because they have conned the workforce on why they have had to start them. Lads who's took their redundancy here starting over there. They have selt their job here and they have gone over there. So that would cause us tremendous problems in the yard if we start to get people coming back in as temps who previously took their redundancy money. That's another aspect. And lads were telling me from Scott Lithgow where they had started enrolling temps that there has actually been fisticuffs in the yard between members of the union.[1] Them that's took the money saying, 'You daft bastard, you should have took yours like I did and I am back here now.' And that doesn't cause no trouble of course! So that kind of thing will go on, lads coming back into the yard laughing at you. Because we went through some bad experiences over the last two years, heart-searching, took some decisions that we didn't like and a lot of things we've done to keep the yard open and these cowboys who walk up the bank with cheques laughing at you, coming back in the yard. Christ! I don't know how they come to terms with the situation. I think in SS it's just total demoralisation. Now they are saying over there, 'For God's sake, hurry up and

1. Scott Lithgow, Greenock, outside Glasgow, a large shipyard specialising in oilrigs. When denationalised in 1984 and bought by Trafalgar House, it had a workforce of 8,000. Now staffed by 40 on a care-and-maintenance basis. It was alleged at the time that it was bought as an asset-stripping move for its valuable riverside site.

close to let me get the hell out of this yard because I am as sick as a cherry at the whole situation.' That's how far down the morale has gone. And that's why it is going on over there; they don't give a monkey's. It's total demoralization.

Rick: The standard of work being sent in by the blacksmith contractors, it's mainly handrails in the engine room and the module. The work that has been sent in is an absolute disgrace and we have had managers admit that it is a disgrace. We got in touch with C— during the week to ask him for a meeting and he said, 'I'll get back to you when I can.' I said, 'I want you to come and look at it yourself, because we've been on to you from day one about the standard that is coming in. It is just appalling,' but he will not discuss it. So the lads in the department decided that they are not going to touch or rectify any work that comes in, it's just going to lie. In the engine room the question was raised have we got to do any rectifications, the joggles and so on which gans on in the engine room, and the management turns round and tells us, 'You do the hard bits and the contractors will send in the easy bits.' We've been asking them for weeks now to at least give us something back.

gannin' back on the stones again

Tony: Casualisation means ... if you are casual then you don't complain about the job, you don't complain about the safety, cause there is always a chance that you'll get kept on, your short-term contract will be extended, and extended. So you tend not to complain and do everything the gaffer tells you, cut corners, do owt, to stop gannin' back on the stones again. Therefore it undermines the safety, it reverts you to the market system where – like we used to be – we'd have a hundred and odd people standing of a morning and the gaffer would come and pick who is going to get a start. Any troublemakers wouldn't get a look in, no chance, no chance.

Pickard: Shut your trap and snap your back.

Tony: They didn't used to be temps, everybody was a temp. That's why it will be even worse now because you will have two categories.

Danny: Somebody once said to me a welder that had committed murder would never get away with it because sitting watching that little blue light you'd gan mad, you've got nowt else to think about. You concentrate on that light, you are just watching the light and

127

everything is going through your mind, all the things … problems at home. It's not a job that you do where you are physically working and concentrating on the job that you do, you are just sitting watching the light, consequently it's all going through your mind …

> At the end of February I interviewed Big Dan, one of the oldest welders in the yard. He also brought along and lent me old Bartram's diary which he had rescued from the fire when the shipyard was closed down.

there's no such thing as a Militant

Dan: There was caulkers, burners, and welders. By the time I finished my time the welding trade had been initiated so you got a welder's card. They didn't say you were a 'caulker-burner-welder'; you were a 'welder' then. Some fellahs, most of them older than me, they got 'caulker-burner-welder' cards, so they could do the three, but all I ever did was just the welding.

Pickard: How long was the apprenticeship?

Dan: You did seven year, fourteen to twenty-one, and if you lost any time you had to do back time before you got proper wages. You see you 'did time', that was the phrase, if you did a year away from the trade through no fault of your own, you had to do that year when you came back.

The first day when you went to work there was noise. Noise and bedlam. There was a lot of men. There's nobody working in the yard now to compare. In the morning, it was literally a mass of men walking along the dock. And then five o'clock it was just a stream of men walking up to the town. Every shipyard. When you look at Trimdan Street, when they come up the lane from Doxford's, you couldn't walk up when they were walking down, there was too many of them. But my first impression was of a mass of men and the noise. The noise especially. I mean I lived on the river and you could hear the noise all the time, but when you went inside it was a different world. It was bedlam. You can quite imagine why all the people were getting these deaf pensions. They should have had them then.

You had drillers, caulkers, riveters, there was squads! They were about the biggest trade of the lot, the riveters. You see there was

128

three men to a squad plus the heater and the catcher, so every squad you had five men. There was more of them than anybody else, them and platers.

I was turned fourteen, because I was on at Austin's for about ten months, and it was no good along there. I got a chance to gan to Bartram's when I was about sixteen.

I knew what to expect because all the family were boilermakers. If you lived on the river, wherever you looked you saw a shipyard. Looking across the water from where I lived I could see Thompson's Cranes, Dickenson's, I could see Austin's then looking towards the dock I could see Greenwell's. If you were brought up with that, it wasn't strange to you, but on face-values it was like your first job. But having said that, you knew everybody that was in the yard, because they were either relations or neighbours, so you weren't strange. Not like now with kids coming in from outside the district, they don't know nobody. But, when I went in there, I had uncles, cousins, so it wasn't really strange. Only for the noise.

Pickard: Did you have to join the union straight away?

Dan: Oh, that was one thing you make sure you do, then you dare not be behind with your dues, you had to pay, if you didn't you got wrong. I mean, more so the shop stewards then ... they were strict.

Pickard: Were you apprenticed to a particular bloke?

Dan: No, well that was the best thing about it then, you got sent with a fellah, I knew the two I was ganna gan with, you were taught the right way. Now they are not. They put the gear in their hands and expect them to pick the job up. You cannot. If you want to be a decent welder you've got to be shown by somebody that can do it, because you cannot pick it up by yourself. But these fellahs, when they saw you do the job and if you didn't do it right, you got a crack! And made to put it right. But the way they do it now, these colleges, is rubbish.

You were sent with them for about a year or two, but you stopped with them, and if you didn't stop with them you got with somebody else, equally as good. There was some good welders in there. There was some bad ones as well, but you knew who the good ones were and you just attached yourself to them. Having said that, the foreman had a little say then, and they would tell you where to gan and – it was piece-work – and you had to go down there and do it.

129

I mean you didn't just gan on and bop off, because if you don't do the job you didn't get paid.

Pickard: How did you get a start?

Dan: It was all a family affair, your father spoke for you, or your uncle or whatever. You never had to wait. The war was on so there was plenty of work. 1942 when I went in. That was the best system, when you got fellahs bringing sons in, cousins or whatever, then you looked after them. You didn't get a chance to be a bad worker because you got it knocked into you.

It was open, when you walked in the yard you looked at the sea. You looked and saw two piers, you could see the two piers, aye, you'd see a beach and three berths. Well it was bleak in the winter, it was a cold place, lovely in the summer.

Bartram's was in the dock, and then literally, when you come out of the yard, you couldn't see across the other side of the dock for ships, colliers, just lined up about six abreast.

And the characters that we had then! You've none like them now. They were great. Now, you would lock them up because they were daft, you'd think they were daft, but they weren't though. They were good people, good workmen. But you had characters all over, man. Now you haven't got them. They haven't got the same kind of feeling for the place now. Then it was a pleasure to gan to work. Not this place, boy. But you see Bartram's was unique in that respect in that it launched into the sea, and sometimes you got sent home, not because of the rain but because of the spray coming up. It was a northeasterly wind blowing a gale into the piers and the top of the yard. Anybody working aft were sent home. It wasn't raining, it was just the spray.

Pickard: Did you get paid if you were sent home?

Dan: No. You had to sign the dole. That time if you were out all the week you could sign on the Saturday as well. You got the extra day. But Thompson, he put the block on it because he said – he was a proper Tory like – he said, 'Don't give them it!' And he got it stopped, the Saturday morning. They spoilt the river, I must say, Thompson's. They tried to implement things other yards wouldn't stand for. They got away with it, where they wouldn't get away with it on other yards.

A lot of the lads got very active in the union. Every meeting there was, there they would gan. I mean the likes of little Danny. From the offset you could tell what he was going to be, Danny. And Tony

130

Carty. Hill! They were all good union men. That's how we've got the conditions we've got. All right you might call them 'militants', I don't call them 'militants'. They are just people speaking for what they want. There is no such thing as a militant, it's only a term used by these people because they don't like what they are doing, that's all. That's why they call you militant. But if you didn't stand up you wouldn't get nowt, would you?

I suppose there was plenty strikes and, all right, we lost money, but we always came out with what we went for. When you struck it was only a matter of principles. Basically you don't want to hold anybody to ransom, but if you stood together you got what you wanted.

If I had had my chance, opportunity, I would have went to sea. I had family seamen as well. But obviously with the war coming, me mother, she said, 'Don't go to sea,' and that was it. A welding job was all right, and I've made some money out of it.

Pickard: Did you ever work away from home?

Dan: Not much, one or two jobs. There was a Scottish firm, Kincaid's, well they came on the river and for a time they used to weld in the yard. I got involved with them, I got to know them, and one time I got laid off for something or other, I wasn't working, and they came back into the town and they knew I wasn't working so they started me as their welder from Sunderland. I had about six year with them. Great. Just moving about, see, at this yard, Short's, Lane's, Bartram's. It was a good job because I was moving all over the river, practically your own gaffer.

Pickard: When you were moving around on the river, was there much difference in the atmosphere in other yards?

Dan: Well one yard, Thompson's, nobody liked to gan in there. A concentration camp with staging, that's all it was. You were locked in. We were spoilt working at Bartram's, they were an open yard, you could walk about anywhere you wanted. There was no gates. Well, there was gates but you could just walk along the beach. There was no railings round, it was an open yard. That's what made Bartram's unique. You didn't walk in and they didn't slam gates behind you...

If something doesn't turn up in the next six months we'll be all flat. I'm nearly retired, but it will bugger the town. I would hate to see it happen because it is like shutting a pit, isn't it? Only more so.

a yank on the piano

Dan: Now Tony's father was a good singer, fantastic. He was a fool, he shouldn't have been welding, he was a good tenor. When we got a launch do, we got a few quid. Gordon Scott, a foreman welder, he was very good with his hands, sketching, and he used to make the bill out. Obvious, *Joe Carty: Mariolanza Carty.* He'd sing all the lads a song, and he could sing, no doubt about it. Then there was another welder, pianist, The Yank we called him: *Barefoot Days.* Another lad called Billy Moon, and The Yank on the piano. Another one called Henderson, Jimmy Henderson: *Al Johnson,* and they filled that place. If they knew there was a launch do on you couldn't get in. Strangers coming down just to join in. There's nowt like that now. You get a load of fights that's all. You see the old barbary coast, on that side of the water [south], and this side, the east end, was just shipyards, nowt else. Everybody knew everybody, so there was never any trouble. You had the two communities, the east end and the barbary coast.

strippers

Harry: We had this terrific black cockney stripper on the other night. She is standing at the bar and this young shipwright kid went up to her and said, you know the old bullshit, he said, 'You know, I thought you had marvellous movements. Can I buy you a drink?' He says, 'Your movements were lovely, I thought you were a great dancer.' And she said, 'Yes, but I've got no fucking tits, have I?' He didn't know what to do.
John: How many was on the stage on Friday? Two. And who organised that like?
Harry: It was organised as a football do. We usually get them from Bradford. They earn some money, you know. At four quid a ticket, and there was an extra pound in for the special show.
John: It's a night out though. It cost me about twenty guilders the last one I went to.
Harry: Listen to that fucker!
John: I tell you what, there is no rip-offs. The stage was there and I was right up the front. There was no rip-offs.
Harry: Any whip-offs?

John: I was going to try and get one organised this year but it's fell through.

Harry: They'll have one at the plumbers' bachelor party. So did you get your leg over in Amsterdam, John?

John: Oh no. We had a look at them, mind. Fucking hell, film stars, I'm sure you have heard the crack about them being film stars, and they fucking are. Fucking beautiful.

Harry: One of the lads that was in the Navy, Alfred, he went to Amsterdam, he was fucking one, and he says she had a lovely pair of tits, 'But,' he said, 'she kept her bra on.' He says, 'I was trying to get into her tits,' and she said, 'No, no, more guilders, more guilders.'

John: It was forty guilders, eleven quid, at the time. That's how much it was when we were there.

Billy: I though you said you only looked?

Harry: We went to a shipyard in Rotterdam. Fucking right outside the shipyard there was a fucking brothel. Sex for sale. Right next to the yard.

John: In Amsterdam, you know where you are and you know the area. If you don't want to gan there, you don't gan there. It's simple as that. It's so fucking mercenary though, there's no excitement.

Harry: One of the lads went down Soho, went upstairs and paid his money and he says, 'She was washing me, you know, and playing with me ring,' and he says, 'I just come me lot all over, and that was it.'

Rick: Hey John, I've just been up to your place and dropped off that coat I promised you.

John: What? When I wasn't there? You shouldn't do that, the neighbours will talk.

Rick: What's the matter, do you think I'm ganna jump on your wife?

John: No, but it'll compromise her.

Rick: I don't think so. But it might have embarrassed the bloke who answered the door.

MARCH

7/3/86

confed meeting: state of the industry

Jake: Swan Hunter's have arranged three meetings this week on the new contract of employment, pensions and wages. Govan: steelworkers working three half-shifts and a Sunday, outfit working no overtime, and a surplus of sixty to seventy electricians. Vickers: meeting at Trafalgar House with management, the company were trying to get the workforce interested to invest in the takeover bid and redundancies have been announced with no problems with volunteers. Ferguson Ailsa: two temporary workers have been paid off with the possibility of more redundancies in June: Yarrow's three hundred and ten redundancies announced, seventy-seven skilled and a hundred and forty-six unskilled and eighty-seven staff. They are also having problems with them bringing in sub-contractors from outside the yard. Ferguson Ailsa: forty manuals and eight staff have been made redundant and they are working on the last order which ends in May; Harland & Wolf have had no change since their last report. Clarke Kincaid's [engine builders], Greenock: there have been two small medium-speed engines taking work through to July/August. Clark Kincaid, Wallsend: now starting redundancies, no work after July. Barclay Curl: some sub-contract steelwork they've been getting from Govan, but unless work is obtained almost immediately then the yard faces closure. Scott Lithgow: M.o.D order been brought forward to help with continuity of work in the yard, the work at the present time includes pipe-fitters, welders, ancillary trades with the steelwork starting to run out very shortly and when that occurs the welders will be transferred into the pipe-fitting areas...

Tony: Now you can see the whole industry breaking up, there is even the departure of the chairman,[1] and we are down to the merchant sector. Approaches from Govan to ourselves suggested

1. Graham Day resigned and took up the chairmanship of another state-owned company, British Leyland.

that, prior to the wage negotiations in particular, we should have a meeting of representatives of the merchant sector. With the approaches to Smith Dock and SS about setting up a company of North East Shipbuilders, then you can see the fears of Govan, or the fears of Appledore with the centralisation of merchant shipbuilding. And M— has telt Govan, 'It's the best news for us because we'll have the central shipbuilding for Scotland, Smith Dock's ganna gan or one of them yards, either A&P or SS in the North-East is ganna gan. We're all right because we are on the Clyde.' You see that sort of thing is being said by the different managements, and also you'll get parochial feelings coming in, saying, 'They are doing that, and they are doing something else or other.' Whether it be temporary contracts, whether it be accepting working on reduced rates or whatever, they'll use one section or one yard against another. It is the old trick, divide and conquer all the way along the line until there is nowt left and everybody disappears, just like we were talking about last week. However, what they've asked for, and we've agreed with it, is that we should have a meeting of the merchant sector yards before then. I said I would test the water, knowing full well I'd already on the table that we were agreed in principle with the sort of meeting taking place just in the first instance to get to know what each management is saying so we are not stabbing each other in the back. Albeit we might not be able to do anything about it, we might have to stand up and say, 'Well my yard first and fuck all the rest of yous.' Sometimes that happens, but there is nowt stopping you protecting your own interests, and your own yards by finding out what the other yards is doing, and where you have common ground. So I said we would sound out on the Wear, for SS and Smith's Docks on the Tees, whether they'd be prepared to attend such meetings. Smith's Dock said aye. It's not a confed decision, the only link we've got there is with the boilermakers, but they said, if the confed turned it down, the boilermakers would still attend in any case. SS have said aye, they'll send four delegates . . .

gis ya card, who are ya?

WW: Concerning the West Yard saw mill, is there any indication when they are going to bring that down? Obviously with the asbestos being involved, there is a safety hazard. Has there been any final plans for an alternative saw mill?

138

Tony: Two weeks ago when we raised it, it was still either the transfer of machinery to the east yard saw mill or the furniture store in the complex. As regards the asbestos structure, we did suggest the best time to do it would be during the Easter weekend when there would be nobody in the yard.

WW: The biggest concern is where they are going to put the micro oven.

Eddy: Chairman, we are having difficulty with the contractors coming into the yard and not reporting to shop stewards when they come in. We've been gannin' about the yard this week, getting the word off other people in the yard, looking at cards. What I am suggesting is that if they came into the yard without reporting to shop stewards first, when we *do* find them and they haven't got the up-to-date card we tell them to leave the yard. We generally give them a day, if they come in the yard that day and they have forgotten their cards. That's if we find them.

Tony: Who are they?

John: The people who come in the yard are the AEUW [Amalgamated Engineering Union] members and we had to stop the job around with the GM [General and Municipal] members. They are coming in to put panels along the storm damage, along at the sheds. I approached O— and said, 'You never telt us they were coming in.' He says, 'Oh, I'm sorry, but the bloke that looks after them forgot to tell me that they were coming in.' I think they had been in a few days previous to that and we are still now having to chase round with Rick Jones looking for the AEUW cards and we now cannot find them. We are not going on the roof to look for them. As soon as you mention union cards they are away.

Tony: The best thing to do is, anybody that you haven't been notified of, just say, 'I haven't been telt that you should be on the site and until I am you'd better get off the site, on the grounds of health and safety.' Because that's what they said, they said every contractor has been sent a letter and been told that he has to report to the gatehouse under the Health and Safety Act. So everybody knows they are in the yard and what they are doing in the yard. Management are supposed to inform us and we are supposed to inform you, all the trades concerned.

Jack: They report to the gatehouse, chairman, but what I am saying is they don't report to the shop stewards.

Rick: Can we not ask the company when they are sending these letters out asking them to report on health and safety that they do it before they pick up their tools, that they show their union cards to the respective trade unions, before they pick up a tool.

Will: We seem to be falling down on the subcontractors as well.

Tony: That's the best way if we do get pulled, until the company tries to pull us under the law – that you by your actions are frustrating their contract to carry out work for A&P. Until we are pulled, then, just act as we normally do. Just say, 'Gis your card, who are you?' If the company is not going to co-operate with us, and it appears that O— is not, then we are just going to rattle them off the site and take the consequences because we are not working with scabs and we are not working with non-union members.

Rob: The staging makers, we approached them and asked them if they were in the union, they said, 'No, but we'll soon join.'

Tony: I inspected two AEUW cards of the lads that's doing the racking system in D Bay and there wasn't even a payment in it, they were brand-new cards, and they had been told by the branch secretary that they didn't have to make the payment until the following fortnight. They were just given cards. There is nowt we can do about that, that's an external organisation of our own, just issuing cards willy-nilly – it doesn't matter who to.

John: Regarding subcontractors and shot-blasters, the other night I was leaving the establishment and these two blokes were coming in with overalls on (clean overalls), looking for somebody from Tyroids. They didn't even know who they were looking for, to start on the shot-blasting. Fair enough they had union cards, but it has to be asked now, are they on the lump? Just coming in the yard and not knowing who the foreman is, or who they've got to report to, to do the shot-blasting.

Tony: You see the thing you do with them, you just say, 'Gis your union card, give me your name, and I'm going to check with the social security to see if you are working or unemployed or what?' That's all you've got to do with them.

Dave: Just to answer John, they were shot-blasting one night, I went over there and checked six or seven people out. They all had union cards and I've got their names and numbers in me book. They are painting now, by the way. Do we have to stop behind after four-thirty every night to check them?

Chris: Maybe have a word with the manager, just to see if it is going on, if they are on the dole. It looked like that to me.

Tony: You try to come to an agreement with the company to get things ... we try to work inside the law. But at times you just say, 'If they're not doing it, well I'm not doing it: we'll just take the consequences.' There is no way we should accept in this yard either non-union members or scabs or whatever. We've never done it before and we are not going to do it now, no matter what happens. If you find somebody, or somebody is reported to you, that is on the site and you've never been telt, just gan over and say, 'What are you doing on the site? What is your job? Where is your union card?' They could be lump-workers and all you've got to do is say, 'I want to know if you've got paid the rate, where do you get your pay slip? I want to see your pay slip to see you are getting paid the same rate as me for doing my job.' Or if he hasn't got a pay slip he must be unemployed and doing the job on the lump. 'Have you got a secondary job?' Or whatever. Now all that sort of thing, it's rife throughout the industry, and it is going on in all the yards throughout the country, this sort of thing. The lad doing the job in D Bay is being subcontracted to the subcontractor and he is self-employed. When I said to him, 'You'll have to pay the skilled rate for the job,' because he is a grade-three AEUW member, he said, 'Oh, it's all right, it's me and our boy, and I'll make sure he gets one hundred and fifty-eight pound.'

John: Fucking hell.

Tony: They are also talking now about the lads not being able to stop work to watch the launch.

24/3/86

A blizzard blowing. Tempers fraying. Jim, the welder, is
out on a cherry-picker in the gale, the sleet and snow
whipping against him. A lot of men taken off the fore-
end as the conditions are horrendous, although a number
of welders and burners are working on some hazardous-
looking rigging, sparks of molten metal blowing all
around and over their mates working alongside or below.
Jim's mate, Dave, is off ill with bruised or broken ribs:
someone was demonstrating to him how to use a new
cherry-picker [mobile lift platform on a long arm] when
they brought it down too hard, throwing him against the
iron rails and bruising his ribs. Spoke to a welder who
told me about moving from berth to berth when finished
working in one sump tank to another. Said a mate of his
went mad, used to sit against the inside ribs, crouched-
up, wearing a skull mask. Described his own moment of
terror: he was working inside the lube-oil sump,
completely inside the box, legs drawn up behind him,
when he suddenly felt he was getting larger. He thought
all of his body was swelling up, his head expanding, that
he would never be able to get out.

The ship to be launched on a spring tide. Saw a tree
washed down the river today. Seals and shags in the
water. No one really sure if the ship will be done on time.
One foreman complained to one of the shop stewards,
Brian, that he was under tremendous pressure from the
management to get this done and that done. Brian told
him that the pressure stopped with him, the foreman, and
would not be put on the men who were having to work
in the most atrocious conditions already.

Spoke to Peter Gibson under the ship. He was going
round patching up, a good job for welders, he told me,
especially in these conditions.

25/3/86

Brian Tate told me that the best time to launch a ship
was on the spring tides. Tomorrow is a full moon and
the tide will be at its highest. Incredible bustle to get the
ship ready in time for the launch. Last night as I was
leaving, a gaffer told me that they would get seven million
pounds when it went in the water. 'What does seven
million pound look like? How big is it? Would it fill your
bedroom? I can't imagine it, can you?' he said in a very
serious voice. When asked, no one will say if they think
the ship will be launched, yet, when pushed, they
obviously think it will. Jim was working twelve hours on
the cherry-picker yesterday, he was in a terrible state
when he got back home. 'No good to anybody. I just had
a bath and went to bed and slept like a bairn till this
morning.' He was working today again on the cherry-
picker, half-way up the vessel with showers of sparks
flying all around him. Although the weather is fine today,
'there is still a strong wind once you get up a-height,' he
told me. Despite working for twelve hours yesterday in
the middle of icy blizzards and gale-force winds, he was
singing to himself at about six in the evening, as the sun
set: maybe a last burst of adrenalin as he approached the
end of his day.

APRIL

7/4/86

Asked about launch parties and were they invited. Representatives of the unions are always invited to the launch party, but this shop stewards' committee refuses because they believe it to be a form of soft corruption. 'They wouldn't drink with us socially, so why should we do it for that occasion. Anyway we consider it to be a waste of money.' The confed refused to visit Japan for the same reason.

A walk-out at Swan Hunter's on the Tyne the day before the launch of HMS *Coventry*. Management dragging out pay talks.

8/4/86

Driving in to the yard this morning I turn on the car
radio to hear a jubilant BBC announcer describe launch
of HMS *Coventry* at three in the morning by management
and the navy!

A special shop stewards' meeting called at 9.30 to
explain a request/demand from management for a team
of specialists to interview the workforce in groups of four
about communication with management and problems
therein. Sounds very much like the measures which the
secret report commissioned by BS recommended. They
want a kind of Japanese system.

Visited the ship for the first time in its new berth, tied
up to the quay. A noticeably different atmosphere since
management have introduced a new regime, 'a purge' the
men call it. No one is allowed to leave the ship before
the siren. Although the work is obviously finished for the
day, and the men gather round the gangplank waiting to
get off the ship, if they do put a foot on the gangplank
they are booked. If they get three bookings they can be
fired. A very noticeable atmosphere of resentment. Two
gaffers stand at the top of the gangplank and two at the
bottom, with three or four white hats [managers] around.
A worker on contract goes down the plank and a roar
of derision goes up from the blokes. What happens is that
all of the men gather at the gangplank and wait to leave
at once. This puts an obvious strain on the plank and it
looks very dangerous indeed when they all eventually,
like children with a school bell, go down the plank
together and in a rush. Without fail the gaffers and white
hats on the quay look at their watches. They themselves
have been standing around, doing nothing else but
making sure that no one leaves the ship.

Management having got the ship in the water at great

expense and with a tremendous effort by the workforce in awful conditions, have now solved their cash-flow problems and can afford to take a more macho stand against the unions.

The welders are under pressure because D— insists that they use the semi-automatic Kempy welding machines. He wants to make it compulsory. The machines overheat and are useless for most types of welding. Obviously, instead of going to the shop floor and finding out why few people volunteer to use the machines, they are issuing a diktat: *Work on the machines or else*. The convener had to dig through his minutes to prove that they had an agreement whereby welders could volunteer to use the machines but not be forced to. A hurried meeting was called in the afternoon with the welders' shop stewards, then the welders' negotiating team went for a meeting with management at 2.30. The meeting lasted until almost five o'clock. They came back looking exhausted. D— suggested they both go away and think about it until Monday. Danny Morgan thinks that it is a tactic to split the solidarity of the yard. They accused D— of planning a campaign of provocation, as outlined in the secret report. He denied it and said that they had sacked the bloke, a technical director, who was responsible for the remarks. 'That useless fucker,' said D.

Apropos the purge, TB said that he, as a safety rep for the union, was going to be going around with a safety rulebook tomorrow as the ship was highly unsafe with wires and cables lying all over the decks, and he'd be sticking to the letter of the law.

Anyone leaving their area is booked.

Bob came to see me in my office and spoke about his son. A good drawer, not motivated, typical teenager, but a very talented drawer, could I help in any way. I didn't know how but arranged to go and see him and the drawings on Thursday.

HMS Scab

BBC radio news: ... is now tied up at Swan's Neptune Yard. From there Malcolm Bergman:

Bergman: The navy's newest warship, the *Coventry*, now stands berthed here at the Neptune Yard at Walker after a dramatic night-time launch from the Wallsend Yard. Dwarfed by the huge cranes here on the dockside the *Coventry* is moored next to the *Sheffield*, another Falklands replacement launched rather differently in a blaze of publicity less than two weeks ago. Both ships will now be doing extensive outfitting work and it will be almost two years before either of them is ready to sail from the Tyne. Swan Hunter's managing director Alex Marsh said he is delighted with the quality of the company's latest ship.

Marsh: I think the *Coventry* is a super ship and I don't believe that our launch last night in any way affects the ship. She's lovely, she's in her home element in the water and very glad to be there. Although no real problems, we were concerned about the high winds but they in the event proved to abate near high-water and the launch went very smoothly indeed.

Bergman: It must be a very unusual thing indeed to launch a ship in the darkness.

Marsh: Yes it is very unusual, I don't know when it was done last on the Tyne, if it has been done at all. It has worked very successfully.

Bergman: So what is going to happen to the ship now that it has been brought from the Wallsend Yard to the Neptune.

Marsh: She is now ready for outfitting, to the last year and a half of her building phase, before she hands over to the Royal Navy after hopefully successful sea trials.

Bergman: What sort of things need to be done to the ship now?

Marsh: Well it is basically completion of the interior outfit, the joinery work, the beds and the pipework, starting the engines and running the engines and things of that nature.

Bergman: Do you believe the way in which she has been launched might just encourage people to place further orders with Swan Hunter's.

Marsh: Well I hope it shows that the company has a determination to succeed and to provide the product to the customer at the right time, and hopefully very good value for money.

BBC: Meanwhile union leaders representing the striking workers whose threat of mass protest caused the surprise launch, are trying to decide what to do next. This morning they turned up at the yard to find the *Coventry* already in the water and the gates closed to keep them out. Management suspended them when they staged yesterday's walk-out. There was little for shop stewards' leader, Alan Wilkinson, to do but tell them to go home and get out of the rain.

Wilkinson: The boat is in the water, we are totally locked out, it would be very unfair to keep you here this morning just to get drenched. Find somewhere dry and return at half one, we are now going into the meeting with the stewards here. We'll make no comment until we come out of the meeting.

Reporter: Can I ask how you feel about this?

Worker: Bloody sick. Disgusting.

Worker: My comment can't gan on the radio.

10/4/86

South Africa

> The confed meeting was addressed this morning by a
> black South African trade unionist, Charles. Work had
> been taken from strike-bound South African plants and
> brought to BTR in England. He was on a quick tour to
> lobby British trade unionists.

Dodds: Using BTR as an example, what reaction, if any, have you received from the workers, the British trades-union workers at BTR?

Charles: I have met two BTR companies, in Birmingham and in Leicester. They didn't respond positively, except that they have promised to start discussing the issue. They also promised to start a collection and send money over. And they will see if there is anything for use in South Africa in their factory and they will try to start boycotting this material. They are not sure what the response will be from the workers themselves, but the group I met there were sympathetic with the workers in South Africa and promised to do something about it, but I don't know what.

Dodds: Can we just get back to the point where you mentioned the scab labour. Can you tell us some more about the identity of the scab labour? Obviously it's one of your biggest problems when it happens all over the country, and surely these people must realise, in South Africa, the damage that they are doing to their fellow workers by being scab labour in the first place. I'm just interested in their motives and their identity.

Charles: Well the biggest problem that we've got in South Africa is that there is high unemployment, and the people are forced out of their cities into the homelands: they don't know what is happening in the cities. They are recruited in the homelands, loaded onto buses, and taken to the work places. The employers keep them in hostels. They will only find out later that there were people working

152

9. Welder entering a confined space on the shell

10. Erecting the bulbous bow

11. Welders (in cherry-pickers) and burners working on the bulbous bow

12. Positioning the propellor

13. Lifting the propellor boss

14. Preparing drag chains for the launch

15. Welding on the bulbous bow thirty minutes before the launch

16. One of the waxed ways prior to the launch

there before them who had been dismissed for going on strike. They have been recruited as strike-breakers.

Mack: Have you got any white people in your union? You say there are forty-five thousand; are they all black people or have you got white ones as well?

Charles: Yes, but they are a very low percentage. It is between three and five per cent white.

Mack: Do you have the same wages?

Charles: No, they are earning more. You see, in the case of South Africa, even if you do the same job as a white person he will always earn more than a black worker. We have fought this with the government and the employers and they have scrapped a local 'job reservation' which they used to reserve certain jobs only for whites. They have scrapped it, but as it has existed for years there is still that gap. It will take a long time to overcome that problem.

Billy: Knowing that you are a hardened trade unionist, did the South African government try to stop you leaving the country when they knew you were coming to Britain?

Charles: They have been very difficult. What they do is refuse to give us a passport. If you apply for a passport and fill in a form saying that you want to go to a country in April, they will delay your passport and you will only get one in September, and they'll know they have stopped you going in April. So what do I do? I just apply for a passport. It takes a year, two years, and so on, and when I get it I just organise a trip immediately. What they are doing now is only giving us a passport for one year, which means every year you have to go and renew it.

Dodds: Will you have problems getting back into the country?

Charles: That has always been the case, but in fact if you are a member of any organisation in South Africa, whether a political organisation or trade-union movement, you have to tell yourself that you have signed a contract to die for your own people. We are risking our lives, my family know this, and everybody knows this. We have to do it. We can't let them get away with this. I can be detained in the airport easily, but they have to say exactly what they are doing. My crime has to be that I call the government our enemy. I have to say this.

Tony: Part of anybody's education is learning how other people have struggles just the same as overselves, not just picking up what is happening in South Africa from the media, but hearing it first

153

hand. What we can do is, first of all, on the BTR issue, see if we have any connection with them: whether they supply us, or whatever. Also, because it is in line with our unions policy, the confederation and the TUC policy, that we support the struggle in South Africa, we'll apply added pressure. We'll see that the secretary writes to our executives, expressing support for the South African Metal Workers Allied Union, and we will also ask the Labour party to put on whatever pressure they can and talk about boycotts. But to me they just mouth support on the question of boycotts. They didn't really organise a campaign within the trade-union and labour movement to actually see that those sort of campaigns against multinational companies become successful. Possibly they start off and then just peter out. One opposite example, of course, is the group of Irish shop workers who only recently were in a long dispute about boycotting South African goods. They stood out like a beacon to every other worker in the international trade-union movement and the international workers' movement. We've got the power and the strength there for combating multinationals easily. It is just harnessing that power.

11/4/86

News came in that some hardwood blocks had been found inside both launch triggers and could have caused an horrendous accident, making the ship capsize during the launch.

Bob took me down into the engine room. It was very dangerous. A rickety unsecured ladder was the only means of escape to the top deck for about forty men had an accident occurred. Not only that but once at the top of the ladder you met a wooden partition causing you to stoop under it by bending double and leaning back over the unsecured ladder to get out. Two decks further down, below the engine there was an unenclosed fire burning, caused by the molten metal which comes from the burners above. Then, below the floor of the engine room grid, the bodies of a couple of men can be seen bent into a contorted position, welding. A shower of molten metal falls on to the stairs above us.

With the lunch-time siren, Bob took me home and introduced me to his son who has just turned twenty and draws very good portraits from photographs with a thick pencil. His parents are worried about him being shiftless and unmotivated; not about getting a job, but about neglecting his obvious talent. His mother did almost all of the talking, Later, in the car, when we gave her a lift to the hospital, she told me this: 'When he first started drawing I found them. I said who did these? And he told me a lad he knew. I said, hey, these are good. What does he do for a living? Nothing, he said. He's unemployed. What, how could a lad as talented as this be out of a job? I asked him. Then he told me it was him that did it.'

21/4/86

where newts spend their adult life

Ronnie: What about suckling?
Cal: No.
Eddy: Talking, walking, shitting.
Cal: It comes naturally to most animals but it has to be taught to humans.
Eddy: Swimming.
Cal: Who sang 'Kissing to be clever?'
Eddy: Noel Coward.
Cal: Boy George.
Eddy: I was getting close with Noel Coward, they're both bent.
Ronnie: Was Noel Coward bent?
Eddy: He used to gan round all the pot-holes.
Cal: Is *phlogiston*, certified by thirteenth-century chemists, a real substance or not? And why? Is it yes or no?
Tommy: Yes.
Cal: Anybody else want to come in on that?
Tommy: I though it was Saint Elmo's fire, like phosphorus that builds . . .
Cal: Well, that's not what it's got here.
Chris: St Elmo's fire is what you see on the rigging on ships.
Cal: What is a snake doing when it sloughs?
Pickard: Shedding its skin.
Eddy: Come on! You didn't have your hand up. I was just about on a par with him with my hand up.
Tommy: I was ganna say shedding its skin.
Eddy: That's what I was ganna say, shedding.
Ronnie: That's all it could be, like. You couldn't slough owt else could you?
Eddy: You were jumping the gun. Put your hand up and wait your turn.
Cal: How many kings named Geordie ruled Britain?

156

Pickard: Five. Six.
Cal: Correct.
Chris: He got it wrong at first.
Pickard: It was before my time.
Chris: Was it fuck! It was 1950 before he died, man.
Cal: Where do newts spend their adult life?
George: In the water.
Danny: In the grass.
Rick: In a marsh. In a bog.
Eddy: Under rocks.
Tommy: No, they don't, do they? Because newts become lizards.
Jimmy: You daft twat.
Eddy: The club, cause you get pissed as a newt for a quid. Did you not hear that programme on the telly the other night about them? They were saying there was three different kinds: I says, 'I know two, the crested newt and the common one.' Our lass says, 'What's the other?' I said, 'The pissed as a.'
Cal: I'll have to give Danny that one, he said grass. What is the blue in blue cheese?
Tommy: Mould.
Cal: Five squared equals twenty-five: five times five is twenty-five. What is the other number when squared gives the answer twenty-five?
George: Three.
Tommy: It's not minus five is it?
Cal: What would you keep in a bandolier?
Tommy: Bullets.
Rick: That was an easy one. I would have got that.
Tommy: It's amazing how they are always easy when I get a one.
Cal: Now this is on geography. I don't want you to give the answer, just in case he says it's easy. So if you know it just keep it to yourself. By what name is the country of Bechuanaland now known? And that's the way you say it as well.

keep them guessing

Tony: To run it down, first of all there'll be surpluses in September in all sections and he's certain to offer certain ones redundancy. And as there is no replacement scheme or BS scheme there will be a mad fucking scramble and then they can pick and choose who they are going to keep and who they are not fucking going to keep. But another interesting thing, in the state scheme it used to be fifty/fifty, that the government paid fifty and the employer paid fifty. From now BS picks up the full tab and that's another disincentive.
Pickard: So they can choose amongst the volunteers who they want to accept?
Tony: But we've got criteria: age and length of service.
Jake: All things like that only apply when you've got something to bargain with, and in that situation they would do what the fucking hell they want to do. And there is not fucking much you could do about it. Because the ball would be totally in their court.
Tony: The only thing we would have would be the ships that have to be delivered, and that would be our bargaining point that we'd still have that number of pounds within our grasp.
Jake: By transferring the majority of the responsibility of the state scheme to the employer, what does that give the incentive to do? Not to employ people on the long-term, so he doesn't get into that situation, into acquiring another fixed overhead. So he'll keep people on short-term employment.
Tony: Nobody ever gets two year, because that's one hundred and four weeks, when redundancy benefit is required. On two occasions he's made no bones about it: what he sees is a diminishing labour force, and they are using more and more temporary people. He says the remaining labour force make their jobs more secure by using temps. And through natural wastage, or whatever, he gets shot of them, that's what he wants. That's what all this is about, about

temporary contracts. It's about setting up the industry and the company for a potential private fucking buyer. He can say, 'Look what we've got. We've got all these agreements, we've got fucking temporary contracts, we've trimmed the labour force down to the fucking bone, we've trimmed all the staff, all the planning, everything is down to the bone. It's a lean dog just waiting to be used. All right, shipbuilding is finished, but if there is an upturn in the oil industry, and they are forecasting next year that the price of oil will start to rise because it cannot keep its low level all the time, then people will start to want to get the fucking transport, or get oil. And I can tell you there is a labour force there, whether it be modules or whether it be fucking crane barges or barges for the North Sea oil-related industries. And say you are paying six pound an hour, or seven pound an hour at a time, and we are only paying three and four and you've got an outfit there can do the fucking lot. Can do any type of welding you fucking want. They can build any sophisticated vessel you fucking want, because they have been trained to fucking do it, and there she is.' I'm not saying it will be here, it could possibly be that fucking yard over there [Sunderland Shipbuilders]. You see there are all sorts of options and strategies they've got. It stands out a mile, if you are ganna take a labour force, and you are ganna take a yard, who would you take? Ours or theirs? They are broke.

Pickard: You wouldn't take an organised labour force, would you?

Tony: No.

Jake: And we'll gan the same way unless we continually do our fucking job, and that means everybody all the time. And not going round forgetting about it. Because he's got the aces and he's ganna come in with the fucking big boot. You are not even ganna see him anyway, he'll get other people to do it and just sit back and wait for results.

Pickard: Where is the administration of the new company, North East Shipbuilders Ltd?

Tony: Over there [Sunderland Shipbuilders]. They are just emptying our offices and taking the stuff over there. The drawing office is bound to be fucking next. I mean they cannot just fucking sit up there.

Jake: I got a shock last week, you know what they used to be like. Pretty compact, with bodies all over. It's fucking not now.

Danny: They used to be in two sections. There used to be the hull section and the engine section, now it's just down to one office, they've cut the partition down and they are just working any-fucking-where.

Tony: P— says, 'The drawing office is a load of fucking shite, fucking rubbish. We've got a load of inexperienced fucking boys in there who don't know their fucking job.' And in a normal drawing office situation you've still got some old hands who'll help the fucking young ones along, but he says, 'We haven't, they are all young ones.'

Jake: I think P— had a relevant point when he said they'd been building SDs too long. I think that is part of it as well.

Tony: I'm waiting to see if anybody is going to get finished. All this re-organisation. I'm still waiting to see if people gan out the fucking door like we did.

Jake: They've got another three weeks before their six weeks is up.

Pickard: What's the six weeks?

Jake: They are supposed to be on six weeks' secondment over there, at Sunderland Shipbuilders, then it's make-your-mind-up time.

Pickard: Then they have an option whether to stay there or lose their jobs?

Jake: I don't know if they went over there with that intention but that's what he's ganna give them. They work over there for less money.

Pickard: So the office staff over here get the same twenty quid a week more, do they?

Tony: I don't know what the difference is, but they get more. Our clerical staff get more, they work less hours than them.

Pickard: If you lot got transferred over there, I mean if anybody was on loan over there from this yard, would they be on that yard's wages of twenty quid less a week?

Tony: Aye.

Pickard: So you wouldn't get many volunteers?

[*Laughter*]

Jake: I imagine they get the same wages at the present time, on secondment, but after that they'll get a reduction or fuck all.

Pickard: Do you think the strategy is to reduce the capacity of the yard?

Tony: I don't know. I can just surmise what the possibilities are.

25/4/86

the Thatcher visit

Rick: Is there owt in the *Journal* about fucking Thatcher coming?

Tommy: Aye, she's gannin' over the water. There's frogmen over there now. I've just heard what the arrangements are: J. L. Thompson's men are getting a full day off, Doxford's men are getting half a day, Laing's is getting fucking nowt. But all the subcontractors on the boat and down J. L. Thompson's are getting a day off with pay. And the fucking gold men's only getting half a day.

Rick: I remember when everybody walked away from her, everybody turned their backs on her.

Billy: They turned their backs on her, quite deliberately at the launch.

28/4/86

Mackem etymology

Pickard: What does that mean?

Eddy: *Macking taffy*? Get with it. You know when a man's horny, gets a horn, and a woman fucking lubricates, doesn't she? *Macking taffy* [making toffee]. You've got to get with it, Tom. You could write a fucking book just with the fucking daft sayings we've got.

Chris: You've been down fucking London too long.

Pickard: You are winding me up.

Rick: Did you hear the programme on the wireless the other day there? Cockney bastards, well maybe not Cockneys but general people down that area, talking about what they thought it was like up here. You should have fucking heard them. They are up here now at the universities, and they are saying, 'It's great, it's much better than we thought. We thought there would be coal mines along the streets and all sorts.' They thought we were all a bit thick up here. They were sincere, and all.

Eddy: There was a Cockney come it with one of the lads from the outlying villages, a fucking pitman boy, he had a scar reet down there, across his two eyelids. He come the lip with him. 'You fucker, thick!' He belted him round the fucking chimney. Every time he hit him a bump came out. He enjoyed his leave. He didn't half enjoy his leave.

Chris: I'll tell you what though, you gan up to Scotland, and Glasgow, and you can see poverty worse than we've got here.

Tommy: Worse place I've seen poverty is Dublin. Bairns begging in the street.

Eddy: These are canny biscuits. Who brought them in? Rick's getting intellectual as well. He'll finish up like Oscar Wilde, him. He'll definitely end up like Oscar.

Rick: There's nothing wrong with educating yourself.

Eddy: This country doesn't count education. It's who you know. You can see it in this fucking yard.

162

Rick: Education and art are two different things really. Fucking art, you've either got it or you haven't.

Eddy: You've got to be a natural.

Rick: Like me and Tom are naturals.

Tommy: I'll tell you what, you'll get further on in art than you will in education. It doesn't matter how many qualifications you've got, if you try to get a job.

Rick: I enjoyed watching Tom negotiating his expenses. Brilliant. No slaver with manager, just sitting there, he shouted a number out and he got it like that. Fucking brilliant.

Chris: What about this festival you are going to organise for us? And haven't we got a producer called Nigel coming up from 'Arena'? Are you going to get a stripper on?

Pickard: Nigel's not very clever on his feet. He'd probably get his zipper stuck.

Rick: They have to be special, not like the ones that get round the club.

Eddy: I'll tell you what you can do, you can audition them, make sure they've got no spots on their backsides.

Rick: I'd like twins that could do a really good stage-act. In fact I was talking to a lad that said, 'Anytime you want two strippers, I can get you two strippers, both twins . . . One of them ties a fucking dildo . . .'

Pickard: What did it cost?

Chris: We were paying them fifty quid each. So can we have something like that Tom for the festival?

Pickard: I'll see if Northern Arts have a ballet fund.

Chris: So Nigel from 'Arena' is coming tomorrow? Do we call him Ducky?

Pickard: Everybody else does. And I'll bring him in for the tea-break.

Chris: Well, tell the bastard he'll have to bring some fucking biscuits.

Rick: Here's a joke for you, Tom. This bloke gans to the doctors . . .

Billy: Tommy, no disrespect, but your fucking jokes is crap.

Dicky: When your old wedding ring was new.

Chris: So who are we going to get introduced to tomorrow? Some fucking ducky producer? Long scarf, white polo neck sweater.

George: Portable beanbag.

Chris: 'The sweat of the shipyard workers.'

163

Pickard: Nigel Williams.

Cal: Hello Nigel.

Dicky: I said to that big mouth-fucker over there: 'If you ever see his wife there's going to be fucking hell on.'

Pickard: Is he sniffing the nurse?

Eddy: Sniffing her? Fucking bacon sandwiches and groceries. He gets the groceries in for her when he's on shiftwork.

Pickard: Are you still delivering the dead?

Dicky: Not this week, I had a rest this week.

Pickard: Where are you drinking now?

Tommy: I'm not. No cash, no dash. All our lads are the same when there is no overtime on.

Chris: This lad here, he's got a meeting with management. Never done it before. What time is your meeting? If he gets on top of you, just say to him, 'Are you still beating up your wife?' If he says no, you say,'Oh you've stopped have you?' If he says yes, say, 'Oh, the rumours is true.' It flattens them if they get on top of you.

George: We went on a union course when we were down at Bartram's, and Henry Williams used to call in a couple of times a week.

Chris: He was fucking good, old Wilky. He used to say the things shop stewards had to remember was: 'Why? What? When? And what for? Just keep asking why? What for? Just keep them on why? And what?

George: Who's going to take the notes?

Chris: Geordie, the trouble with you is, you are too tense. Before you get up there you should just get into a few lotus positions, get cooled down. Just keep your cool with him. You know when you've got him on the go when he starts mumbling and playing with his pencil. You know that's when you've got him. Get him to commit himself.

George: He cannot commit himself, he'll have to gan to S—. He says, 'I'll have to have a word with S— and I'll let you know.'

Chris: Don't lose your temper and swear, like I do . . .

confed meeting: Thatcher and the Chinese take-away

Tony: I'll report on an informal basis what the yard committee has been doing. On Friday we had a meeting with Thatcher at Newcastle airport. There was representatives from Sunderland Shipbuilders there and we had two. When we spoke to Thatcher, my impression was she was very patronising to say the least, she agreed with everything we said, she agreed that the shipbuilding market was in a very steep decline, and that she sympathised very much with us and that she assured us that her government would do everything possible it could to see that they secured orders and put a smile on our faces, she said, for our families and for the communities we lived in. On specific points she mentioned two Chinese ships, and the possible further two 22,000-ton container ships. She said one pair was in an advanced state of negotiation and that hopefully they would put a package credit facility together linked with what they call aid and trade provision, ATP, that would be as good as or better than anybody could put together in the whole of the world apart from Japan. I'll comment on that statement later. We didn't know and nor has it ever been mentioned to us that there was a possibility of Chinese orders being placed with British Shipbuilders or being a possibility. And she said, 'You'll probably know more than I do, on them ships.' Well, we knew nothing so we didn't say anything. We asked all the relevant points that we've all made before, about incentives to give British owners the incentives to order in British yards, scrap-and-build policy, even stockpiling ships if it came to it. She made the points that there are too many ships swimming around to stockpile. She accepted that everyone was buying orders, that it wasn't a question of fair competition, it was a question of states deciding that they would buy an order to place in their yards to keep their yards running. She said that they'd sought to increase the intervention fund and that would be subject to a later report. They had in fact achieved nineteen per cent on every ship intervention fund, that they've got it up to twenty-three per cent. All right, they did that but we are looking for subsidies in the region of thirty to thirty-five per cent on the ship. She said, like I've indicated on the Chinese ship, that there would be credit facility made available that would beat anybody else in the world. She also said that she'd be looking at the FSK [military ship] ... the defence budget was running very high and it wasn't probable that they

165

could spend any more money from the defence budget for the FSK. As I say, she sympathises with our problem and the government would do everything possible to help us. I think there was only two things that were different, that came out of that: when she said that they would give softer credit facilities, they would make it easier in particular for Third World nations to order ships by inclusion of the trade and aid provision. That means they give them soft interest and also make other arrangements with them on trade or aid, whatever they can do for the infrastructure of that country, building bridges, etc. That would all be part of that provision. 'And,' she said, and without a doubt the four of us all took her to say the same (these are the actual notes I marked, I've got underlined), 'no one will beat us on credit terms and other things.' I took 'other things' to mean aid and trade like she'd said, because when she said ATP I didn't know what she meant, and I was going to ask her what she meant, but she came back and when she mentioned ATP she looked at her civil servants, and said, 'I mean by ATP, aid and trade provision,' then she qualified that and said, 'apart from Japan. We cannot beat the credit facilities that are being offered at the moment by Japan. We'll beat anybody else's terms for new orders.' It seemed to be a little bit of light at the end of the tunnel, a change in government policy if you want to put it that way. And also two possible Chinese ships. So that is which way we stood when we came out of the meeting.

When we came out of there we went on to have a meeting on Saturday morning in Sunderland Labour Club, arranged by the constituency party and met Denis Skinner, who is a national executive member. We met him on the best way to launch the campaign, particularly getting support within the Labour Party, and with the view to getting what they call a 'supply day debate' which is a major debate on a particular issue. The opposition is only given, I understand, twenty supply dates a year and they are very loath to use them on, as they see it, peripheral issues, or issues they think are not a major embarrassment to the government. That's what supply days are all about. Anyhow we have met, myself and Peter, along with brother Stores and brother Mores from SS, we met him for a short time and he advised us the best way to get the supply date. Also to draw to the attention of not only our own unions but also the national executive of the Labour Party.

We then went to the Houses of Parliament on Monday night and

166

the debate started on British Shipbuilders' borrowing requirements; to increase that amount of money by two hundred million pound in the intervention fund. Naturally the opposition party wasn't going to object to the increase of funds, so it was just a question of debating the issue.

I've made photocopies of the debate for you to study.[1] In the debate the MP from Govan mentioned the two Chinese orders, so they were also aware of them but they had never said nowt to anybody else. Also the minister made reference to the two possible Chinese orders and that they were also using provision of trade and aid to make the credit facility more attractive. They pinned the minister down by asking was it a change of government policy, what she told us on the Friday? And by mentioning that the subsequent press statements that appeared from the government departments disputing what she'd said to ourselves. The departments have said that there is still no change in making the credit package up to what they normally do. As you'll read there is a bit of a contradiction during the debate, first of all he's saying there is no change in policy and on the other hand he is saying they will use, for the merchant nations, trade and aid facilities to give a better package to any prospective owner. Really they had the minister on the ropes because all he was saying was contradicting himself in what the government was prepared to do. He said each possible order would be looked at on its own merits. But there was facilities for British Shipbuilders to gan and ask that this order or whatever order, to be made a special case and the government would see what they could do. Mind, by saying that, the question was asked, as you'll see, how many times has British Shipbuilders approached the government to look at a particular order in the past year and say *make it a special case*. And the ministry reply was *none*. On not one occasion has British Shipbuilders ever approached the government for extra aid. It could be they didn't want extra aid for orders because they were going through a restructuring exercise.

We had a meeting with Smith and Brown who I thought put up a competent reply to the government. They had the government ministers on the ropes on this question of what actually Thatcher had said. They thought it was important to keep her in the limelight, keep her linked with any campaign, and what she said that led to

1. *Hansard*, 28 April 1986, pp. 685–716.

the press report, and what she said about Stena ships. So they said we should keep what Thatcher said in the limelight and ask British Shipbuilders if they had any approaches to the government for extra aid. Ask for a meeting and just ask the question: *If not why not? Why were approaches never made for extra aid?* Ask the company how much they know about the Chinese order, how could we be affected by the Chinese order, is it a possibility and are we in with a chance of a two ships, possibly four ships, situation. Also they said, because there is some ambiguity in what we were saying and what Thatcher and her advisors were saying, that we needed to put down exactly what we interpreted what she said, and in fact give them copies of our notes, and then the three of us would agree a minute of what she actually said regarding soft credit facilities. Because immediately we come out of the room, Clay said, 'What did you understand her to say about credit facilities?' And we all said the same: that she said that they could put a credit package together better than any other country, and after consulting with one of her advisors, apart from Japan, and they would use the trade and aid provisions to make us attractive to prospective owners from the Third World. That's what she said, and that's the change in policy. I remember her saying 'we know other countries fiddle the books the way they structure loans': for example we know for our owners there is an eight-year moratorium period, eight year to pay the loan back for a ship. But the Italians, the way they do it is fourteen year. So there is no question of who is going to get the order in them circumstances. Eight year or fourteen years to pay the money back. She said, 'They are not the only ones that manipulate figures. We can do it also.' To my mind that's what she said, and the other lads understood her to say exactly the same.

So we then are looking to write direct to Kinnock. We met after that another national executive member, Margaret Becket, and she said that possibly we should be writing not only to our union but direct to Kinnock, and Whitey [secretary of the Labour Party] and any other member of the NEC who may be sympathetic. Let them all know that there is a problem in shipbuilding.

That's the up-to-date situation and what we intend to do. We are on our way. But with all the problems we have in doing that there are a lot of areas and MPs who are looking to their own area. You got the impression in the debate that people who didn't have merchant shipbuilding in their constituency were using that debate

168

to get in and argue about the AOR [naval auxiliary ship to replace Falklands' losses], about naval work for Swan's. There was very few Tories with shipbuilding in their constituencies: the only one is Neville Trotter and he wasn't even present. There are that few of them. During the whole of the debate I don't think there was any more than sixteen MPs in the chamber. The majority were on the Labour benches, the likes of Clay, Milne from Govan, Bob Brown, all the shipbuilding MPs.

May Day May Day

Danny: There was a meeting at the trade council and one of the things that came out of it was at the May Day rally on Saturday. They hoped there would be a big turnout of shipbuilding workers and that somebody would speak about the shipbuilding crisis at the rally, or at the end of the rally.

Tony: Well at the end of the day, we've got to provide speakers if organisations ask for them. Just laying it on the line. There is plenty notes that people can have, if they want to speak. Because possibly, depending on which way the campaign's developing, we cannot do it all. OK, I'll do it, and possibly Jake, and some of the other lads, but you are going to have to learn and be able to stand on your feet yourself and put a few words together because we all cannot be in the one place at the same time.

Jake: Just on that point, by virtue of what we have done over the last five days, we've met Thatcher, we've met Skinner and we've met John Smith, and various other MPs. But at the end of the day it is only us that can do it. Don't get it wrong, it's not going to be easy. Smith said himself that there are very few MPs, even Labour, let alone Tories, that are not loath to pick the tab up on shipbuilding. They are not interested in it. So it is against that backdrop that we are going for publicity. And if we have meetings they'll expect shop stewards to attend. I was disgusted on Saturday morning that there wasn't more shop stewards there. Because if you want to save the yard, if you want to have a campaign, if we are going to do that, we are going to have to be physical about it and attend meetings and support speakers on the platform. Danny Morgan spoke on Saturday morning: he did it not because he wanted to, nobody likes getting up there and making contributions. But it has to be said, it

169

has to be done. And people are going to have to support. Because if you are not gannin' to support, tell us now that we are wasting our time. We've got to get it together and we've got to transfer that down to the shop floor and as a unit we've got to get that together and make sure that we get as much publicity and as much gain out of this as we possibly can. I'm telling you now, everybody I talked to feels the same way: we are going down the tube. So we can either lie down and get our bellies tickled and gan, or we can stand up and fight. I would impress on you, please, support wherever you can and whenever you can.

MAY

8/5/86

there's no truth in the rumour

Dicky: The safety office a few weeks ago told the nurse, 'Don't use the same one all the time, because they'll start to notice one or two things.' But she says, 'What is the point?' She gets the list, now it might be, say, Tommy Somebody or other, so she'll bleep him. Now he might be round on the quay, on the ship, so she's got to give him time to come off the ship, come to the nearest phone and phone to see what she wants. Then he might say, 'Oh, I'm too busy.' So she has to put the phone down and then bleep someone else on the team, and has to wait till they get to the phone and find out to see if they can do it. Now all this is taking time. The original concept of getting the ambulance was to get the injured person to hospital as soon as possible, which she knows will be done if she bleeps me. That is why I'm always getting bleeped. I rest my case.
Pickard: Is that a brief outline?
Dicky: If you interview the nurse she'll tell you all these things herself.
Chris: Don't ask this bastard to talk to her, he'll drive her nuts.
Pickard: You thought that I'd have a nervous fucking breakdown, but it's ye that's fucking cracking up.
Chris: You're thick-skinned you know, we really don't want you. Do we, Dicky?
Dicky: I don't mind, he's writing a book and I'm going to be in it.
Chris: He's not ganna write a book. There's been no fucking mention of a book. Tell me when you've heard a mention of a book?
Dicky: He's a writer isn't he? He's not going to put it in poetry, is he?
Chris: Well, go on then, ask him when the book's coming out.
Dicky: Are you writing a book?
Jake: Don't fucking spoil it for him, he doesn't want to have to start work now.

173

Dicky: Are you writing a book?

Pickard: I'm supposed to produce a booklet.

Chris: *Booklet?*

Pickard: Well, pamphlet.

Chris: *Pamphlet!* Our bairn could have done one.

Dicky: I thought it was the day-to-day running of Picky's.

Chris: No, he's taken the fucking piss out of us. If he went on 'What's My Line?' he'd confuse the fucking audience; nobody knows what he does.

Rick: You never question an artist, you know.

Chris: He's lived off our fucking backs.

Pickard: Pass them biscuits.

Chris: Tommy done his maiden speech and he's expecting to be compère on the Sunderland fucking Empire. You, you daft cunt, you thought he was writing about shipyards and individuals.

Dicky: What do you want to interview the nurse for?

Chris: He just wants an interview with the nurse to see if you fuck her. 'Can I ask you a personal question, my dear? Is Dicky giving you one?'

Jake: Here, it's all over the fucking yard.

Dicky: I know, it's serious.

Jake: You should behave yourself, man.

Dicky: I asked Geordie to call them out of order at this morning's meeting but he just sat there laughing.

Chris: Dick, people realise ...

Dicky: No, people *assume* ...

Chris: Well, you've got to try it. Even she knows that now.

Rick: Before long, you know, she's going to blow you out, if you don't have a fucking go at her. She's not going to put it with you for ever.

Tommy: It's always his bleep when the ambulance is wanted, I've noticed that. It's never any fucker else.

Dicky: I've already explained that on tape.

Rick: She'll turn to somebody like Joe – or somebody like that.

Chris: I don't think she would.

Dicky: There's a good programme about the North-East next Monday on Channel Four, Pickard.

Chris: Here, when he fucks off down London, he's not worried about the fucking North-East, man.

174

Rick: Lying back on his beanbag.

Chris: I'm fucking sure, man. He's just living off us.

Dicky: Have you got your car in the yard?

Pickard: Aye.

Dicky: There you are, you see what I mean? The poor nurse cannot get hers in; priority.

Jake: You're giving people room to talk about you.

Dicky: The safety aspect, that's all I'm looking at, purely and simply the safety.

Jake: Do you wear blobs, like?

Chris: Well Dicky you've fucking . . .

Jake: Shot your lot by the sounds of it.

Dicky: I think I'll start tomorrow's meeting off, at the safety committee, by making a statement, a public statement, that there is no truth in the rumours that I'm fucking the nurse. And that'll be minuted.

[*Dicky's bleeper goes off.*]

Chris: Oh, there you are.

Pickard: There goes my pacemaker.

Chris: Keep it quiet. Tell her she has to be interviewed by the poet.

Dicky: (*Picks up the phone*) I thought he was a writer, not a poet. Are you a writer or a poet? Hello, Doris. As you know, there has been a writer in the yard for six months, and he wants to interview a few people including yourself.

Chris: He's from *Fiesta*!

Dicky: Well he's asked millions of questions but we don't know exactly what he's going to write about. She will do it gladly, for a fee.

Chris: For a feel? Oh, she can have a feel.

Dicky: I don't know, it depends on the photographs he takes. I suppose he wants to know about a nurse's job in the yard, what kind of accidents you have to deal with. How many accidents are there, and how often do they happen, things like that. Anyway, what do you want?

Chris: Fucking hell, there's probably a bloke lying there bleeding to death.

Rick: Just a slow walk round.

Chris: What does she want?

Dicky: Somebody to go home in the ambulance. I'll see you later.

Chris: You fucker, he's not daft.

Jake: Is he bucking her or what?

Dicky: He says he's not. But if he's not, he's an idiot.

Pickard: Is she nice?

Jake: Is she fuck, she's horrible.

Chris: I'd fuck her.

Jake: You'd fuck a frog. 'I'd fuck her.' You'd fuck me, you big twat.

Chris: She's a tubby little thing.

Tommy: I find her pleasant.

Chris: Big tits.

Tommy: Pleasant lass. Hey, I've been talking to the radiographer, and he said the background levels of radiation on the ground in the yard is doubled since last week. He's got a Geiger counter. And they've got little tabs, and every so often they send it away to get a reading and see how much radioactivity they've been exposed to.

Chris: Are you bringing that up at the safety meeting tomorrow?

Tommy: There's nowt to worry about. Peter Walker [Secretary of State for Energy] has been to Sellafield this morning and there's nowt to worry about. John Selwyn Gummer [Conservative Party Chairman] was going to make a speech about his kids drinking loads of milk and eating lettuce, and he's been stopped.

14/5/86

the river is fucked

On 14 May 1986 at a national meeting with the SNC,[1]
British Shipbuilders' new chairman, Philip Hares,
announced a savage packet of redundancies and yard
closures to the delegates who had come to hear the
management's response to what he called a 'very
ambitious wage claim'. It sent a shudder through the
merchant sector: three yards to close and one third of the
workforce to be made redundant. A further programme
of subcontracting was thrown in for good measure. The
unions and others in the maritime industry firmly believe
that this will mean the end of the merchant sector.

I listened to British Shipbuilders' cruel news on the car
radio as I drove in to Austin and Pickersgill's. A shipyard
is a big and sprawling place but the mood can change in
an instant and affect the whole plant. Morale is an almost
tactile thing which can be tasted in the air like the toxic
fumes of the iron powder rods. Walking across the yard
to the fitting-out quay I was stopped by a labourer.

Frank: It's a waste of time, this place now. There'll be loads finished.
October, I think it starts. The river's fucked! No chance. The unions
cannot do nowt about it. Definite. Shame, like, but that's the way
it goes.
Pickard: You've got to put up a fight, surely.
Frank: If you had something to fight with, fair enough. But they've
got no orders coming in. We've got a boat to finish fitting-out at
the quay, another one to be launched over there, about eight weeks
time maybe. When that one goes off, there's nowt. Only a barge.
She wants fuck all up here, Thatcher. She wants nowt. She doesn't

1. Shipyard Negotiating Committee: a national body of trade union representatives.

like the North. She gets no votes out of here, so that's it. Simple as that. The river's fucked.

we've just got to fight them all the way

Paul: There's a mass meeting on Saturday. You see, what the SNC had said was that they are pressing the Labour Party to give us a supply day so there can be a debate on shipbuilding. And on that day, provided the feeling was there, they'd be calling for a one-day total stoppage, the day of the debate. Across the merchant sector. The feeling on the shop floor now is for a stoppage. The feeling is there.

Bluey: Don Dixon [MP for Jarrow] has booked a big committee room so possibly the Labour MPs might be addressing the shop stewards.

Paul: Being a working-class boy it's my ambition to go down there and see the boys' club they've got. Fucking education.

Pickard: I was in for the first time a week ago. It's like a cathedral and has a faintly sweet smell.

Paul: Those working lads will be able to go down there and sit in that fucking gallery and watch them cunts perform, or not perform.

Jake: They are certainly fucking corrupt.

Paul: What we're getting when we go round is: 'The others are going to accept,' that Sunderland Shipbuilders is going to accept.

Ronnie: They're not.

Pickard: I thought the proposal was to keep two yards open here.

Ronnie: They want to build ships over there and for us to build the lumps.

Paul: Prefabrication, build the units here and the ships get built over there. We just become an extended manufacturing base, that's all. They've had five options, five scenarios. They knocked the first two back and went for the third option, which was to shut one big yard, which was the South Bank Yard [Middlesbrough], keep one facility in Scotland which is Govan, and keep the two yards on this river, and the two smaller yards. From there, if no further work becomes available, then we go to the next scenario – four, which is the closure of Austin and Pickersgill's. They've said that, Picky's is the next one to gan. So that will leave you the big yard in Scotland, (Govan), Sunderland Shipbuilders, Ailsa will be left and you'll have the Appledore place in Devon. Then scenario five: by the end of the year if there is no more orders and everything goes down the Swannee, the whole lot gan.

Pickard: So have they issued compulsory redundancy notices in Smith's Docks?

Paul: Yes, they've just wiped them out. One of the things in the report-back this morning, they were saying a lad from Troon Yard was saying that he was under the impression that it was the other yard in his area that was closing and he went in saying to the other stewards and officials that was there: 'No, it's not my yard, it's the other one in the area.' He gans into the meeting: boomf! And he's saying, 'Nar, it's not, it's not our yard.' But he was told, 'It is, you're finished, you're shut.' They said his face just hit the bottom; you can imagine the lad just sitting there going through turmoil, trying to tick over, and they just say, 'Your job's wiped out and all your members is wiped out.'

Pickard: Do you think Smith's Dock will resist closure?

Paul: I couldn't say.

Pickard: Is the national union giving any reasonable kind of leadership?

Ronnie: No.

Paul: At the minute, the first thing they do is reject the document totally, because they cannot accept that the merchant shipbuilding capacity can reduce from ten thousand people down to five and a half thousand and still be maintained as a viable industry. You cannot. If there is any kind of upturn in the industry those five and a half thousand are not going to be able to cope with it. Therefore the orders may go abroad, or to Harland and Wolf, or Vickers. You've got five and half thousand men in the merchant sector, you've got that many men in Harland and Wolf, you've got that many in Vickers, so they can turn round to us and say, 'Well, unfortunately you've been decimated that much that you cannot cope with the extra input that's coming into the yards so therefore they'll have to go to the other yards and the naval yards, and they'll build them.' We'll just be wiped out.

Pickard: Just like somebody planned it.

Paul: It was planned from Day One when they were ganna denationalise all the naval sector yards, you could see it. We were left to survive on our own, the loss-making parts of the company. We've just got to fight them all the way.

16/5/86

confed meeting: don't rock the boat

Tony: There will be a meeting of the yard committee and the council. It has been arranged for Monday at 2.45, regarding which way we now start to pursue the campaign to maintain the shipbuilding industry and what assistance the council are prepared to give and how far the local full-time officials will be involved in that.

Chris: Just on that point, Mr Chairman, reading the press last night, I think it is essential now that we've got to act together, but when you see MF quoted in the press saying, 'There will be no industrial action,' and things like that, when they are going to decimate the industry! That's a ridiculous situation. No doubt we'll be going out in the yard this morning and the lads will be saying, 'Well, are they going to take any action over the river?' If they are going to make press statements I think they should either tell yourself, or we've got to get together as shop stewards for all of the river and make somebody the spokesman, so at least we know what we are saying to the press. Because last night where he was saying 'We cannot go on strike, we've got to be good lads,' I interpreted that as 'we are the good lads and we'll get the ships'.

Tony: Well, he's totally out of order. He was party to a decision and he was a member of the SNC when they took that decision, and I've got the resolution, I wrote it down, he was in the same room as me when Ferry went over it. There was no dissenters. No dissenters, not one. Now I mean, we've got a meeting with him this morning, with an MP and Sunderland Shipbuilders' shop stewards, and we're going to have to know where we stand because clearly it only needs one yard in the whole of British Shipbuilders in the merchant sector to dissent and then it's in, and you just have to battle your own corner. And we'll make our own decisions. All I'm interested in is A&P and we do the right thing. I've never cared what they do over there, in that sort of situation. If that's what they want to do, and do nowt, well, good luck to them, but I know

180

my national officials and the SNC have said which way they are approaching the problem and we'll gan down that line. At the end of the day, like I say, if one yard remains, then there'll be no strike or nowt. It's a national strike, and what Ferry said was, 'I've got to know before I call a national strike of the shipbuilding industry for a minimum of one day that the troops is there to support me.' And that's our job that we've got to do, we've got to find out whether the troops is prepared to come. It's a call for one day of action, but if it was going to be full call for strike action you know full well that every union then would demand its own autonomy. It's not a question of whether there's going to be a ballot, there's got to be a ballot anyway, you got no option, it's the law. The unions are abiding by the law when it comes to industrial action because they have seen over many unions get their funds sequestrated by the courts: NGA, the mineworkers. And they know full well that they have got to go to ballot. So it's not a question of 'Will we get a ballot to call a national strike?' All that is rubbish. All we are asking for at the moment is one day off in an orchestrated way throughout the country to draw the attention of the country to the question of British shipbuilding. That's all they are asking for.

Roger: Well, Mr Chairman, I'm very reluctant to get involved with them at all, because on their past record and on the record of last night's papers, as Chris has pointed out, I'm very reluctant to stand side by side with them people, I'll tell you straight. And I think my members on the shop floor are of the same mind.

Tony: Like I say, we are, unfortunately, being drawn towards them, we cannot stand as A&P because we are North-East Shipbuilders Ltd now.

Roger: That's what scares us, Chairman, that we are getting drawn towards them and it starts to rub off on us.

Tony: What we've got to do is try to control the situation, and I'll be going and asking them this morning what he intends to do.

Jake: The morning's meeting of the two yard committees has been requested by Bob Clay so he can be put in the picture about what exactly happened on Wednesday. Now, what we are saying is, we aren't being drawn towards SS in that sense, all we are asking for is that we reject British Shipbuilders' wages and conditions offer this year, which I think everybody in here agreed unanimously,

181

without the prerequisite that's put on it. And also that we support unanimously the SNC. Now, that's all we are doing, and if they do something different, as Tony said and I agree with him whole-heartedly, if they do something different then it is their fault. All we've got to be seen to be doing is that we do things right. And if any yard or subsidiary is going to let the side down, then Christ I only hope it's not going to be A&P. As long as we can be seen to be clean that's all we are asking for. I don't see nowt wrong with it. I don't know, maybe he'll say this morning that he's been misquoted in the paper. It's happened before.

Harry: I don't think we'll have any problems in this yard, Mr Chairman, because there is quite a few blokes asked me when is the date.

Tony: On the question of the shipbuilding debate again, we've got notified yesterday that the Opposition has agreed to use one of the supply days to debate shipbuilding in the House of Commons. Unfortunately, or fortunately, depending on which way you look at it, on the one hand it is on Wednesday from seven o'clock at night, on the other hand it doesn't give the SNC much time to get a feedback from subsidiaries to call the stoppage on that day. I don't think they'll be able to do it. And we've also got to take a decision this morning: if there's not a national stoppage, shall we organise a lobby from this yard?

We met informally with R— and S— yesterday, after refusing to meet P—. He said that he just wanted to talk informally to clear away any misconceptions that I had when I complained that nego-tiations had been carried out through the media with British Ship-builders and that details of the offer had been put in a pamphlet and given to our people while negotiations were at a very early stage, which had never been done before. The proposals for nego-tiations had been put to the members at the same time as they were being put to the SNC, and the tactic was to undermine the negotiations. I think it has backfired on them, I don't think the lads will be able to stomach the things they asked for. He said he needed just to clear the air as well, as to where he thought British Shipbuilders stood. Also that he just needed to tell us about the order book situation. He said he wished we had attended the meeting with Mr P, because Mr P (and they were all confident) was going away and he would be coming back with work for us. So there was no need to worry. 'We are going to be all right and we

182

are going to survive, blah blah blah, so don't, whatever you do, rock the boat.'

Kenny: We haven't got one to rock.

Tony: 'So don't talk about strikes or any form of disruptive action at this time because we are convinced that we are going to get work.' I told him that the only time I'm convinced we are going to get work is when the steel is in that stockyard, like I've always said. How many times have I been told we are going to get this and get that? Notional orders. I find it is better never to take any notice of them than it is to think that you are going to be all right and there is going to be work there.

On the question of British Shipbuilders' attitude to negotiations he said that he is 'convinced that British Shipbuilders didn't leak that information'. He said, 'I'm convinced of that.' He said, 'I think we've got a mole in Whitehall.' We must have another Anthony Blunt that's dealing with shipbuilding. Anthony Punt.

The mass meeting tomorrow starts promptly at nine o'clock.

Under any other business, I'm also proposing something for the lads from the NGA who are in dire straits now. It's a peculiar case altogether, they've not even been allowed the right to redundancy or nowt, they've just been all sacked. So what I'm suggesting is that after the meeting tomorrow we ask for a voluntary collection for the NGA, bearing in mind that they were supposed to be here this morning to address us. Is that agreed?

shop stewards' office: mass meetings

Tony: They've got a mass meeting in Middlesbrough Town Hall and they're recommending the day off on Wednesday. Channon is coming on Friday and he has refused to meet them, so they are going to block the road.

Danny: Appledore: a one-day national stoppage and a lobby of Parliament. He says we've got a hundred per cent support.

Brian: Fucking smashing.

Danny: That's what we'll have to do, get out and into our lot before we get to the meeting and tell them, Govan, Ferguson Ailsa, Smith's, fucking Appledore, they are all fucking hundred per cent out. Smith's is in the worst position, they are closing down, they've got nowt to lose. They are walking out today for a mass meeting at the

183

town hall, and they are going to recommend that they are out next Wednesday.

Journalist: What are these scenarios that British Shipbuilders are proposing?

Danny: Scenario three involves a permanent capacity reduction from the current level of 800,000 man hours per month to 500,000, by closure and EML's (Economic Manning Levels). Facilities closed under this scenario would be one large yard, Smith's Docks, one small yard, Troon, and part of the engine-building facility at Wallsend. Now then, if that doesn't work they move to the next one which represents an additional step down and the shipbuilding industry will be settled on one yard in Scotland, that's Govan, and one in the North-East, that is the Pallion yard at SS. So we have gone, and you have roughly halved the position as it stands at the moment. And then you move to the last one: this scenario assumes little or no orders are won and that the corporation are forced to proceed with a programme of progressively closing the merchant shipyards during 1986/7 as the work runs out.

Journalist: Is there any reference in there to the newly formed North East Shipbuilders Limited?

Danny: Well it is only a few weeks since the NESL said there would be no further redundancies within that group. Now here we are just a few weeks later with fourteen hundred people being made redundant and a yard closed on Teeside, and nearly a thousand being made redundant in the two yards on the Wear. It was only February when we had a meeting with the managing director about it when he said it would be beneficial to all of us and that he didn't foresee any changes in working conditions or pay. Now here we are with one yard closing and the other two yards losing nearly a thousand people. So that is what NESL has done for us.

Journalist: What is the story with the ex-chairman of British Ship-builders?

Danny: The one about Day is that he was receiving £80,000 per year plus bonuses and for that he got eleven per cent of his target and fucked off to British Leyland. So he done a hell of a fucking job for himself, him. He didn't do very much for us, mind.

There is a classic example: under the Labour Party, in 1976 Graham Day was appointed as chairman of British Shipbuilders for when it was nationalised. The only reason he didn't was because of the carry-on of it going from the House of Commons and the

House of Lords, backwards and forwards, and the bill was delayed so he fucked off. Now what was the Labour Party thinking of when they were prepared to put a fellah in who is appointed by the Tory government, and butchers us?

Pickard: He was complaining the other day saying he only got £80,000-a-year wages and thought he deserved a lot more.

Danny: The other point is the fact that since Day came into power we are now a hundred in the pay line. I got into an argument last night, a fellah comes in that has got a little painting and decorating business, while I was sitting talking to this lad from one of the other shipyard unions about the industry. This bloke chirps in: 'What can you expect, your fucking low production and high wages, it's bound to come to an end sometime.' So, 'you fucker,' me horns came oot and I went reet off. He never supped his pint, he left the cunt. I gave him a right lashing, you know. We know it's totally untrue. Wages is part of the industry, and it has got to be a vital part of the industry, without the wages nobody wants to work in it anyway. They'd rather get out. We've always believed it is the employer's responsibility not only to get his production, not only to build his ships, or whatever he's manufacturing. It's also his responsibility to look after his workforce. And that means by paying them a reasonable wage and looking after them and giving the best conditions they can achieve. All they can think about is butchering you every time. It's fucking crazy. You've got the local management here continually gannin' into lads here, screwing them rotten all day every day.

Robert: Hundred per cent Appledore.

Tony: Off a Wednesday?

Robert: He didn't know about Wednesday but he said all right because we are lobbying. So he said we are all right we are definitely on, hundred per cent. Dick Mathews [Appledore yard convener] phoned. They had a mass meeting yesterday. He said it was a hundred per cent.

Tony: What about fucking Clarke Kincaid's from the Swine [Tyne]?

Pickard: River Swine. All clear on the River Queer [Wear].

Paul: I think he wants to try on the Mackems.

Tony: What you on about, like?

Brian: He's determined to end up in the sleck. Aren't you?

Danny: What we are saying is, at the moment, just to survive, unless the government put in a softer credit facility for owners to take that

185

option up, then we are not going to get any ships and we are not going to be anywhere, anyway. All right, the long-term argument is that we are not in that situation at the moment, but the situation at the moment is that, if something is not done and done very quickly, we will be. People say the next Labour government will change the policies, and bah bah bah, but we are not there.

Pickard: The Type-23 frigate for Swan's looks like it is in the far and distant future. In this morning's paper it said that the Ministry of Defence have asked them to get their estimates down. But my mate on the *Shields Gazette* phoned up somebody in the M.o.D. on Wednesday and asked what was happening with the Type-23 frigate and he said, 'Well, with the new white paper on defence, Trident comes first,' and he says it will be at least a year before they place an order. So he got back to Swan's managing director and asked him, 'What would happen if you don't get a Type-23 frigate for a year?' And he said, 'Unofficially, we'd all be on the fucking dole.'

Journalist: Don't you think a strike would be the most effective weapon at this point?

Tony: It wouldn't be reet for me to fucking lead the lads on fucking strike for fucking months and months on fucking end knowing at the end of the day they couldn't fucking win the cunt. And who is going to support us, like? The same cunts that supported the miners! No fucker. Same cunts that supported the printers. Nobody. At the moment you've got a political campaign. What I'm saying, at the moment the SNC have asked the lads on the shop floor to give us authority to call action the minimum of a day, and once they get that authority they are going ahead.

Jake: As Tony has explained it, any confidence that was there in the trade union movement after the miners' strike, it's gone. Trade union leaders are now not prepared to enter into any kind of long-drawn-out strike.

Hill: We'll lose the technology of the sea, never mind owt else. Maggie will pass a law to stop us swimming. Keep us out the water.

Brown: Just as well with the shite coming out of Sellafield.

Hill: Officers have got to gan abroad to Hong Kong to get fixed up now with a ship. So has seamen. There are very few seamen out of the home ports now. They have got to gan abroad to get a contract. I'm talking about chief engineers and senior officers having to go abroad to get a ship out to sea. The marine colleges are just going to disappear as such.

186

Pickard: Given the ramifications of that, can't you involve the seamen's union.

Hill: Everybody.

Jake: We've involved NUPE [National Union of Public Employees] because they've got a conference next week. And NUPE realises, especially in this area, that the shipyards is the biggest employers. You can involve all kinds of public sector workers. That's all you can do. You just hope you can highlight it to such an extent that they become totally embarrassed and they've got to back off. One of the biggest sectors that involves us is warship building: because they could effectively close the merchant sector down. Especially if they get it down to five and half thousand. Any future capacity for merchant ships can be built in them yards. Swan Hunter's, Cammell Laird's . . .

Hill: You are cutting down on the surface fleet anyhow, with modern technology and forthcoming wars and everything that entails. Of course, surface fleets in a nuclear holocaust – they wouldn't last an hour. It would be only them under the water that had a chance.

they need you when there is shit to be thrown about

I walked past the doomed plumbers' shop to the quay. I
climbed up the steep gangplank to the boat and
descended into number one hold to look for Dave and
Jim. I had to pass a lot of blokes who stood around in
groups. There was no obvious enthusiasm for work now.
I climbed up the rigging and made my way along the
scaffolding to where Dave and Jim were working. When
I approached them they stopped work and greeted me,
Dave with a smile and Jim with a sad shake of the head.
I commented on the apparent mood of the boat.
'Everybody's demoralised. Look at him down there,' Jim
said, pointing to a man sitting below us in the hold. 'He
knows he hasn't got a job in a few weeks' time. Finished!
He's a good worker and he's been took out of his own
trade and he's doing everything that they ever wanted
him to do.'

He paused while we looked at the man. His tools lay

at his feet and he was gazing at nothing in particular.
Jim shook his head bitterly.

Jim: He's never known anything like it in his life.
Dave: Funnily enough I was working over at Laing's and it got to
a situation where everybody was like him. You're that fed up you
don't know what you're going to do next, what was happening the
next week. You didn't know whether you could afford to save up
for a holiday, or if you were going to be on strike. You couldn't
settle yourself, you know. Now this yard, when I come over here,
it was a totally different atmosphere; everybody worked together –
had a bit carry-on, you know – and you got through your day. But
you can gradually see this place going exactly the same as Laing's.
The redundancies, everything that's going on. You cannot see any
future in it, can you? Course they want you to use these iron powder
rods which you know damages your health. What can you do?
You're just pushed into a corner where there's no way you can win.
Jim: The faces, man! You can see them on a morning: they've got
no interest in coming here now. Like I say, you don't know if you
can afford a holiday, a little car or nothing. There's nowt left for
us, is there? Nowt at all.
Dave: It makes you see why those places – in Bristol and that – turn
to violence to release their frustrations.

Is that what it is? You get pushed that far into a corner you've
got to do something violent to let them see how bad it is for you?
As long as you keep quiet they just think, 'Oh well, they're happy,
they're not saying fuck all, they're just accepting it.' Have you got
to turn to *that* to fucking get your point over? It seems to be the
only way. It makes you think that. We're not advocating violence
one little bit, but you can honestly see how people turn to it.
Jim: Yes, that's probably the reason for it.
Dave: The whole human element is forgotten in this system. They're
always on about money and profit and things like that, but what
about the people? People's minds and bodies, the whole principles
of life? All we want to do is come to work, do a fair day's work,
but we're not allowed to. They're talking about more redundancies.
They've actually run this yard that far down now, that we're running
about looking for a hammer so we can get on with our jobs. And
they say that we haven't leaned any way to try and help! You
bugger, we go and do somersaults to try and get the job away.

188

We're not even supplied with a two-foot rule or a hammer or nowt, we've got to go and borrow them to further our job on.

Then we get slagged off by the press. They want to get down here and just see what it's like.

In fact, I'd do what the Jarrow lads did! If it would mean anything I'd walk all the way down to London. And we should pick all the unemployed up on the way. We'd have three million people standing outside of Parliament. Just let them see how many people there are and what it's about.

Jim: It's terrible, this area. It doesn't bear thinking about, the North of England, does it? It's just going to be a fucking wasteland.

Dave: Obviously, Tom, strike action is no good. It's been proved now off the miners and the print workers. The only way we can do it is to show them through our Members of Parliament who we've voted in and elected to let them do our fighting for us in Parliament. That's all we can do. We cannot go out on strike. What have we got to strike with?

Jim: There's another thing we always get slagged off for, striking. I've never been on strike very much in my time in the shipyards. Have you, Dave? We get run into the ground for it. They say we're always anti-management: *anti-management*, you bugger! We've give up on loads of things to get this yard going.

Dave: It's right what you say, Jim. Soon as we go out these gates they could just say, 'Right, you're sacked,' and you lose all your redundancy money. You got to think of that, like. There's them lads at Liverpool who occupied the yard, they were jailing them when they went out. What do you do?

Jim: If we could just get an election now and let the people show their feelings.[1] I can never ever see this woman getting in again. I'm not blaming just her. I don't think it is just her, she's in the front line, Thatcherism and all that. It's government policy this, and it's time we had these out.

I've never been politically minded in my life, but I can see what's happening here, man: twenty-odd per cent on the bloody dole up here. Twenty-eight per cent in Teeside. Well, that's criminal that,

1. Thirteen months later, in the 1987 general election, the local Labour MPs did increase their majorities with an increased poll. In Newcastle, another ship-building city, the Tories lost what seats they had. There was a massive regional vote of no confidence in Mrs Thatcher's government, but to no avail as they came back to power with a majority of 102, with seats won mainly in the South-East and Midlands.

isn't it? It's took everybody's pride off them. I would like to know how many's going to top themselves over these yard closures, cause I bet there's plenty.

Dave: Look at those lads at Smith's.[1] They're told, 'You're finished, you're working your notice!' Down there it's bad enough anyhow, the last place where there's any work at all, and they just shut it like that, without any feelings or anything.

Jim: What else can they subject us to now?

Dave: They stop this and you cannot get that. It's bad enough for us, but I've got two little lads and I don't know what they're going to do when they grow up. I mean they're even cutting back on education, closing a hundred and odd schools down.

Jim: Hospital, everything connected with ordinary working people. We cannot afford to go into private hospitals. They want you to go into BUPA. We've paid our stamps, we're not getting anything for nowt. Ordinary people means nothing, that's what I think. This country at the moment, the way it's going!

The people that's getting affected by all the redundancies, cuts in the National Health Service, schools and everything else like that, are the same people that they want to go and fight for them in a state of war. We're the first fuckers that has to go there. We're the people now that's getting subjected to this. When the war was, in 1939, my father had to go, and a lot of other people. These fellahs that's telling us what to do now didn't have nowt to do with it; they weren't in the front line. And it'll be the same for us. We get penalised like our forefathers did. They don't want us now, but by God they'll want us when there's somebody hoying bullets at us. That's what it amounts to. They need you when there's shit to be flung about, that's when they want us.

Dave: They want you to fight for your country, yet in peacetime you cannot go here, or you're trespassing there, with private land and all that. You've got no fucking country, all you've got is a little bit house . . .

> We climbed down the scaffolding and, as I looked around the deep hold at the small gangs of men, they all, without exception, looked as though they were waiting to go to a funeral.

1. Smith's Docks, at Middlesbrough, the last shipyard on the River Tees, was later closd in May 1987 with a loss of 1,500 jobs in the yard alone.

Jim: It's shock. They don't know what's going to be happening to them. They're living in fear. I've heard people now saying that they're contemplating taking redundancy that I never thought in me life would talk about it. Just to get out of it and try and find something else.

Dave: We think it's going to close in October.

Jim: They're good lads, good workers. They're living in fear of it now. They're saying to themselves, 'Should we take a chance and see if we can get a job now or what?' It's not because we want to get out, it's because we fear that there'll be too many on the dole by the time we do get out.

> We began to climb out of the hold to the gangway on deck. Jim drew my attention to the men who had gathered there, like schoolchildren, to wait for the buzzer before they would be allowed to leave the ship for their morning break. We joined the back of the crowd.

Dave: Not so long ago we were working on the fore-end, fucking snow coming down and all sorts: they didn't chase you out of the road then, they left you alone. All the trust, it's just gone. It's totally gone. We were doing favours. We weren't saying, 'Look, it's too bad, we're not doing this.'

We really were taking risks, the staging wasn't up properly, for instance, but we tried to help because they wanted the launch on time. We were working in conditions that were totally ridiculous. But now they want you on the boat until five to nine. That little bit five minutes extra. There's no give and take.

Jim: They treat it like a factory, but we haven't got factory conditions. We haven't got central heating and air cooled in the summer, we're open to all the elements. These forget all that. It's all very well for them sitting in Parliament and that, saying this and you've got to work this. If they come down and see what you actually did, they might have another idea. If they could see what we are actually doing, and the things that we've done to help them. They wanted to do away with demarcation and all that, we've done it all. We've been doing it for years, and they're saying we'll not do extra. We do two and three trades! We always have done, to try and further our job on, we've always done it.

191

By now most of the men on the boat had gathered at one
of the two gangways and were waiting for the buzzer to
go. There was a low angry jeer as a subcontractor, who
obviously felt that he was not required to observe the
'purge',[1] walked down the long gangplank. The noise
followed him to the quay and beyond as the minutes
ticked towards 8.55.

Dave: They just treat you like bairns now, man, keeping you on the
gangway like this.

Moving forward a little we found ourselves standing
directly behind a couple of green hats (gaffers). Jim
winked at me and spoke in a voice intended for the
foremen's ears.

Jim: The other day it was chucking it down with rain and even the
foreman was having to stand here waiting, getting soaked, until the
manager saw fit to come out of his office where he'd been sitting in
the warm all day. The foreman used to have a bit of respect for us
and we had it for them, but they've taken that away. No trust.

The foremen pretended not to hear and continued
showing us the back of their necks beneath the green
hard hats. I turned to look at a piece of graffiti written in
chalk on the pink steel bulkhead: SAY NO TO REDUNDO.

Jim: That's right, Tom, we want a job. And we're not frightened
of work either.

The patience of the men ended just before the whistle
went and they began to move down the gangplank, too
many at once, to the quay. The plank began shaking and
I was nervous about mounting it with the rest, but
followed Jim and Dave down. As we walked towards
their bait huts the buzzer began an ear-piercing blast.

Jim: You see, it's a big decision to take your redundancy. You go

1. The 'purge' is when management work to rule and insist, for instance, that
no one can leave the boat or their place of work until the buzzer goes.

192

home to your lass and your house is in a turmoil. Do you take your redundancy, chance getting out now, before the glut, and get another job? On the other hand, if you wait until the end, so you cannot reproach yourself for selling your job, there might not be any work left to get. The jobs will have gone. So it's a catch-22 situation. There's just no way out for us.

Dave: We don't want to be on the dole and milk the system, we want to be putting into the country and not taking out. We're not allowed to. Surely it's got to be better with me working and paying taxes, stamps and everything else, than it is hoying us on the dole. It must be. Even if we're subsidised it's still better than them paying us full dole, isn't it? This country! I can't believe what's happening.

> As we walked past the plumbers' shop, which was about
> to be demolished, I saw someone had written on the wall:
> FIGHT YARD CLOSURES.

Jim: Great Britain! They took the *great* out of it. If them say the shipyards is finished, let them finish them. But give us a job. What else can we do, we just want to work, we don't want to take everything out of the system, we want to put into it.

mass meeting at the Empire Theatre – blood money

Tony: On the question of what is being related in the media, again I must say that I've never known us, all of a sudden to have so many options of work. After last month when we met P— and pressed him continually on the question of whether there was orders in the pipeline, in negotiation, and he said that the best he could hope was the possibility of a further barge. Now, because of the new situation, we've got six ships from China, twenty-two-thousand-ton bulkers, four reefers, we've got four from Cuba and ferries and what have you appearing from all avenues. I'm mentioning this because you should be very wary of what you believe is a possible order for A&P. All I can say is that I know what BS plans for A&P are and we'll discuss that later. But always remember the week that you've got a ship is when that steel's in our stockyard. No other time. Up to that point in time they're only ideas, and that's what been floating around at this moment in time, only ideas, what they term as 'notional orders'. We recognise that we've got a ship when she's coming into the stockyard.

To go on to BS wage negotiations and conditions on the 14th of May. I think at times BS have leaked on the question of wages and job losses in the industry but I don't think it's ever been done in such a ruthless fashion as it was on Wednesday last. The leaking of information to the press from the day before totally devastated a hell of a lot of lads who'd been told that their plant was to close. And I've never seen a reaction like it, when I talk to lads from Clarke Kincaid's, from Smith's Dock, who before they went into the meeting were saying: 'It might be true, but I don't think it is, because our management was assuring us that we had our Cuban ships at Smith's Dock, and we're going to build them so it must all be one big mistake and we'll get it cleared away when we see British Shipbuilders this morning.' They got it cleared away all right. They

194

were told straight, 'You're finished, lad, the lot of yous.' And never have I seen on lads' faces such total despair as what I'd seen on them lad's faces, in particular from Smith's Docks. And that's how brutal negotiations were. They talk about thousands of jobs, and they talk about closures just like a drop of a hat with a string and numbers of men's lives and families just hanging there, and being told, 'You're finished.'

There was three hundred and twenty-five from Ferguson Troon, closure; Smith's Docks, one thousand two hundred and ninety-five, closure: Clarke Kinkaid's, three hundred and sixty, closure. Total one thousand nine hundred and eighty. Further redundancies on top of that: Austin and Pickersgill's and Sunderland Shipbuilders – within the new North East Shipbuilders Ltd, nine hundred and twenty-five; Govan, four hundred and ninety-five; Appledore, ninety-five. One thousand five hundred and fifteen, a grand total of three thousand four hundred and ninety-five jobs.

They told us that we'd be notified that redundancies had to take place on 1 July. If not enough is achieved by voluntary means by September then he would introduce other means. And that other means is compulsion. It must be the total reduction of the labour force down to five and a half thousand by March 1987.

They've introduced what they call BS Enterprise Ltd. It's ten million pound put aside by that company set up by BS to help redundant shipyard workers set up their own businesses by giving them grants or giving them consultation, by helping in any way they can to set up their own private businesses. What it's gonna do just doesn't come through to me. I've seen that many of that type of thing in the steel industry and the mining industry; they set it up in the end as a sop. They say they are butchering the jobs but they are trying to do something on the other hand.

Breaks: strict starting and stopping times, all breaks, and abolition of the afternoon tea-break. Also, new working practices will be introduced with the introduction of team leaders. Team leaders will cover people, possibly twelve, if the Japanese syndrome is anything to go by. You've got teams varying from twelve to eighteen with a team leader with the responsibility of seeing that team produces its function of building a ship or whatever. And they are going to introduce team leaders into that area. Team leaders who will be selected for their leadership. And we are all well aware of people who we call whiz-kids. A whiz-kid for every eighteen. They will receive seven pound ninety more than the skilled rate. There is also a compulsory transfer system which has to be accepted, that within seven days you have to agree to be transferred anywhere in the UK, and that you must work on a contract of a maximum of six weeks. You have to gan within seven days and, if you refuse, then your pay will be stopped. It is quite clear, it says you will no longer be paid if you refuse. The subcontracting that they require, and what we've already gotten in Austin and Pickersgill, is extensive: when you listen to the list, just think where you work and what you do, individually. Lofting: all lofting will be subcontracted that's in the steel area. All piece part preparation will be subcontracted, all hatches, watertight doors will be subcontracted. If necessary, panels and units will be subcontracted. In outfit: joiners and modules and electric installation, pipe manufacture also. Extra staging, painting, ship cleaning. In overhead areas: all electrical and mechanical maintenance will be subcontracted. All office and yard cleaning will be subcontracted. All canteens will be subcontracted. All external transport will be subcontracted. And further changes in working practices will be required, in particular self-servicing, and all to be agreed locally...

So what we are saying quite clearly is that British Shipbuilders' proposals and projections for the industry, as far as we're concerned, is just a non-runner. We're not in this game of life to take blood money, and that's what it is. We're not in this game to see another lad who's in exactly the same circumstances as ourselves gan down the road with his redundancy money in his pocket, or nowt in his pocket, or whatever, and for us to reap the benefit of that. Because that's a short-term outlook, and it's our turn next. The NSC are also recommending rejection and the shop stewards have discussed the resolution from the SNC and are now recommending it to yourselves. And it reads:

'The SNC totally rejects BS's projection of five and a half thousand jobs for the future of the industry. This would lead to the total demise of the merchant shipbuilding industry. The SNC will respond with a strategy for the retention of the industry and will immediately instigate a campaign to achieve the same. The SNC will demand a statement from government that they intend to maintain and support UK shipbuilding and give the assurance that they will not be undercut by any other country in giving credit facilities to get ships. The SNC requests the authority to call a minimum of one day of national action to support the political campaign to save the shipbuilding industry.'

We've managed to get a debate in the House of Commons, a supply day: that's a special day for our industry being discussed on the floor of the House of Commons and part of the political debate takes place on Wednesday. And so our first stoppage day will be on Wednesday. A twenty-four-hour stoppage. We are also making arrangements to cover that event.

Just to bring you up to date so you know exactly where the rest of the industry stands after we've took our decision now, on the question of rejection of the document and support for a one-day stoppage: Clarke Kinkaid, Wallsend, reject and stoppage; Smith's Dock, reject and stoppage; Govan, reject and stoppage; Ferguson, Ailsa, reject and stoppage; Ferguson, Troon, reject and stoppage. Clarke Kinkaid, like ourselves, is meeting this morning, and SS are meeting after us: so we'll know the full picture exactly of whether we've got a national stoppage or not. It appears that we are all on together.

21/5/86

London

Conversations in a pub on Gray's Inn Road with shipyard
workers from Smith's Dock (Middlesbrough).

'We've been told it's going to close down. The rumour that was
going about the yard was they've got another four orders for the
Cuban ships and Sunderland shipyards are going to get the orders,
which I think is a disgrace.'

'Do you think it's true or something to divide the workers?'

'We've been told it's true, because we're going to go down the
road regardless. We've built up a good reputation with the Cubans,
we've got four ships on the stocks there now. One is almost
completed, one is almost ready to launch, another one is three-
quarters of the way built, and they are very pleased with them. So
Smith's Docks themselves sought the order, and now it looks as
though it's going to be snatched and put in the Tyne. Of course
everybody here is disgusted.'

'Smith's Docks have been bought and that's the end of it. It
means it will close down and get re-opened in a couple of months
time after next year. On contract labour. British Gas are buying it.
They've been there drilling, doing a few excavations so it's obvious
that's where it's going. It could be storage...'

'The whole town must be pretty angry?'

'She said it's closed and that's the end of it, isn't it?'

'Presumably you think there is a chance of stopping the bastards,
otherwise you wouldn't be here.'

'You've just got to try, haven't you.'

'The only way to stop her is to strangle her, for me.'

'Talk is cheap. Talk is very cheap. And there is going to be a lot
of bother, a lot of bother over this shutting. Because that's all we've
got left in Middlesbrough is a shipyard. Talk is very cheap. Actions!

198

We need actions! We need a lot of actions. Talk is very cheap. Action!'

'There's only one way to take her, and that's by the neck with both hands.'

'You must be pleased with the response today? The national stoppage.'

'We stick together, us lads, because we've got families to think of.'

'Let's face it, on the Monday before they told us about the closure, half of us here were in a seminar telling us how to cut costs. It costs them thousands of pounds to put chaps through that education, what they are going to do, what new job rotas we're going to have to work, flexibility, and then on the Wednesday they turn round and say, "You are going to close down." What's the point? These pamphlets that they issued to us on the Wednesday, they never just printed them on the Monday or the Tuesday, they've been printed months. We got a leaflet in December telling us how many was going each month. Before they came all out we were told there was five hundred going. One hundred and fifty in May (in the drawing office, they were finished), five hundred at the end of July and six hundred and fifty at the end of the year. They knew it.'

'When they close the yard I can't see us getting a job anywhere now, because everywhere you go it's just flat. She's flattened the lot.'

'What else is there in Middlesbrough in terms of employment?'

'British Steel but there's something in the papers saying that is going down. ICI announced the other day that there was going to be cuts, three hundred and fifty jobs going in three year. There's nothing at all. And cuts in the railways as well.'

'They put us through them seminars, then they turn round and kick you in the teeth and say that you are closed down. To me it was a waste of man hours and a waste of time – because they must have known it was closing down. And I would like to know myself how much Maggie is getting a backhander out of this. She surely can't sleep on a night, not after this. She's known and everybody has known.'

'How true is it about the Cubans being over in Sunderland?'

'It's the first I've heard of it.'

'We know our director has been over to Cuba negotiating about these four Cuban ships.'

199

'These four, five ships that they are going to get now, whoever builds them they won't be able to sleep of a night, because we won them and we should build them. They shouldn't be able to sleep of a night because it really is disgusting. I'd just like to know how she can go to a bed at night and sleep. It's like it's said, there is definitely a dividing line: the South is getting richer and the North is getting poorer. Every week it's job cuts here and job cuts there, but London you can walk into a job centre and get a job tomorrow if you wanted one.'

'This lot here will have some different views for you.'

'Yes, we got a bit of a shock all right. It's political this, that's all it is. They're saying it's not advisable to travel forty miles down from Sunderland to bring all the gear down. They are talking a load of shite. What they are doing is they are packing our pipe-fitting shop up, fitting shop up and the joiners up – transferring all that up to Sunderland. It's all going to Sunderland. So now they've decided to shut our yard and take it all up there. It's a load of balls, man. Political, that's all.'

'All our working life has been in that yard. It's ridiculous.'

'When they amalgamated us with Sunderland shipyard it was all a con from the start.'

'Roger Spence has done more work in that yard than any director in British Shipbuilders. We've been told now that we have the other Cuban ships but they are going to Sunderland.'

'Do you believe that?'

'Yes, I believe it. What else can I believe?'

'Roger Spence won them orders and they are going to Sunderland. Now he's out the way and his fucking workforce is out the way. And he's done all the donkey-work.'

'We're out of work. It's all wrong.'

'Personally, I don't think this [the demo] is going to do anything.'

'That fucking government is hard to move.'

'So is fucking chewing gum.'

'I'd like to see her on my wages for a year, see what she fucking thinks of that.'

'They were going to close British Leyland's. There was a hue and cry about British Leyland, and they didn't close it because of the Tories. Because the Tories were involved.'

'Tories have no seats round our place, that's what it is.'

'Because we are a Labour constituency, that's what it is about.'

'Ninety per cent of the North-East are Labour and that's why she's hitting the North-East.'

'How am I going to feed my fucking racing pigeons now? I'll have to kill the poor fuckers.'

'You look at where the damage has been done on the redundancy scene, and it is all Labour seats. No Tory constituency has been hurt, except in dribs and drabs. The big hammering has been done in Labour constituencies.'

'You get these young lads here who have been used to money every blasted week, they go on the dole and that's when they start thieving, isn't it?'

'Don't worry, she's going to employ more coppers.'

Outside, the Austin and Pickersgill workers began
unwrapping their banners.

the march

Dave: They are saying now, when we get back they want us to transfer some of the steel from our yard to Sunderland Shipbuilders. We are off pay if we don't. From Friday ... I can't see us doing that.

There was some energetic singing of 'Here we go, Here
we go,' varied with choruses of 'On the dole, on the dole,
on the dole' to the same tune. The police chief refused to
let Smith's Docks have a banner at the front of the march
but an incredible chorus of 'At the front, at the front, at
the front' built up until he gave way and the banner was
allowed. A long and angry march made its way down
Gray's Inn Road to the Strand, passing NGA pickets
outside of the *Times* building. Even with the anger there
was a great deal of humour. Chris told Dicky to keep
the banner up.

Billy: The nurse won't be pleased if you can't keep it up.
Chris: It's not true he's knocking the nurse off.

201

Maggie, Maggie, out, out, out,
Walk on, walk on,
walk with hope in your heart and you'll never walk alone

It starts to rain heavily and the entire march begins
singing 'I'm walking in the rain' for several verses. In the
Strand, the march comes to a halt outside of an
employment centre. The shipyard workers change the
chant to:
Gis a job, gis a job, gis a job,
We went here, we went there, we went every fucking
where.
The workers united will never be defeated,
Shut ya mooth, shut ya mooth, shut ya mooth,
If you hate Maggie Thatcher, clap your hands.

The march terminated just behind the National Theatre
and was addressed by a number of MPs and trade union
officials. When it was announced that Neil Kinnock, the
leader of the Labour Party, could not be present to
address them either there or at the lobby, there was a
great cry of anger, then a chant of 'We want Kinnock'.
They didn't want him because they loved him but because
he was the official leader of the Labour Party and he was
too busy with other things to attend and give his personal
support to a campaign which meant the life and death
of an industry which in some instances was the only
industry in the towns that these men and women came
from. Kinnock evidently felt that the expulsion of
Militants could not be postponed, even for this.

the lobby

The demonstration wrapped up its banners and walked
to Parliament. In the large central lobby a shipyard
worker from Smith's Docks was talking to a colleague
from Sunderland.

Jim: That's what I didn't understand, because Middle Dock is right
at the mouth of the river, all the stuff comes up from Sunderland ... The other problem is, I said to the manager, 'What are you

going to do about it? Are you going to close it?' And he says, 'I am meeting the local authorities tomorrow,' (because they pay three hundred thousand pound a year rates,) and, as I understand the situation, unless they destroy the yard, flood it, knock all the cranes down, they have to pay rates on it. So they may have to destroy the yard. It's crazy. So I said, 'Are you prepared to sell it?' And they said, 'Well, sell it, but not to anyone who is going to open it as a ship repair yard.' You can't win, can you?
Jake: What about healthy competition?
Mack: That's capitalism.

> Inside, further apologies were made for Neil Kinnock who was too busy to show up.
> Although there were many heartening speeches by MPs to the lobby of shipyard workers, when I turned to look at a few of the lads I knew from Sunderland, there was a profound depression registered on their faces.

in the pub waiting for the train back north

Dave: You know I gan up the club with me father every Wednesday night, and he gets talking about me grandfather and different things. He says me grandfather never had a full-time job, he never worked full-time. He was a fisherman. He worked in the mines a little bit, but he never had much employment. He was a fisherman, and what money he made was by selling a few fish. In the summer he had a couple of boats and he'd take people out and he'd make his money that way. When he took people out there was never any accidents, never anybody hurt. A couple of money people found out that there was somebody making a few bob out of this. So he had to pay a thousand pound a year if he wanted to take the public on. He had to get life-belts and all sorts, everything to stop him. Then you get this bloke coming along who knows sod all about the sea, with a big boat and life-belt and all that. Me old man says there was more accidents with that idiot because he didn't know when the tide was out and he was hitting the rocks and people were getting hurt. That's just totally the way this country is: it's a prime example of the way they've gone.
Jim: Here, have a look at this cloudy pint. I went out to the back

yard for a piss, and when I came back I said to the manager, 'There's about fifteen dogs running round your bitch.' He said, 'Oh, aye, it's in heat.' I said, 'Well, go and pour that beer over it and you'll have no more bother...'

Dave: We come off the job and were standing on the deck and the foreman says. 'Right, you can gan.' And Jimmy ran down first and got to the bottom and a manager, the bastard, stopped him and said, 'You're off too early.' He says, 'You'd better see the foreman, he told me it's all right to go.' He come out of the office at four o'clock. He hadn't been standing out in the fucking rain all day working. He's in the office all day till four o'clock, then he comes out. I mean how can you respect a bloke like that?

Jim: It was pissing down with rain. I said, 'Did you think I'm fucking daft, it's pissing down with rain, I'm not standing up there and getting wet, man.' He says, 'You shouldn't have come off your job.'

Mick: When I asked Jacka if he was coming on the demonstration he said, 'I'm not really a shipyard worker, I've only been here seven years.' I think he was the best of the lot, apart from Sam Rain who said, 'They can shut them down if they want for all I care.' I had no answer to that.

Tommy: What happened to him? He seemed very adamant at the welders' meeting, yet he hasn't turned up.

Jim: Davy said to him: 'Are you coming down with us, Sam?' 'No,' he says. So he says, 'Do you mind me asking why you're not coming? Have you got an excuse?' He said, 'I don't need a one.' I says, 'OK, fair enough, if that's the way you want to be.' He says, 'No, I just don't give a monkey's if it closes or not.'

Dave: After that he says, 'I'll be out cutting the grass,' and Jimmy says, 'Aye, next year you'll be out eating the bastard.'

the British Empire

Ron: I gan down there, I'm a skilled man in the shipyard, I'm working, using me skill for everything, doing me job. Now I could be sitting in the house getting just as much money from the dole as going down there and using me skills, and getting fucked about by gaffers and daft fucking buzzers here and buzzers there and buzzers every-fucking-where. I can get just as much money sitting in the house as going down there and getting fucked about.

Gordon: And another point, it's not a question of racism, it's a question of priorities. This government, and by the way the Labour government, is pouring millions of quids outside this country to various black countries. It's out my pocket, his pocket, your pocket, and all these people that's down here now. It's a fact like. Can you turn that off, I am a racist, I hate fucking darkies.

Pickard: We fucking sucked the blood out of those countries for years.

Gordon: Who fucking did?

Pickard: The British Empire.

Gordon: I fucking never, my fucking parent never. That's the first argument you get back: 'You fucking sucked the blood out of our country.' I fucking never!

Pickard: That's the point I'm making, *they* aren't the enemy, it's them twats!

Gordon: My fucking parents were probably getting knocked on the head in the High Street and took away to be sailors.

Pickard: Pressganged, shanghaied. So we've got a common enemy, that's what the point is.

Gordon: I've never sucked the blood out of anybody. They say, 'You sucked the blood out of us,' but I fucking never sucked the blood out of any cunt!

Pickard: That must mean that we have a common enemy. It's a class fucking enemy, not a fucking race enemy, it's a fucking class enemy. Because it's the same bastards that fucked them that fucked us, and are fucking us now!

the debate

Tommy: It appears the Tories were in a bit of disarray. Sir Edward du Cann certainly lashed the Tories for their failure to help the shipbuilding industry. Channon was an absolute disgrace. His own side were laughing at him. There was only three speakers, Channon opened the debate, John Smith, the Shadow Industry Minister, got up and spoke and then Edward du Cann. We had to leave at that. It's a pity we had to leave. That goes for all the lads, we were all loath to leave, it seemed to be a good debate.

Ken: Quite honestly I think Channon is a wanker and shouldn't be

205

allowed to be a minister. He showed himself up. Tom, put that fucking tape off.

Pickard: Fuck off, it's me job. I'll tell you what, I'll put the microphone in my buttonhole and you think of it as a bouquet.

Ken: Smith asked him how much government money had been spent on merchant shipbuilding, and he couldn't answer. He just sat there dumbfounded.

Tommy: He's the old-monied Tory, Eton background, the Guinness family, and he's got more money than sense. His own side were laughing at him. He just didn't come over at all. Smith came at him when he went on about enterprise boards. He said, 'We've redundancies in the steel industry and we've had steel enterprise boards set up, we've had redundancies in the mining industry and mining enterprise boards put up, and another, and now you are going to set up a shipbuilding enterprise board.' He says, 'There are that many enterprise boards set up in our area we don't know whether we are coming or going. They are still not creating work.' Du Cann lashed him. If he'd been one of ours we couldn't have asked for better. The way he got up and the way he pulled the government policy on shipbuilding to bits had to be seen to be believed. He was good, very good. The trouble is, we know we'll win the argument, but when the division bell gans and the lobby gans we know which way they'll vote.

There was only about thirty or forty Labour MPs but about a dozen Tories.

Ken: The argument was made that if people came in from the outlying districts and went to Parliament and saw the way the MPs act, they wouldn't vote for them. The complacency of people! Like Tommy is saying, a dozen on each side during the previous debate, and when it come to the vote they all crawled out of the woodwork and there was a massive vote.

JUNE

2/6/86

I still have nightmares about that

Mack: When we were in London, he had no shower in his room, so I says to him, 'Dan, you can use me shower you know.' He comes in and gets showered, and gans out. I gans in after him and gets showered, I gets a fucking shave, fills the basin, swills me face, gets a towel: it's his fucking underpants! He'd left his fucking underpants on the fucking side and I'm wiping me fucking face on them. I thought it was the fucking towel. I still have fucking nightmares about that. I threw them against the wall: and they stuck!
Pickard: Long John's were they?
Brian: No, short Dan's.

on the ship

Alf: There might be Nissan cars in here next year. They might be storing them in here. They reckon they've bought the quay. So I have heard. That's what the rumour is. They've acquired all the land around the fitting-out quay. They aren't going to use it any more. The next ship is being fitted out down at Palmer's Hill on the other side of the water, further down. They are only going to build the accommodation module down here.
Pickard: Is there a noticeable change in the atmosphere?
Alf: He's done a good job, P—. He's conditioned everybody to be sick. He wears you down so you get that apathetic about the situation that when the crunch comes and he says, 'I'm very sorry, lads, but the yard is going to have to shut,' you are going to turn round and say, 'Oh well, that's it, we don't care.'

Nobody here really cares. Build a fucking ship in seven weeks, we can!
Pickard: I really noticed when I came here, the speed that last ship was got together. I couldn't believe my eyes.

Alf: Aye, and what about when we were building SD14s? Seven weeks. That's from the stockyard to the water and going on sea trials. They were popping off them berths, by hell. Off that one and on to the next one, do that one and off that one and back on to the next one. They were going out like that. And we were building twenty-six-thousand tonners. Some Tyneside lads, from Swan Hunter's, came when we were working on that one that's at the quay now. The one you are on about, the one that flew up. And he says, 'When's this launching?' I says, 'The 26th.' he says, 'The 26th of when?' I says, 'This month.' He said, 'You're kidding, aren't you?' The fore-end just wasn't there. He says, 'You'll never get this.' I said, 'Oh, we'll get it.' And that's the one you see. I was working in number one hold at the time and I tell you we were diving all over. The SD14s at Smith's Docks, it took eighteen months to build one. Seven weeks here.

John: There was a bloke in the pub, when I was working at Doxford's yard, the new covered-in yard, and he was bragging to these blokes about Pickersgill's. He says, 'Aye, we can launch a ship in seven weeks.' He was baffling them, they knew nowt about ships. But I was sitting at the next table drinking me beer. He must have seen me looking, and he knew I was from Sunderland, and he says, 'Isn't that right, Picky's can launch a one in seven weeks?' I said, 'Oh aye, that's true, and they can sink a one in thirty seconds and all.' One of the first went down in thirty seconds, after a collision. All the fore end was fucking burst wide open. It takes seven weeks to build them and thirty seconds to sink them.

Harry: I know, the *Sigma*, a forty-five-thousand tonner, was brought back off the Australian coast. Me uncle sailed on a ship built at Bartram's called the *Wear*. I remember it, I was only a schoolkid at the time, it was tied up in the docks, waiting to go, brand new. It sailed just in ballast, it was going to America. He was an experienced sailor and he said at the start there was a storm and nobody slept, they were all with their life-jackets on, brand new ships. The officers were down looking at the ship. He said that, if the storm hadn't of abated when it did, they would have brought it back. It had to be towed in. Brand new, it had to be towed in.

Alf: I'm going to tell you two stories. One is I've talked to a lad who was a seaman, merchant seaman, and another one was telt to me by a bloke who worked here and his brother-in-law is a second officer. They have both been on SD14s on the Atlantic, and they are the best boats they have ever been on.

John: When I was working at SS, one of my neighbours was a sea-going engineer and his mate worked for Bank Line, and SS were building ships for Bank Line at the time.

Alf: I know the ones you mean, they had a new bow on, they just swept down like that.

John: *Cedar Bank*, that was the first one. I was talking to Dennis, and his mate was home, and he says, 'It's a pity we couldn't have gone out with you for a drink because he sails on that ship you have just finished, the *Cedar Bank*. He says, "It's the fastest Bank boat I've ever got."' They were built to last.

Alf: You couldn't get any better than the fucking SD fucking 14. Fifteen-year-old and fucking selling off for seven million, and it only cost a hundred million to buy.

John: The Banks were superior.

Alf: Superior to what?

John: SDs. They had to be, man, they cost a lot more money.

Alf: The SD14s were only workhorses, man.

John: The Banks were, they were tramps.

Alf: They were a worse tramp than the SD14? You can't get a lower recommendation than that, can you? I think you are trying to kid me, ye.

hurdy-gurdy

Alf: I'll bet you are fucking pleased you didn't get a welder's job in the shipyard. I'm talking about having to work inside double bottoms and confined spaces. The time you would have started, there'd be no extractors. They only had hurdy-gurdies, what do they call them, a wind-blown propeller, aluminium outside casing with like a propeller in the middle blown by air. Fucking hell. If you got a couple of them on, you fucking knew about it. They used to have my head going like that: booooom boooooooom. You couldn't think, you couldn't fucking hear. I think that's why I shout. Here, one day I was sat in the fucking double bottom, and we had them yellow trumpets things: what they used to do was, one blowing in one end of the fucking tank and another one sucking, or blowing out. I was sitting there, there was heat in the tank like that off the

211

sun, the fumes that were in the tank coming up like that! And they were going straight out through the extractor unit. They were loaded on the top and coming back down again.

John: Best thing they ever got rid of in the yard was the caulking.

Alf: You know Dante had us in the unit over there, and it was the far-end unit where the bilge sweeps come up like that! There was about five spaces and we had a seam to do. He put little Harry in the one right next to the tank, then he put Les in one, then he put me in, and Huey. You need space, they are only small, for to do the seam. Can you imagine five welders in a little fucking unit like that? We got the first one in and we were busy back-filling it up, and he puts a fucking caulker on the outside! *DRRRRRRRR!!!!* I says, 'Fuck you!' and shot straight out the fucking hole. It's bad enough working in the fuckers without putting a fucking caulker there.

London

Billy: But the feeling you got. When we came round the first corner, then up the street and round again, and when you looked back and when you passed the *Times* office! 'Fucking hell,' I says, 'hey Mack, you should fucking see them behind here.'

Dicky: I didn't realise it was so long.

Chris: Is that what the nurse said to you?

Billy: I felt proud walking through London, fighting for me job.

3/6/86

Rick takes his lot

Paul: He said last week, 'I'm fucking sick, it looks like there is no future, they are trying to get shot of us, I'm going to look for another job and wrap up as steward.' All right, he's wrapping in, just fucking off, fair enough, but he's selling it.
Pickard: You don't know that for sure.
Bluey: He's a scab until proven different. He's guilty until proven innocent.
Paul: We don't use their form of justice, mind.
Pickard: He'll have to resign from his job with me, as poet's mate.

it used to be a pleasure

Burner: It's fucking awful now, isn't it? How long have you been here?
Pickard: Since January.
Burner: You'll have noticed the bloody change in the place. I'm not kidding you, at one time it used to be a pleasure coming here. Ships used to get turned out. It used to be a good laugh.

burying Rick

Cal: We've just had the longest meeting of the outfitters on record just putting other people on the committees that Rick was on. The committees he was on! You'll have to put him in the class traitor section of the book. I feel a poem coming on: is that because I'm on the arts committee now?

213

Eddy: The plumbers' shop is empty. Everything is gone. The blacksmiths' shop is just a shell now. They've cleared out most of the shops. Could have been a bomb in here. You see that bloke over there? He's one of our members, he's looking around for a tool where his old bench used to be.

Plumber: This is just the start, this. Terrible man. This shop was the best, well the men were anyway, the best fabrication shops on the River Wear. In the North-East. Because some of the lads that worked in here could be put against anybody. They would do any type of fabrication.

Eddy: I tell you what, you'd have to gan a long way to find better lads at doing the job of fabricating. You see this stuff here? It is York Alborough pipe.

Plumber: That's £80 a metre.

Eddy: When the previous Oldendorf boats came here, they do their salt water with aluminium brass. That stuff. And the management wanted to subcontract it out. And for eight months the stewards argued with the management that we could do it. At the finish we done it. And the lads that flanged it up ...

Plumber: There wasn't a pipe wrong, not one.

Eddy: ... done three ships of it. The managing director, which was Carter, and the manager, Carroll, came round and shook their hands, they had done such a good job.

Plumber: The Germans were over the moon with it.

Eddy: But the foreman at first didn't want the job, they didn't want nowt to do with it ... And what we done in here, you wouldn't get taught in night school or college. I'm telling you.

Plumber: You see those big wooden pads with the holes in. They are to make templates with, they take them on the ships and they make a template to fit two ends. Now that template used to come back here and it used to go on this block and these lads used to make the pipes up. It was all silver solder welding. It used to be taken on the ship and it used to go plop straight in. Now they are doing the same templates and over at Doxford's they can't make it to a template. They've got to break a sketch down, give the lengths of pipe, give them all the angles, and everything, and they are coming back wrong. They won't fit. There wasn't one scrapped on the three Oldendorfs that we done.

Eddy: Whatever you put on paper or a template here, you got it.

Plumber: Because the lads were that good at their job, plus the fact that it is expensive pipe, you couldn't afford to make a mistake with it. But over there I don't know how many they've had back. And we have had to alter them. Put them right.

Pickard: Why are they doing it?

Plumber: Because they haven't got the men capable of doing it. These lads used to set it up on the blocks, set them to the face plates and everything, they used to be dead on. If you take a template, bearing in mind that it is all stiffened up and that's where that pipe's got to go, and you bring it back and put it on a block and you set it up to face plates, and you mark through your holes, when the templates are taken off, the blocks are all set up and when the pipe goes on it is spot on to the holes. It can't be any other than right, but the subcontractors cannot do it. A template is no good there.

Eddy: We've never had any wrong. Foolproof.

Plumber: Take it on to the ship and put it straight in. Now they are taking them aboard, getting them wrong, taking them off, chopping and cutting them till they get them right and putting them on again. It's costing not two times, it's costing four or five times more . . .

I do fire-bending, smaller pipes, where the job is too tight for fitting, where we have to pack them with silver sand and fire-bend them. They cannot do it. They don't do that over there. I wish you could see an example. There is one next door where they butt-welded and we would have fire-bent the pipe all in one.

Eddy: You see we try and make a neat job as well. There was one time here when we were doing nine ships at one time. One in the river, you had the berths full, and you had drawings coming through. At one time we were doing nine.

Plumber: And not a ship late either.

Eddy: That's not so long ago.

Plumber: We could still do the same if they gave us a chance. There is none of us frightened of work that's worked in here. Any of the old gaffers would tell you . . . they were over the moon, they would never bother anybody.

Eddy: Come on, I'll show you where we are now. You've not seen fire-bending? When he's bending a square bend you can have a look. They are doing away with the skills slowly but surely. As Tommy says, where we would do a fire-bend and make the job look

215

neat, now they are just cutting. They buy bends in, what we call factory bends. They are just cutting them and butting them together and the job is manky. It's just a fucking manky job.

Plumber: To us, when you have to cut a pipe and buck-weld it, it's come from over the subcontractors and it's wrong. If it had of been done in our shop in the first place, we could have done away with all those joints where it could leak, and the pipe would have been offset to start with. It would have been all right. Twice the work and at what cost by the time you take into consideration transport, everything else?

Pickard: You must feel pretty demoralised?

Plumber: We are. We know the workforce we've got, they are quite capable of doing anything these people want us to do. These are the people that's caused all the problems, not us. We've never had a ship late, man. We've kept up with all the work they've ever given us, haven't we?

Pickard: But if they start jamming the ship with duff jobs like that, won't it damage the reputation of the yard?

Plumber: But the point is: is this what these people want? It makes you think that.

Eddy: It's not the subcontractors that get the bad reputation, it is A&P. It is always the parent company that gets the bad name. If a contractor puts a job in on your ship, he doesn't get the blame. The owner blames A&P. So the bad name gets known in the world.

Plumber: When Robert Atkinson was chairman of BS he didn't want any contractors, he wanted every yard and BS to be self-sufficient, no contractors at all.

Eddy: Then all of a sudden the leadership was changed and now we've got contractors. But we were more efficient when we done everything ourselves. We couldn't be beaten. We got three Queen's Awards.

Plumber: That's within the last seven year, so you cannot blame the workforce. We've always worked. Not frightened of work. What sickens us is the demoralising. But maybe that's what they are after.

Pickard: What do you think will happen to you?

Plumber: That's anybody's guess. Nobody is sure of their future here. If it closes, that solves the problem for everybody, doesn't it?

Pickard: But at the minute you've no idea of what is going to happen to you and they've not told you?

Plumber: They'll not even give us a breakdown for the people that's got to go. It's supposed to be starting from the 1st of July and the first batch should be out by September. Then the next lot will be the end of the year, January or something. They want a thousand men from the two yards. I cannot see them getting it, so what is going to happen from there? They know what's going to happen but they won't tell you. They knew five year ago what's ganna happen.

It's quite possible it could open again, private. But you've lost all the conditions that you've fought for over the years and you've got to start from scratch. You'll have to use things that you normally would never use. Fine iron powder and low hydrogen. Well they are using low hydrogen, but not to a great extent. It is all in the open but these will want to use it in the double bottoms and confined spaces and all sorts. You just sign your own death certificates as far as we are concerned ... I think the Tories will get punished. It would take a hell of a lot to get us back into shipbuilding.

Pickard: They say that there's never been a shipyard re-opened once closed.

Plumber: Well, it could go private, but, even so, I would be too old to get into it. I'd be finished anyway.

Pickard: How old are you now?

Plumber: Fifty-one. So there is very little work for me, unless I can find something else.

Pickard: Do you find it worrying that you don't know what is going to happen?

Plumber: These people that have mortgages, especially young people, it's going to be devastating to them, because when they do get finished they'll have nowt to pick up, redundancy-wise or anything like that. You are talking about youngsters that's paying two hundred and odd pound per month on mortgage. So where is that going to come from?

5/6/86

Dicky's dog-tag skagged

Dicky: When you take me photo, Pickard, can you make sure me dog-tag is in the picture.
Billy: Why do you wear daft dog-tags like that?
Dicky: Because I'm in the fire-fighting, and if I get caught in a fire and there's just a skeleton left I want to make sure...
Billy: It's made of plastic, you daft bastard.
Chris: You fucking wally.
Eddy: It's Bakelite.
Chris: If the body's ganna burn, the skeleton will fucking burn.
Dicky: What about during the war when they wore them?
Eddy: They were metal.
Billy: Isn't it time you got a bit more active?
Dicky: If I think it's a good enough cause, I give it me full support.
Billy: What *you* think is a good enough cause? But what about what your members think?
Dicky: I'm not one of these that gans along because everybody else does it. They proved that with the miners. I said that if I think it's a hundred per cent worthwhile fighting for it, I'll give it my support.
Pickard: Did you not support the miners?
Dicky: It was the way they went about it ... Just cause Scargill wanted it, and that's what bollocksed it.
Eddy: If you are going to say they got beat, what bollocksed the miners' strike? What knackered it?
Dicky: Eh?
Eddy: She didn't beat them, or the police.
Dicky: Well, what beat them?
Eddy: The scabs. The scabs fucking done it. If it hadn't of been for the scabs, that strike would have been over in a couple of weeks.
Dicky: You can't call a miner that's been out for ten months or so a scab.

Eddy: It wouldn't have lasted that long if they'd all fucking come out.

Dicky: Well, why didn't he call for a vote and see if they wanted to come out, instead of being dictated to?

Eddy: Everything he said has fucking come true over the years, man.

Dicky: Winston Churchill was the same...

Eddy: Winston Churchill should have been skagged with hot shite.

Billy: Are you finished? Now chuck this stupid fucking dog-tag away.

they lay down their tools

Pickard: So the worst scenario then, is that you are just here until the barge is finished and that's it, and the place is just closing down around your ears.

Catwalk: If there is no further orders.

Pickard: What would hapen to you? Would you be transferred across the water?

Catwalk: I can't see it. I wouldn't want to go over, to tell you the truth. Different life over there.

Pickard: What's the difference?

Catwalk: Men's attitudes, not bothered whether it stays open or not. They're not bothered. It's the way he's driven them into the ground where they don't give a shit now whether it stops open or not. There's lads here that's willing to fight for their jobs, willing to get mucked in. Go across the water and you'll see them. I was over there twice a fortnight ago: all right they'll work when the foreman's there, but as soon as the foreman turns his back they lay down their tools. Lads that come over here say it's like a holiday camp, not because they're not doing any work, it's because of the relaxed atmosphere, you can enjoy yourself, have a bit laugh and carry-on. The work is still getting done, whereas over there they are all miserable and they're doing nowt. Everything is a chore to them.

Pickard: Are you saying they don't have the same pride? Cause it's obvious here that people are proud of their skills.

Catwalk: He's demoralised them, hasn't he.

Pickard: How is that done? How would he go about doing something like that?

Catwalk: It's the way he's gone over the years. Giving crane drivers higher wages than the rest of them, agitating the situation. Low hydrogen, iron powder rods, arc air gouging in the shed, demoralise them. He just tells them to 'accept it or you know what to do'. That's the line they've took instead of standing up against him, so the lads there that's left are just demoralised. They just think to themselves, 'What's he going to do to us next?'

Pickard: Have they never bothered organising?

Catwalk: They've got no leadership. At a meeting of Save Our Shipyards there was two hundred turned up out of the whole workforce and fifty of them were shop stewards. That shows the interest they are generating over there.

Pickard: How many turned up from here?

Catwalk: We get about ninety per cent for meetings like that. We get a good turn-out. He's just worn them down; they've been out the gates on total strike, they've banned overtime, but after twenty-four hours it's back on again. He just treats them like shit. They've never stuck together over there, it's always one bickering against the other.

Pickard: They haven't got a confed?

Catwalk: No. He just works one off against the other. There won't be any shop stewards from Picky's over there.

Pickard: They wouldn't get in?

Catwalk: I wouldn't think so.

Pickard: So when they make the final selection of who goes over, the rest will be made compulsorily redundant?

Catwalk: It's looking that way, but there again we're not talking about compulsory redundancies.

Pickard: You're not?

Catwalk: We're not, as a union, we're not. Them might be thinking of it.

Pickard: As a union, or a confed?

Catwalk: As a confed over here. What the union decides in the near future all depends on what response they get off the rest of the yards. As you said, to resist it we've got to be a hundred per cent, when you get yards going the other way we are all fucked, aren't we? They'll just give them the earth and pick the others off one at a time.

Pickard: So what would most of the blokes do?

Catwalk: I've got two brothers-in-law and one brother, they've been out more than three years, the lot of them now. One's had a job, full-time job for about four weeks, or three full-time jobs lasting him a total of four weeks, and the other one – he's had six months' work in three year and our Allen's had none at all. That's just my family, what I know of, like. So you can say a total of seven months work out of thirty-six is not a lot.

Pickard: I suppose if they had orders they wouldn't tell you?

Catwalk: Oh, he wouldn't tell us. It sets the depression in, 'We haven't got any orders.' People talking about strikes and that, lads get sick and hope they get their redundancy, he gets the numbers he wants and all of a sudden he's got an order. I think that's the plan, wear people down, keep them on the bottom, these orders is coming through one at a time, that's how it's went for the last three or four year, get people depressed and that, 'Oh, there's no future here.' He gets the numbers he wants for the redundancies, he got ninety-five per cent of them last time and then he turns up with an order.

Pickard: And he brings people in on contract as well?

Catwalk: We must have a hundred lads in on temporary transfer. Plus contractors.

Pickard: What happens to the lads from Appledore?

Catwalk: They're still here, and from Clarke Kinkaid's, Swan Hunter's ... all they'll be interested in here is the steel structure, everything else will be subcontracted, that's what they're talking about ... I can't see any shop stewards going over there. Even the bad ones has a little bit more savvy than the ones over there. With atmospheric tests and things like that, they don't seem to care, they just take the management's word for it: 'It's all right, get on with it.'

Pickard: Do you get tests off your own bat?

Catwalk: We tell management what they've done, and if it doesn't get done, well, we dinna do the job. They have to prove to us that its within the TLV [Threshold Limit Values].

Pickard: What's that?

Catwalk: Something like Total Living Values. They used to do tests on American marines, twenty-year-olds, and see how much fumes they could take before it starts to affect people. And that's what they work off. But it just so happens that the Russians' is fifty per cent less than ours. And now our health and safety executive is

221

saying anything above fifty per cent of the recommended level we should be wary of.

a bowl of rice and a nest of bastards

Noddy: it's the fucking naval yards, man, that's our backbone gone.
Pickard: Do you think you'll beat them?
Noddy: Who us? No way we'll beat them. There's nobody beat the bastard yet, is there? The miners couldn't beat her, lad.
Pickard: They were turned round though at British Leyland.
Noddy: Aye, and who's gone there now? The same twat that ran this place. You watch in a few years' time and see where British Leyland is. It'll be cut into little fucking pieces. That's what he was brought in for, that bastard ... They spend millions here on computers, makes no difference, they'll close it down. As long as they are saving money a year they don't give a fuck about that. A fucking villain, a fucking villain.
Pickard: I tend to refuse to admit defeat. It's getting a bit tiring though.
Noddy: Oh, you've got to try and fight them, like. But I watched the miners. I've watched them all, and they've all fucking gone under. How much did it cost through the miners' strike? Millions, fucking millions, you fucker: as long as she beats them. What's come out of it is all this cheap labour now. All this cheap labour, fifty-pound jobs, that's what comes out of it: part-time jobs, short-time fucking working jobs. That's what come out of it. They are a nest of bastards. This cunt for another five years and the working man will be on his fucking knees. He'll be going along for a fucking bowl of rice. She's a fucking villain. They'll grind you into the fucking ground. The only people that can beat her is the likes of the civil servants and the telecommunications and all that lot: when they threaten, she shies off. Vickers, what happened to Vickers? They were on strike for three weeks, what happened to them? Eighteen per cent pay rise. They've got orders there as long as your fucking arm, haven't they? That's our backbone gone.
Pickard: Looks like the naval yards will join in, especially Swan's.
Noddy: They're not a naval yard any more, are they? That's been sacrificed for fucking Harland and Wolf, purely political. They didn't want another three thousands Protestants running the street,

did they? Purely political. We were convinced we had three fucking meat-boats coming here; Boyars stepped in and they went to Harland and Wolf. No fucking danger, boy, they were coming here. There was a lad from Swan Hunter's told me, he says, 'You think you've got them but the steel is already going into Harland and Wolf,' and it fucking was! And the orders went; no messing. She knows what she's doing; a very shrewd woman where the unions are concerned. She picks the telecommunications in the Post Office, put that to one side so she can take the Post Office on any time she fucking likes. Drive them into the fucking ground. Villain, man villain. She crucified the unions since she came in. Some unions is helping her and all, with their fucking heads in the fucking sand. She prepared for the miners' strike, how we didn't fucking see what she was doing, I don't know. She was buying coal from Australia and all over the fucking place, stockpiling it. She had millions of tons stockpiled, you fucker, when that dozy cunt went on strike. If he'd gone about that the right way and took them all out he would have fucking won. He would have fucking won, boy. Aye, you fucker.

I can't see them keeping open. Honestly I can't see them keeping open. They were going to take that vessel at the quayside, they were going to take it down there, down to Palmer's Hill; what for? All the gear is up here. Everything has got to be transported down there now ... It has to go down to Palmer's Hill or, he says, 'Heads will fucking roll.' He's ganna sack managers. Right, it's ganna go down. What for? Why does he want it down there? He wants it down there out of our control. He'll put any cunt on it down there, I bet a fucking pound to a penny. Half our lads have fucking come back up here, and them that's down there – he just does what he likes with them: two bowls of fucking rice. He's in sole command now, isn't he. He's ruling by fear, he's got all his managers shitting themselves. Before, [during a dispute] they'd turn back at the gates: he phoned them up and telt them and they came in. He said he'd sack the fuckers. He's ruling by fear, man, he's a fucking villain.

Pickard: He's the one that introduced the 'purge'?

Noddy: Yes, he first started it at Sunderland Shipbuilders and he's brought it over here with him. I think I'll be finished. There is nowhere else I can fucking gan. I'm not ganna hump my box over the fucking country at my fucking age, fifty-four. Fuck that! I did enough of that. Living in fucking caravans, no friggin' good at all, that. With bastards like him, 'Why don't you emigrate?' or 'Why don't you move fucking South?' If we all went down South, it would be great, wouldn't it? You flog your house here and you move down and it wouldn't make a fucking deposit for a house down there. It's a fucking fact, boy.

Doctor Death

Chris: Here you are, you can do an interview with a lad that's taken his redundancy. A boy twenty year old.
Pickard: Why'd you take your redundancy?
Lad: I've been forced out in a way.
Pickard: What's your trade?
Lad: Fitter.
Pickard: How long have you worked here?
Lad: Nearly on four year; I served me time here. Been out me time about four or five months.
Pickard: So what suddenly prompted you to take drastic action like that?
Lad: Well, for the past two to three months I've been lying about doing nothing.
Chris: You cannot say that, you daft twat!
George: It's the foreman not giving him a job. I asked him. I've asked the foreman to give him a job and he's just refused.
Pickard: Why?
George: He's just got his own reasons. The foreman reckons that when he does give him a job he'll not do it. And if he does do it he only does it half-heartedly and wants to be took off the job and put on something else. What he told us was that he thought that he was trying to pick his own job; what job he wanted to do, when he wanted to do it and why he wanted to do it. That's the main reason why he'll not give him a job. That's the top and bottom of it.
Pickard: So is that why you're leaving?
Lad: Purely and simply cause he'll not gis a job and I've got nowt to do, just standing about doing nothing.
Pickard: So it boils down to a gaffer in the sulks?
George: That's about it.
Pickard: Can't you do anything about it?
Chris: We've saved his job about ten fucking times, man.

George: He's been nearly going to get sacked about three or four times.

Pickard: If he says you work half-heartedly and keep chopping and changing, is that a load of bollocks?

Lad: If he would give me a job I'd do it, but he'll not. He doesn't like is, full stop.

Pickard: Have you got another job?

Lad: No.

Chris: He wants to be an undertaker.

Pickard: He should talk to Dicky. Why did you want to be an undertaker?

Ron: Reckons he'll get a good living out of it.

Lad: There's a good living in it. You go to new towns and that, springing up down South, go there, set up there. You might have to wait a bit, but . . . you gan into the new towns, young people and that. After a while they'll start kicking the bucket.

Chris: His name is Doctor Death.

Pickard: In the SDP, is he? Are you qualified?

Lad: No, not yet. I've got to take the exams, an embalming exam, get a diploma at the end of it, man. Before I started here, I served me time at the Co-op, I was working there for three or four months.

Pickard: Dying on the divy.

Chris: Did you hear about Rick taking his lot?

Pickard: Now that brother Rick won't be around to take any more stick you'll need a new scapegoat in here. I got fucking whacked with the broom next door the other day.

Eddy: We use verbal.

Chris: I'll bet he'll not sleep the neet, Rick.

Eddy: I walked over the yard with him, last neet when I was gannin' yem. I said to him, 'When you leaving?' He says, 'Hopefully Friday, I've got a few things to sort out.' I said, 'Have you got fixed up?' He said, 'Oh, aye.' I didn't ask him what or where. He says he felt fucking awful. I said, 'Well if you make your fucking mouth gan and then if the time comes . . .'

Chris: Nobody has made his mouth go more than Rick. I don't think he wants people to know where he's going to work, cause they'll start laughing.

George: Chris knows where he's ganna work.

Chris: I'm saying nothing. But people will laugh when they find out

225

where he's going to work. He asked me not to disclose where he's ganna work.

Pickard: His wife is having a bairn, isn't she?

Chris: She's expecting, yes. But people will laugh when they find out where he's going to work and that's why he doesn't want them to know.

Pickard: He's going to work at Tesco's?

Chris: Very near. If you lot actually knew where he was going to work you'd shout different things at him, that would really embarrass him.

oh my name is Walnut Jim

The singing welder: As I wake up in the morning feeling tired
　　　　　　　　　　listless knackered and run down,
　　　　　　　　　　'cause I'm a fucking welder
　　　　　　　　　　ain't never made those double bottoms
　　　　　　　　　　for the summer time.

Then a bit plucking on the guitar. I'm not great, I just like a bit plonk on the guitar when I'm feeling down in the dumps. I nip up stairs in the bathroom and plonk plonk plonk, like Ken Dodd used to say ... I used to write songs about welders when I used to work down there, little ditties. I never kept them; just in the mind. I used to do daft little things like Walnut Jim, the gaffer:

　　　　　　　　　　Oh my name is Walnut Jim
　　　　　　　　　　I'm a welder through and through
　　　　　　　　　　I'm canny when I'm sober
　　　　　　　　　　and I'm happy when I'm blue
　　　　　　　　　　I'm welding for a living
　　　　　　　　　　its a load upon my mind
　　　　　　　　　　and when I take a day off
　　　　　　　　　　well I'm only tea and kind
　　　　　　　　　　For I'm an electric welder
　　　　　　　　　　and I'm working down the deck ...

19/6/86

selective overtime

Eddy: It just brought me in mind, when we were talking about selective overtime, there was a bloke working for them, a labourer, K—, a big bloke. Anyhow, there was little Alun, hard case, ex-merchant navy, found out K— had worked a friggin' Sunday and we all came in of a Monday and got to know and we started friggin' calling him. And K— was a friggin' big lad. 'Get on you big cunt, working Sunday, saying nowt to no fucker.' Anyway, one word further on, K— stands up and Tommy says to Alun, 'Go on give him a friggin' crack and when you've done I'll kick his friggin' head off.' K— backed off. That was just for a friggin' Sunday. Terrible, man.

Beak: Didn't you use matchboxes to get a Sunday in?

Eddy: The gaffers used to come along, 'Have you got a match? Have you got a match?' Get your matchbox out with a dollar in. Two half-dollars. I didn't know what they were on about when I first went there. The foreman says to me, 'Got a match?' I says, 'Here,' and handed him the box. He opened it and says, 'Hey, there's nowt in here.' I said, 'Friggin' hell I've just bought the twats.'

Chris: And you've got to think about the sites, you'd got maybe five or six hundred men working for you.

Eddy: Working all neet, over at Doxy's, fitters, we got the job done before half-seven and said, 'Come on, let we fuck off.' He says, 'No, it's dodgy.' So I said, 'The job's done, we may as well go,' and we went. The bloke came in on a Monday, 'Hey, next time I work all night like that I'm stopping for the proper time.' 'How's that?' 'When I got home the fucking gaffer was in the house.' Blokes used to gan on nightshift and the gaffers used to sleep with their wives. It was done loads of times, Chris.

Chris: Get away and shite.

Eddy: Hey, I'm telling you.

Dave: Chris won't want to work half-shifts now, 'Who's been in here?'

Eddy: I knew two blokes, good mates, you cannot trust no cunt: 'Where are you gannin'?' He says, 'Down to Butchers along Trimdon Street, get in two pints. I'm bursting for a shite but I'm not ganna use the shithouse here.' He's away, up their lass. Oh aye, trust no cunt, I'm telling you.

Beak: When I was working down the Dock, men who wanted to work a half-shift would have to do the gaffer a favour. The gaffer said, 'You want to work a half-shift?' cause the money was bad without it. So he says, 'If you want to work a half-shift, you'll have to get us some coal.' They had the beach down there for sea coal so I paddled down, took two bags down, and cleaned up everything in sight: friggin' stones, rocks, coal, the friggin' lot. I finished in about ten minutes. He came back the next day and said, 'I don't know what you've put in that friggin' bag but it's banging off all over the shop.'

Pickard: You mean you had to get him two bags of sea coal before you could work a half-shift?

Chris: You've had an easy life, Pickard.

Eddy: There was some funny things happening, some funny things. They're coming back, that's the fucking trouble.

Chris: We were up in Glasgow for a meeting, and you can see it getting worse.

Eddy: Depressing, that fucking place. How the fucking hell Harry Lauder can sing 'Glasgow belongs to me!'

George: It's further up the league than Sunderland in the worst-place-in-Europe league.

Eddy: The Scotch boy says to his father, 'Give is fifty pence, Dad.' His dad says, 'Forty pence, what do you want thirty pence for?'

the engine room: labourers

Bill: The stories you get off him: 'There's twelve ferries to be built.'

Pickard: There is a rumour going round. A gaffer told me.

Jack: According to him: 'There's accommodation, crew of six, generators on after-deck, and a further twelve.'

Pickard: I've seen a plan.

Bill: What, to be built here?

228

Pickard: Tony is putting out a bulletin tomorrow. I typed it up for him. He's just saying up to now it's a rumour and just to be careful because it's absolutely not confirmed.

Bill: It was announced last weekend, by all the crack . . .

Jack: Did you hear about this afternoon, labourers gannin' in the sheds?

Bill: This is our last ship. When we gan down the river, we finish. We're in the big shed.

Jack: Where's the two hundred and twenty-eight labourers ganna come from?

Bill: What they want is short-term fucking labouring. They don't want full-time labourers.

Pickard: So you come in on short-term contracts?

Jack: They want everybody to do their own housekeeping, that's what they want. And maybe have a labourer come along, pick the muck up and hoy it into the bin. They just want everybody to sweep their muck into a pile and get it straight into a skip.

Bill: It's going to be a full-time job doing that, isn't it?

Jack: I'm fucking sure.

Bill: I think we'll just get blathered like what they are doing now with these contract painters.

Jack: All outfitters will gan, definitely. They want shot of them because it's fucking cheaper getting a contractor in.

Bill: Apart from that, the fucking onus is on the contractors then.

Jack: Aye, but the company is still responsible for the ship, and if there is any fault they've got to pay it.

Pickard: I've seen some of the blacksmith stuff that was contracted in, it was fucking terrible.

Bill: That's right.

Jack: There's our lads, could have all this top casting in a day. We've waited three days for that length there.

Bill: We've waited ages for this! About a fortnight ago we were still waiting for a pipe that had been sketched, the sketch sent off in January, we waited five weeks for a pipe.

Jack: If they'd left it to our own plumbers we would have been all finished in here.

Bill: You know them quality samplers? That's what he says. That's what his job was, to come round and find out why, so they can refer it back. He doesn't work for BS, he works for British Maritime Agency. He was doing a survey for British Shipbuilders, and that's where all this is supposed to be going back to. We telt him that it's taking that fucking long for the gear to get here that the job is just getting out of hand.

Jack: It's getting further and further back.

Bill: Like one lad said, a fucking apprentice, by the time you sketch the pipe up, you get the cunt sent away, the sketch, and the time you get it back the electricians are there, the fucking plumbers are there. Every cunt is there to do their job, and you've got to scrap it.

Jack: Aye, reshape it. You've fucking got to send away for another one.

A heavy tool fell a short distance from us.

Bill: I've seen fucking gear come down off here.

Jack: Hammers and all sorts, you know. Wedges coming down. If he's working down here underneath him and his job's coming along and burning, welding, owt, fuck you. He just starts burning above you. You might be under the fucking floor and you cannot find space, you cannot fucking get out of the road. If he wants any welding, the welding is done. The welders aren't fucking working and he wants some burning done he'll take the machine off the burner and do it himself.

Pickard: Is he a gaffer?

Jack: No, he's a workman. Over-active thyroid gland.

Pickard: How old is he?

Jack: Fifty. He's what you call a river, he rives at this cunt and rives at that cunt. He wants me to gan on the funnel with him when they put the funnel up. He knows what he can fucking do as well, gan and get fucked. There's a tank to gan in there before the funnel gans on. Let him put the cunt in himself.

Pickard: Do labourers work all the time with the same trade?

Jack: Yes we do. It's no good me gannin' with a fucking plater, I wouldn't have a clue what's gannin' on. And it's no good a fucking plater's labourer coming with us, because he wouldn't have a fucking clue about what's going on. He might as well not be there. Especially with these two, it's no good any cunt coming on who hasn't got a clue. It takes you a while to learn it.

Bill: That's it. When I first started here with the fitters, with D— and fucking K—, they didn't tell us a fucking thing. That's the fucking truth. I had to try and figure the cunt out meself. What was happening and how the lads were fucking doing it, or how to fucking do it. They didn't give you a fucking hand, if you got a job they would come round and take the cunt off you and push you to one side. That's straight that.

Bob: Oh aye, I know there are a few like that.

Bill: So, at the finish you just had to keep an eye out, see what they were doing and try to pick the cunt up.

Bob: Aye, some of them wouldn't tell you nowt.

Bill: They are two canny lads. As long as they got on with their job they didn't give a fuck if you were standing watching them and doing nowt.

Jack: It's the same in other trades where blokes couldn't read and write and yet no way anybody could tell them how to do that job. He knew it inside out.

Bill: I've fucking argued with that. Fucking lad who used to gan to school couldn't fucking write, they've got boys coming out of school now with 'A' levels, 'O' levels, GC fucking Es, or whatever they call them, and the blokes that couldn't write their fucking name turn out first-class tradesmen.

Jack: He would do that job and not even a gaffer could tell him how to do it. He would just tell him to 'fuck off I'm doing the job, not you'. And he wasn't the only one; there was hundreds of blokes like that, especially the oldish ones. There was nobody could tell them how to do their job.

Bill: That's what makes me laugh about these lads with their fucking degrees, man.

Jack: There's those two that's working with me! Fucking hell! I wish the two cunts would get married and it would solve all our fucking problems. You get a bloke twenty-seven year old passing a bloke forty just cause he's got a degree. This bloke's been fucking years and years in the same game and he's still fucking doing it.

Bill: And this bloke is coming asking you, 'How do you do this and how do you do that?'

Jack: To me, that's the daftest thing ever done in this yard. He's made G— foreman driller: he is over fitters, plumbers, painters, all the trades. On the barges, he's above all them trades, and in the pumproom. The plumber was gannin' up to him and saying, 'How do I do this?' and he was saying, 'I don't know, you'd better go and see your own gaffer.' Yet he was the one you were supposed to consult.

Bill: They haven't a clue. It's like everything else they bring out, it

231

doesn't work. And we get the blame. We try to tell them but they just ignore us. They gan and spend thousands and thousands of pounds and it is just wrote off. You go and ask for another tanner an hour and they chop your hands off.

Jack: The same with them Kempys, isn't it?

Bill: Aye, what was it? One hundred and fifty thousand pound for the Kempys, there was fifty they got in. And they are no good. Them welding machines where the thing moves along by itself, they are useless, they are not built to do that type of job. I was looking in the store just before Christmas, and there was two hundred welding machines. They had them six months, out of fucking date. How much had it cost for them? They just hoyed them in the store and stacked them up. There is a load up at Sand Banks, there is a load up there, and you know they are brand-new machines in there, and there is not one of them working. They have been taking bits and pieces off them and putting them on the others. Brand new, never been used. Taking pieces off them, instead of taking the machine out, no taking pieces out. And they gan on about cost-cutting! I'll tell you what, there is about fifty to sixty machines up there and there is not one working, and they are all brand new.

Jack: You are talking about hundreds of thousands of pounds, all down the fucking drain.

Bill: What are they doing to the fucking welders? Fucking little pots so they can toss the ends of the welding rods in. House-cleaning. Crackers, man. Two hundred and fifty tins or something. How much was it they cost? Two hundred and fifty poundsworth of empty tins. Packing jobs up for every cunt. M— is one of the buggers; field engineer, isn't he? No good with his fucking hands. He was kept on the shop floor on the boat – he's got a degree, he's a foreman field engineer.

Jack: That's what I mean, they come and ask you what to do. I told K— the job up there, I said, 'You'll have to release that right along because there was too much plate.' I says, 'Release right along and you'll lose that plate into that one and all you've got to do is fair it up.' He only re-started. He put a jack in and he's even bent the frame! I'll tell him nowt more, he can find out for himself.

I have been instructed

Pickard: Is it a strict regime over the water?

Dodds: Aye, they've got to even ask the gaffer to leave the job for a shit or something like that.

Ken: It's getting like that here, now. Half-past four you stop work and be on the job again for quarter to five, that's a quarter of an hour tea-break! Fucking hell ... That's what he said when he come up here a few minutes ago: 'Mind, after this, anybody here before half-past six will be booked.' I said, 'What do we have to do, just appear at half-past from nowhere?' He's the manager. So I went across and I says, 'All right, officially half-past six, fair enough, I accept it. But we are right away round here and we expect three or four minutes to be allowed to get from here to the locker-rooms for half-past six. Like, for instance, the sheds: they've just got to walk out of the shed and they are in there, and we've got to walk all the way round from the ship. So, be reasonable with two or three minutes.' He said, 'I've been instructed ...' That's all they say to you now: 'I've been instructed ...' I said, 'It looks like we'll have to see the organ grinder all the time now.' He just laughed. I said, 'Well, we're not ganna stand arguing with you, you've got your job to do, and I've got my job.' He says, 'Fair enough.' So we've been up and had a look around and I've noticed in number two hold all the walkways are blocked up in the 'tween decks so I'll stop all that in the morning. Get that put right. That's our only weapon to fight on: safety.

20/6/86

confed meeting rumours

Tony: On the future prospect of orders we are hearing rumours about twelve roll-on roll-off ferries and a possible further twelve. I have made enquiries in the drawing office. They have got a drawing of a ferry which is about sixty-nine metres long. She weighs about fifteen hundred ton, she is a propelled ferry. There are no detailing drawings, so it is just like we've done hundreds of drawings before of different types of ship for owners' requirements, it's in that embryo stage, if you like. Naturally twenty-four would be thirty-six thousand ton of steel, and it is proposed delivery at one every month. So that would be two years' work. But, like I say, the company neither confirms or denies it, they are just saying nowt about it. They will play politics with the order, like they always do, they'll play politics with the orders in the situation we are going through. But that doesn't get us round our problem, and Philip Hares has said on two occasions, he said when he met the councillors and MPs, he said it again the day before yesterday to the select committee[1] that it doesn't matter what work we get we have still got to cut by the three and a half thousand and three yard closures. So how we get round that one, the question of redundancies, of a thousand from both yards, is still the problem. It doesn't matter if we do get orders, that is still our problem, because up until now we've only got a hundred and ten volunteers. I cannot see them (SS) getting eight or nine hundred over there. So we are still going to have a problem and our policy is unchanged that we will defend anybody with all possible means at our disposal that wants to work at A&P. That pledge still stands and that action will be carried out. So that's what I'm reminding the membership of, that is still our policy. Anybody that wants to work here will receive the protection of the rest of the yard.

1. Minutes of Evidence, 18/6/86, British Shipbuilders and 25/6/86 Dept. of Trade and Industry. HM Stationery Office.

Tony: The BS Enterprise Board: the North-East office will be in Depford with a regional director and there will be counsellors. They will try to use trade unionists to train them to be counsellors on their enterprise committees, consultative committees, helping people to set up, possibly, subcontractors who take their redundancy money, set up a paint or subcontracting firm, then to come back into the yard and do your own subcontracting. Immediately this sort of avenue was opened we immediately said, 'As far as we are concerned, we reject, in total, BS projectives for the industry. And that includes BS Enterprise Board, we want nowt to do with it.' We see that as being part of the plan and part of the strategy and we shouldn't be collaborating with that in any way. The council seem to be saying, 'We've got to accept that there is going to be costs.' They seem to have accepted what Philip Hares said, 'All right the yards on the Wear are going to survive albeit with reduced capacity.' They have accepted that there are nine hundred and twenty-nine have got to gan. We haven't, and we have telt them quite clearly that nobody should be having anything to do with that. There was people, I thought, trying to make niches and avenues for possible councillors who were also shipyard workers to be a given a full-time job on this consultative committee. But we have put the block on that immediately. It is not union policy of any of the unions of the confed and it's not the wishes of the members, and them individuals cannot wear two hats. They cannot be a councillor and also be a shipyard worker on that committee. They are either one or the other. So they backed off that situation, and that was the only other point that we had to report in, although they were saying as a council: 'If there was any funds available to help the community blah blah blah ...'

starting and stopping times

Tony: On the yard committee meeting he is again back with his starting and stopping times. And because he went into the complex on Tuesday night about six o'clock, five to six, there wasn't anybody on the ship. The repercussions of that is that he is coming down hard now on enforcing the rulebook. But not only does he want to enforce the rulebook, but he is now talking about discipline within overtime working. He knows if he pulls anybody during overtime on ship, for example, 'Where are you going? You're not supposed to be here.' You just say, 'I'm clocking off,' that's what the normal reaction is.

Rod: With S— aboard the boat, by the way, at ten past four, there was a flap on, as you can imagine. We eventually got off. They were there waiting again at quarter to five. Feelings are running high. Some of them are asking direction, but I've just been saying, 'It's up to the individual, if he don't want to work the shift-work that day, just stop it. You know what to do, you know what the company's at, you know what they're after, it's up to yourselves.' But I can say the feeling is running very high round there at the moment.

Tony: I think that gans for everywhere in the yard. It's running high over the complex and the shed, all over. You see, you have to control that direction of your members, and say, 'Look, we know what we are doing, and if it comes to it we'll have a go, and you've got to back us up fully to the hilt.' Don't gan and shout in your little corners, 'We shouldn't be doing this and we shouldn't be doing that.' Because when it comes to the time you have to say, 'Aye, we are working no overtime. And that any other gauntlet he throws down we'll have to pick up.' So that's what you have to say to them. We have telt him, we are going to abide by the rulebook, that's what it says. We'll have to put it into procedure ourselves and say we are asking for an extra five minutes, it would have to be our reference, and we'd have to continue doing it in any case while it went through procedure. So we might as well just say, 'Watch your start and stopping times within the overtime, watch your overtime programme,' and then say, 'We'll call a mass meeting.' We know what it's all about, there's no need to have a long meeting, just say, 'Do you want it or do you not?' And at the end of the day we'll make a recommendation. And we'll give them direction when the time comes.

Eddy: Chairman, last night S—, at five past four, stopped two of my members taking a welding cable over the electricians' shop to get repaired. They were off the gangway with it, they hoyed it off the back and they had to gan back on the ship. He's talking about disrupting production. I mean it was five past four. All right, he might of thought they were doing it for a skive, but if he had of

236

seen the heap of cable! Nobody was doing it for a skive. As you know, if you can save ten minutes or so before your break, after break gives you a canny start when you start again.

Willy: In the course of a safety inspection he was talking to the lads in the stockyards, and he was saying he's got two hundred and thirty, five-metre-long, bulb bars in excess, just lying in the stockyard. They were ordered in wrongly for 1432 ship. They get on to us about saving five minutes here, there and everywhere. Think of the cost of that! And that is probably being multiplied all over the yard, because the lads have been cleaning the sheds out and as you gan along the riverside road you'll see two skips full to the brim with pipes which must have cost tens of thousands of pounds to manufacture, bends and flanges. They were just stuffed in the skips to be took away. And they get on about saving five and ten minutes.

in the shed: it eats into your fucking body

Catwalk: It's just that the iron powder rods give off more shit and more fumes. It appears that to increase productivity you've got to kill people. There's five million on the dole so, if you kill a few with the fumes and shit off the rods, why worry, there's plenty on the dole will take their place. Same as the woman who pulled me up on Saturday. She got on to me, she was a bit upset about the union, because her husband was a welder and he had died of cancer of the stomach while working in the shipyards. And the same year that he died, about nine welders in the North-East died of exactly the same: cancer of the stomach. My own father was sixty-four when he died, he was a welder. He had stomach ulcers. Finally he died of a massive stroke. He had been off work for two years sick before then with angina. There are not a lot of welders get to retirement age. Mickey Dodds, the burner, has been a shop steward for seventeen years and he has only been to one retirement do, I think, for a burner. None of them reach retirement. It just goes to show what a great environment we work in. It's the same with the welders. They talk about an increase in productivity and they just poison people to get it.

Pickard: The nurse said that when the pressure is on, on the ship, when they launched the last ship, she had a fantastic number of people coming in for Bisodol, for stomach complaints. For anxiety, stress. A lot of the foremen came in for Panadol, for headaches. She said, at the same time, when the announcement was made by BS about the redundancies, she got a rush on of people suffering from anxiety and wanting the stomach powder.

Catwalk: It's all part of the wearing-down process, I think. To reduce the numbers in the industry, to get back to gypsies again, where you travel all over the country looking for work. A little bit here and a little bit there; finish you when they feel like finishing you and start you when they feel like starting you. Like it was thirty or forty year ago, standing outside the gate waiting for the foreman to come and say, 'I'll have you, I'll have you, I'll have you. The rest of you can go home.' That's what it's getting back to. People on short-term contract so they can finish when they want, no holiday pay. They are sacking them on the Tyne now, on the repair yards through there. My friend was working there, and when he was coming up for holiday pay, they paid him off. They said they'll start him back again after the holidays. Tyne Ship Repair, privatised. Another lad, a painter, he is working on the job, and a big barrel of paint fell on his fingers. By the end of the week they had somebody else to fill his place and he was paid off because he was unfit for work. He had broke his hand. No longer required. Unfit for work. They just paid him off and started somebody else on.

Pickard: Will he get compensation?

Catwalk: He'll have to take it through the union. He hasn't got his job. No long-term sick in them places. If you aren't better in a fortnight, or a week or so, they just pay you off and start somebody else. That's what happened to my mate. Soon as he got near his holidays they paid him off with no holiday pay or nothing. 'On your bike, mate, I'll see you in a few weeks' time.'

Pickard: It's savage. It eats into your fucking body, it's physical. The class war is really so physical. I was speaking to the nurse – I've got an ulcer, but the idea of it on a huge scale in a place like this, where it's part of the production process so to speak, is horrendous.

Catwalk: It sickens you.

Catwalk: I think we'll see Nissan here for, the most, five year. They are getting a foothold into Europe, then they'll be across to France or somewhere like that.

Pickard: They'll go for a country with low wages, like Portugal, or Turkey if they come in.

Catwalk: When they build the Channel tunnel, we'll see where all the work goes then. But they might not be here in five years, or when they build the tunnel. Ninety per cent of the market is in Europe so they may as well have the factories over there. If you've got a milk round and there is ninety per cent of your round here, and there is ten per cent there, you don't build the depot there.

Pickard: You don't keep the cows over there. True.

Catwalk: The South-East of England might be OK, but there won't be much up here.

Pickard: Could you move down there and get yourself a job?

Catwalk: I'm not too keen on the place, but if there is nothing else we might have to. I think there'll only be nuclear power stations up here.

Pickard: Are they building another one up here?

Catwalk: Well, they aren't building them in Downing Street, or near the Houses of Parliament. I've got a kid of ten and he gets on about it, nuclear power stations and acid rain, all the shit being poured over the environment. He's only ten year old. I think he'll join the Greens when he's eighteen. He's very perturbed by it all. And he is only ten year old. When we go into the country he is saying, 'It must be great living out here, away from it all, away from all the fumes from the factories and the power stations and things like that.' He gets on about the acid rain. I've been surprised some of the things he's come out with. He listens to the news and that. You think he's not listening but he picks it all up. He gets worried about all these things, nuclear power stations, acid rain, and what's going to be left for them, like. That's a kid of ten. They might have a better world if they all thought the same, and not just people in it for the money who are only interested in their own lives and not the ones that's got to follow.

Pickard: The lads are knocking off. There's not a lot of enthusiasm left.

239

Catwalk: A damn sight more than there is across the river. I'm told they've got four hundred volunteers for redundancy over there. It shows you what the morale is like. They'll be lucky to hit a hundred here. It shows you what a nice place it must be to work. You should try and get in over there and ask the lads what's happening. Get their feelings. Here it's a better environment, the lads are happy, they get stuck in over here. Over there the thumbscrew's right down on them, so that they do as little as possible.

Pickard: Do they have the same pattern of overtime over there?

Catwalk: No, that's how the management can work one off against the other: if you are bad lad you don't get any overtime.

Pickard: But I presume they must get better productivity out of here.

Catwalk: We say we do. It was suggested a few years ago that nobody could touch us.

30/6/86

iced coffee in the complex

Paul: You have to be on the ship at five past one without having to face a penalty for being docked, losing time and money. If you are not on the job for five past one, then you will be warned and taken through the disciplinary procedure, which is a bit of a contradiction if you can come into the gate at five past one and not get warned, but if you are not on the ship at five past one you are going to get warned and possibly end up getting sacked.

Pickard: What happened when you went upstairs?

Paul: It was a waste of time, I never won one.

Pickard: You argued every case?

Paul: I argued every case and never won one. The lad requests his shop steward, obviously we listen to the lads, what's happened to him, what's his excuses for being late and all the rest, and then we gan upstairs. It depends on what state he is, in the warning procedure, if he has been warned in the past. At first, it is a warning off the foreman and then it can be a fucking warning off the manager along with the foreman, then you gan to the next one in the procedure which is the manager and the personnel, which is your final warning. Obviously the next one and you are on your bike. They can actually sack you within a day, no bother.

Pickard: How long does a warning stay on the books for?

Paul: The first one for three months and your final for six months. It is supposed to be took off your record after three months and six months respectively. We were fucking phoning up there, asking for warnings that lads have received previous and the bastards up there still had them on the books, nine months, fifteen months later. Still reading them out and still giving the foreman that information, that he has been warned fifteen fucking months ago. Fucking hell of a warning, isn't it? If he gans for a cup of tea early, fifteen fucking months... One lad summed it up in a nutshell, young fucking L—, the manager said to him, 'Well, have you got anything to say?' He

241

says, 'No, because whatever I say, I'm just wasting my fucking time, you are going to book me anyhow, aren't you? He said, 'Aye.' L— said, 'That's right, it doesn't matter what I fucking say, I'll still get booked, because you've been telt off higher management!' That's all that me and Danny got out of them all the time: 'I've been telt off my superiors to do this. I've been telt,' all the time. Not interested in the individual case. They were actualy standing here with the manager, and the manager was saying, 'Right, who's he? He's mine, go and book him. Who's he? Yours, go and book him.' And then you had the same fucking manager, the audacity of the cunt, he had two foremen standing over here, and a couple of lads coming off the gangway early, the manager is going up the gangway, and the manager, the creep that he is, gans to the two lads: 'Here, lads, get yourself back up on the boat, there are two foreman over there and they are right cunts, they'll book you!' Lovely people, aren't they?

Comrade Glemp

> Confed meeting addressed by Stefan, a Polish shipyard
> worker from Solidarnosc.

Tony: We would like to think that Polish workers are in struggle to achieve a socialist state, not as the press in this country would have us believe, that the workers in Poland are struggling for a return to capitalism. Tell us what the main feeling of the overall Solidarity is, what they want instead of the present regime.

Stefan: It is a very big problem inside the movement ... First of all you have to make a difference between what all the workers were battling for during Solidarnosc time, and all kind of political wings and political movements. You remember that the main economic, political slogan demand of Solidarnosc was *workers' control of factories*. Those factories in that country belong to the working class. But there is a new bureaucracy, many people call it the 'Red Bourgeoisie' which has replaced the workers. The main point of the official programme of Solidarnosc is freedom. Economically speaking, it's workers' control in the factories as the basis of a solution. That is something very working-class and very socialistic, I imagine. But I have also given you examples of pro-capitalism

242

methods and decisions put into practice by this communist bureaucracy. The problem is that over many years socialism in Poland has been identified, in the minds of the people, with concentration camps and repression. Now the workers have a close relationship with the Church: the Church is a political institution. For example, the Church is the only legal force allowed by the government. Never has the Church had so many legal newspapers. Workers' papers are illegal and people are in jail for publishing them. The Church has all the freedom because of the Pope. To do what? To say to the workers, 'OK, you are in times of struggle, but don't have a general strike, don't try to take control.' That is my opinion. Many workers are very confident in the Church because they are Catholic. And also because when those secret police murdered Popieluszko. Why was he killed? He was killed because he was struggling to maintain Solidarity. The Church hierarchy was trying to pressurise Solidarnosc to be silent. And Cardinal Glemp, you know how the workers are calling him? They are calling him 'Comrade Glemp' because 'comrade' in Poland is a synonym for someone in power, and they call him 'Comrade Glemp' because he is too close to General Jaruzelski. Now if you had speaking here, for example Walesa, or the wings of the intellectual democrats, or moderate wing, or other wing, they would say to you that the Church is very good as a moral symbol of Poland. You have many workers who try to separate the Church, but you have to understand that the Church has a role also. And there is also another question; you know when the socialist ideas, over the years, have been assimilated with the establishment, then the workers say, 'I am not socialist. If this is socialism, I am not a socialist.' But then if the workers do not find an alternative role and method of running society then you have a wide space and somebody else will occupy the space, and the Church will occupy the space. Now it is true that Walesa made this interview on the news saying that the British miners are influenced by Moscow. But now they begin to understand because Thatcher and Reagan, they normalised relationships with Jaruzelski, they accept him now on the international stage. They make many visits and they have said Solidarnosc is over. Walesa has been criticised by workers' wings in Solidarnosc. But Walesa is a symbol of unity in Solidarnosc, and, in spite of some strange positions he takes, it is necessary to defend Walesa if he is persecuted because he is a symbol of our Solidarnosc.

Tony: We have had visits in the past from Polish workers. We had a speaker from the Szczecin yards, Edmund Baluka and I knew Edmund from 1974 and from the early days when he went to jail. Perhaps you could tell us what happened to him? We wrote to the Polish authorities saying that Edmund had never – because he was accused of treason – Edmund had never committed, as far as we were aware, any treasonable act towards Polish people.

Stefan: Edmund Baluka came back to Poland in April 1981 after exile. He went out illegally. There was a big scandal. He wanted to live in Poland but the government did not allow it. It also happened in my case. I was also in exile, I came back to Poland illegally. Baluka was one of the people put in jail after the military coup. He had a trial and he, at his trial, defended quite well the workers and socialist ideas and socialist movement. He suffered very much in prison. He is now out and in France. He is married to a French-woman and I know Baluka ... I found that baluka represents another workers' wing inside the movement and we are in touch with other shipyards in Szczecin and abroad.

Tony: If you could give us his address when the lad takes you out of the yard, we'll correspond with him.

Stefan: I should like to lend you the translation into English of a document in support of the striking Slask miners ...

Tony: On the question of the miner that has been jailed, would it be helpful if we wrote to the Polish Embassy from this committee, expressing that we would like him to be released by the authorities? That's one thing at least we could do.

Jake: Would it also help if we wrote to our union executive to get them to bring pressure to bear?

Stefan: It is good that the letters and pressures happen. But I want to inform you that there are many experiences of twins: mine twins, shipyard twins. In Govan shipyard I wrote to the secretary of the shop stewards proposing that they discuss twinning with Gdansk or Szczecin shipyard and we discussed that. Because together with Baluka we can arrange it with Solidarnosc official representative to organise and exchange letters and people? Especially also the sacking of the NGA. It's not generally known in Poland what is facing workers in Britain.

1. In 1971 Edmund Baluka led a strike in Szczecin which led to a nine-hour meeting with Gierek. An ex-sailor, Baluka was elected president of the regional branch of the metalworkers' union.

Jake: Is Govan now twinned?

Stefan: They are discussing it. I sent a letter.

Tony: Well, send the same letter to ourselves and we'll discuss it. He wants a photograph of us for the paper which they publish in the underground in Poland, to demonstrate that there is sympathy with the Polish working people.

Pickard: Our lass will be surprised if she sees me in the Polish underground press.

Tony: Well, if the Russians don't get you, MI5 will.

Jake takes stick

Danny: You were that pissed, if a fly had of farted, you would fall down.

Paul: I'd get blown away if Jake had of farted.

Pickard: Chris says he had to sleep in the same room as him in London.

Paul: I'd demand a separate room, the tales I've heard about him.

Jake: As long as you don't get a tail up you, that's when you should fucking worry.

Paul: That's what I'd be frightened of if I had the same room.

Jake: You see! You've got me name shit all over, you, you cunt.

Tony: Shit all over, how's that?

Jake: Nobody will sleep with me now, through you!

Tony: It's not just me, man. My arguments are fucking backed up totally by Chris who was forced to sleep there,

Jake: But anybody sleeping with *you* would also agree with me.

Tony: How's that, like?

Jake: Because you fucking snore like a fucking pig, toss and turn.

Tony: That's you, man.

Jake: I've never fucking seen anybody sleeping with their fucking arse up in the air. I don't know if you were trying to tell me something!

Tony: It's a load of shite.

Jake: It would have been.

Tony: You are just saying it, you are just talking to take the grannie off me.

Jake: Take the grannie off you?

Paul: Playing tents?

Jake: I don't know what he was doing. Fucking up on one knee.

Tony: All I have said has been confirmed by fucking Chris.

Jake: Oh man, you can speak of sobriety with Chris, can't you?

Tony: I had to lock you in the hotel room or you'd have been wandering round the hotel in a drunken stupor: your body is still active while your mind is fucking numb with fucking drink.

Jake: Describing yourself again?

Tony: Oh no. I'm talking about you. Your body is still active and your fucking mind's that numb because you are fucking puddled. You don't know what you are doing.

Jake: What you on about?

Tony: A state of drunkenness, paralytic. I'm telling the fucking truth.

Jake: Shut your fucking hole, man, Doctor Death!

Tony: Who started this conversation?

Jake: You! You went round telling everybody that I was fucking rotten . . .

Tony: I'm not, man. Chris is telling everybody.

Bluey: Is it not true, like?

Jake: How the fuck do I know, I was asleep.

[*There is silence for a while.*]

Tony: That's what Ron says, 'No matter how much it costs, we are getting fucking single rooms.'

[*Some quiet chuckling. Jake taps his plastic spoon on the table.*]

Jake: He's there with you, and ten minutes later he's telling everybody a different story.

Tony: All plumbers are the fucking same.

Danny: Uriah Heep! Walking round the sheds like Uriah Heep.

Pickard: Who?

Danny: You!

Pickard: I'm the only one who doesn't make any comments about your diminished stature and I get all the stick.

Danny: Creeping Jesus, you fucker.

Pickard: Just because I took a photograph of you working so you had some proof that you actually did it.

Danny: What a fucking liar he is! And don't you open your fucking mouth, arsehole!

Jake: As long as you don't open your arsehole.

JULY

1/7/86

women

Rab: Name some of them that's any good ... Golda Meir? That bastard in India?
Jacko: Jackie Onassis.
Rab: You fucker...
Jacko: Eva Peron.
Danny: Mary Poppins.
Jacko: Joan of Arc.
Rab: What you on about?
Pickard: Ellen Wilkinson.
Ronnie: Lucrezia Borgia.
Jacko: She was a fucking good one, mind!
Pickard: She was all right.
Jacko: Go an' fuck.
Ronnie: Who?
Pickard: Ellen Wilkinson.
Jacko: Bessie Braddock.
Danny: Betty Boothroyd. Gwyneth Dunwoody.
Mick: Our lass.
Pickard: Boadicea.
Rab: They want special sections here, special sections this and special sections that. They want all the fucking privileges...
Jacko: I was thinking about that one last night, at the constituency, alternating between a male and a female. Does it mean if a year a female has to go, or we cannot get one, we cannot have a delegate?
Rab: But they've got their own section. They can go from their own sections can't they?
Paul: We'll have a men's section. Why is there no men's section?
Jacko: Because they are minorities, aren't they?
Rab: Women in the union are the biggest set of fucking bullshitters, reactionary, right-wing set of cunts you could ever meet.

Pickard: It's not because they are women, it's because they are reactionary.

Jacko: No, it's because they are fucking thick.

Pickard: So are plenty blokes.

Jacko: But he's got a different perspective on things, a bloke. He's more fucking practical.

Pickard: Get away and shite.

Ronnie: The worst pay and the worst conditions are in plants where the majority are women.

Pickard: But I bet the majority of their union leaders are fucking men.

Rab: Aye, that might be so, but you see them operating in the union and they back the hierarchy up to the hilt. There is not a bit of a fucking rebel in any of the cunts.

Pickard: There is in Poland: Valentynowicz. She was the leader of the Solidarity strike in the Lenin shipyard. A crane driver.

Jacko: That's one.

Pickard: Rosa Luxembourg.

Rab: I'm talking in general about the trade union movement. You can pick out a load of men like that.

Jacko: Brenda Dean.

Pickard: Nelly Dean. I still think you cannot generalise.

Jacko: Basically they are thick, women. Do you not think that basically they are thick?

Pickard: No.

Ronnie: Course they are. If you tell them a joke, you've got to explain the punch line and that.

Jacko: [*looking reflective*] I must have just gotten a thick one.

Pickard: Maybe your jokes aren't funny.

Rab: Well it must be just working-class women that's fucking thick, then.

Pickard: How do you jump to that conclusion?

Danny: According to you.

Jacko: It's four to one that they are thick.

Danny: The worst I've met are middle-class women. Load of fucking shite. Fucking middle-class conscience, you fucker!

Pickard: Do you prefer middle-class men?

Danny: Not really.

Rab: I've told you before, middle-class women going round saying, 'You've got to be able to do this, and have your own career, have your own fucking job.' They are that out of touch with reality you just cannot grasp . . .

Jacko: They start from the standpoint that every fucking woman that is married is depressed by her husband, and that's not true . . .

Pickard: Oppressed?

Jacko: Eh?

Pickard: Depressed is probably truer . . .

Jacko: . . . most working-class women and girls when they leave school have only got one thing in mind, and that is to work for a small period of time and then get married and look after a house. Then you get all these people running around stamping the tables and saying, 'No, no, it's wrong, it's wrong what's happening to them, they need their chains lifting off them.' It's a load of crap.

Rab: They should never get married in the fucking first place, should they, if they want a career, if they want to pursue their own lives, as they say. It's no good getting married and having fucking families because you are not going to do it that way. Because we are out at work all fucking bastard day.

Pickard: The blokes could take care of the bairns.

Rab: Without a doubt, I would do it. If our lass says to me, 'I've gotten a job for fucking two hundred pounds a week, but it means there's nobody to look after the family, would you pack in work?' Fuck aye, I would. I'd fucking dive at the bastard. Daft cunts saying to me, 'It's that male chauvinism that makes you want to be the breadwinner, and leave the household.' It's a load of fucking shite! It is. It's full of crap. I'd look after our house, do domestic chores and home management about a hundred times better than our lass can.

Pickard: How many bairns have you got?

Rab: Four.

Pickard: I can just see you being the gaffer in your house.

Jacko: In fact I'm thinking about getting myself a boyfriend.

Rab: But when she was in hospital, when we had the fourth kid, she had a broken leg. She was in a couple of months and I had to look after it for another two. I had that fucking house running like a clock. I was finishing by fucking half-past ten in the morning, washing, meal on the stove ready for them coming in. Everything. I had nothing to do after that.

Jacko: She was in four and a half months, just coming out at weekends, I had no problem. I stopped at me mother's.

251

Danny: You'd just be a fat useless cunt, you.

Jacko: That's right, I am. I suppose if I had to do anything, I'd fucking do it.

Danny: You've got to do the cunt. She says, 'You've got your boots on the wrong feet,' I'd tell her umpteen times, 'They should be on your feet.'

Jacko: She'd probably be better at work than you are, because you only fucking annoy me.

Pickard: Are there any woman welders in the union?

Rab: Because the company decided that they were that much of a distraction, causing that much fucking upset...

Jacko: People trying to stick it up them at the fore-end.

Rab: ... that it wasn't fucking worth it. It's only '75 when we had the last one. That's labourers.

Jacko: There is still some in now, they bring them in as contractors to clean the ship up.

Jacko: We plow the field and scatter the good seed on the ground.

Rab: You gan in the pub and they want to be on the dominoes all the fucking day...

Jacko: No swearing!

Rab: ... but then when you start swearing, oh no, you cannot do that. They want to be treated like women. In the first instance, they just want to be equals like men, then all of a sudden it changes and they want an extra packet of privileges.

Pickard: Our lass doesn't want equality, because she thinks the balance is in her favour.

Jacko: It's us that wants equality. Where else can you get a system, you don't get back in the house until fucking five o'clock, two nights you work overtime, on a Sunday you gan to work, and on a Friday night when you get your recompense you gan home and give it to somebody? Us want our fucking heads looking at. It's a fucking hell of system, that.

Pickard: You get your meals and your bedding washed and your bairns looked after.

Jacko: I could stay in a hotel.

Pickard: I think Thatcher is a good example.

Rab: Good example of what?

Pickard: From the point of view of her class she is a fucking star. In terms of her functioning as a career politician she is fucking brilliant.

Rab: Do you think we would turn one out like that for our class?

Pickard: Do you think we couldn't? It's a pathetic statement if you say we cannot. Mind, we haven't got a fucking bloke that...

Rab: There's not one that I fucking know, in the politics, in the unions or the Labour Party...

Danny: At the GMB [General, Municipal and Boilermakers]: 'Eee, I would like to say that the North Regional Congress was absolutely smashing, we had a lovely banner on the front: Freedom For All.' I said, 'Listen to this shitbag here!' That's what you've fucking got to put up with at meetings. A load of fucking shite.

Rab: Definite different species, I think. It was just a quirk of fucking fate that we have to fucking copulate to reproduce.

Pickard: A quirk of fate?

Rab: We should be able to do it without the bastards.

Pickard: Do you prefer the company of blokes to women?

Rab: Aye. The company...

Jacko: Unless they get their knickers off, and that is different. If it's a fornicating session then obviously...

Danny: Will you behave yourself, man.

Rab: In the club, if there is a big company of men out with their wives, all the wives sit together and all the men sit together.

Jacko: You've only got to look at them when they are courting: what happens if you gan to dances or whatnot? All the tarts dance together round their handbags.

Rab: You gan to funerals, weddings...

Jacko: There's a room full of men or a room full of women.

Rab: You couldn't listen to their daft fucking patter all fucking night! You'd gan round the fucking bend!

Billy: It's fucking clever, you gan in the fucking club with your wife, and you are sitting there you don't know what the fucking hell to talk about.

Jacko: The first ten minutes you talk about the people coming in, 'Look at that cunt there, I've not see him for a long time.'

Rab: *You* don't usually start talking until you've got a gargle down your fucking neck....

Jacko: Then she'll say, 'Shut up, you...

Billy: 'Eeem, you haven't got the bingo books.' Fucking hell!

Jacko: Last Saturday morning: *Blackbeard the Pirate*, Robert Newton.

Rab: He's a fucking topper. Playing Long John Silver again?

Jacko: No, he was Blackbeard, the pirate.

Rab: But the roles are all the same.

Jacko: He gets a fucking ball in his neck and he is sent to the fucking surgeon: 'Come on, sawbones, get it out!' He's drinking the fucking grog and a bloke comes up to him and he says: 'Captain, Captain, we are under fire,' and he gans, 'Ha, ha, and I'm out of the line for I'm under the alcohol.' I was rolling about. Our lass says, 'You're fucking barmy.'

Rab: Every role he's played he's always been the same, man. I seen him in a fucking gangster film and he was just like Long John Silver!

Jacko: He's a fucking topper.

Rab: Who's the other one like that, where all his fucking roles are the same? One of the top fucking actors?

Jacko: Michael Caine, he's like that.

Rab: No man, he played Julius Caesar and the likes of that. All Shakespearean stuff.

Jacko: Laurence Olivier?

Rab: Aye! he's the fucking same in every one he's in.

Jacko: Never changed for forty year.

Rab: And they keep saying he's a hell of an actor! And that other little cunt, that keeps falling asleep when they are interviewing him. Little cunt. He's on 'Spitting Image' ... he keeps falling asleep. Sir John Gielgud. Fucking toppers.

Jacko: Is he dead now, him?

Danny: I hope so, they buried the cunt.

Jacko: That's what you get yourself wrong for.

Danny: What I get myself wrong for?

Rab: We're just common people, man.

Pickard: So give me some shining examples of twentieth-century men whom women should aspire to.

Paul: Connolly.

Pickard: Billy Connolly?

Rab: Connolly, Marx, Lenin ... There's a fucking load, man.

Paul: There's never much mention of Larkin in Desmond Grieves's book. Never much specifically.

254

Pickard: Scargill? I bet you'd find as many women...
Jacko: Covering the British trade union movement...
Rab: Only one of them any fucking good: Sylvia Pankhurst.

they don't want you to work

Pickard: How long have you worked in the yard?
Ken: Eleven year.
Pickard: How do you like it?
Ken: Not very much. It was canny, years ago, not now.
Pickard: How old are you?
Ken: Twenty-seven. I served me time here. But it's crap here now.
Pickard: Why?
Ken: Management.
Pickard: How do you see the future?
Ken: Well, once all these pay-offs have been done, when you weigh it up, it's obvious: they don't want you to work. They want to be fucking you about, having you doing this and that. If they want you to get the work out they just leave you alone. All right you're fucking off five minutes early, but you're on the job, you're doing the work. But now: 'Do this, and you cannot go there, and you've got to knock off at this time.'
Pickard: Why don't they want you to do the work?
Dave: There's no fucking work is there?
Ken: Yes, this fucking ship here is the worst I've worked on. It's a terrible ship this.
Pickard: When does this ship get away?
Ken: Next Thursday it's got to go down to Palmer's Hill to get finished and fitted out.
Pickard: Will people from here go down there?
Ken: Aye, and that's when the trouble starts. We get more money than them down there.
Pickard: Would you be expected to take less?
Ken: No, but if any of their lads come to give us a hand, they expect to get more. All the accommodation unit is getting built down there, it's supposed to be. But apparently they want our money: the ruling is: anybody working on there is on our money. They're going to put together all the money they get, put that together and make

255

sure that every man gets a percentage of the money. That's what they said at the meeting.

Pickard: You are supposed to have high productivity in this yard?

Ken: Used to be. One year Bartram's built thirteen ships: SD14s, and SD18s, bulk carriers. And there was no purge or nowt on.

Pickard: There was no purge before they got the last one here launched, was there?

Ken: That proves me point, when they want you to do any work they leave you alone.

3/7/86

abusing the fresh air

Alf: Last year I went to the doctor's, I had a bad back from lying against the plate. The doctor says, 'How have you gotten your bad back?' I said, 'Lying against the cold plate.' He said, 'What were you doing on the table?' I said, 'A plate in the shipyard.' He didn't have a clue what I was talking about. He thought I was talking about a dinner plate.

Pickard: What air comes in here? Is it just the extractor?

Alf: There's nowt to push air through. There's no circulation. It's dead air.

Bob: We work up at the fore-end, under the engine room. Once they started welding, the fumes off the welding!

Pickard: Do you spend the whole day in it?

Alf: Aye. We've stopped for the minute with the burners being down. It's killer fumes off the burner. Aye, these are killer fumes. They expect you to go and poison yourself.

Bob: It's been going on for years and years, nobody cares.

Alf: If you locked the dog in a car on a day like this for five minutes you'd face a thousand-pound fine: but they're prepared to put us in there.

Bob: You've got to leave windows open for ventilation for a dog. There's no ventilation for people. It just doesn't make sense, man, working them type of conditions. If they could blow fresh air in ... there's nowhere to blow the air.

Pickard: You're sealing off the seams, aren't you?

Alf: We're closing up all the time. And that's the only breeze you usually get, and once you seal them off, that's it, finished. It's just dead. You're breathing it all the time.

Bob: When we were over at Doxy's, the management puts us up on a charge for abusing the fresh air. For coming out of the double bottoms and having a breather: 'abusing the fresh air,' they said.

257

Pickard: They wouldn't stay down there for very long.

Alf: Half of them's never worked in shipyards. They gan to college for a few year, come back top dogs, and then they don't know what they're talking about. It's all paperwork what they know. They just think you do plates the way you do paper in the drawing offices.

Pickard: I took a lot of pictures of the bulbous bow. That was fucking horrendous, the confined spaces people have to get into there. I saw some of the lads doing it when it was on the stocks as well.

Alf: I had a mate took alight on one of them when he was down a few years ago. He still gets nightmares. You had to wedge your head and shoulders in, put the screen on top of you, somebody would pass your pliers in to you, with the rod in, and you'd weld on top of yourself with it all dropping and that. His overalls took alight, and he didn't realise it till it was all over, and on his back. They had to pull him out by his feet, cause he couldn't even get himself out. That's when they started to supply leather coats, after that. You used to have to go to Jacky White's and make your own leather coats, and pay for them yourself. You got two aprons supplied, then you had to go to Jacky White who had a bloke who used to put them together with press studs. If you didn't you had nowt.

Pickard: He caught fire?

Alf: Aye, caught alight. Then they didn't supply you with overalls so you just wore anything.

Pickard: How long ago was that?

Alf: In the seventies.

Bob: There's a few killed with falls and that.

Pickard: I've heard of a few people who threw wobblers in the double bottoms.

Bob: Have you seen them when they're overcome with paint fumes? They fight to gan back in. They're like drunk, you cannot get them out at all, they fight cause they want to stop in. Something takes over, and you've got to get them outside and slap them about and get fresh air and they have got to be sent home.

Pickard: You mean they resist coming out cause they think they're all right?

Alf: Something clicks up there and you think they're trying to hurt you. And they've got to try and manhandle you out of the manholes.

Pickard: How do you know when somebody's suffering from fumes?

258

Bob: His eyes start to roll. It's just like a drunk, he starts singing and falling about. Something takes on with them paint fumes. You're not supposed to work in them. Once it takes over, you don't know when it's starting, it just takes over and that's it. Weird.

Pickard: So you do something for your three hundred quid a week?

Alf: You must be kidding. *Three hundred?* You just get that for your fortnight's holiday. That's all you work for. All the year round for two week. Enjoy yourself and come back to the hole again. Makes you wonder if you'd be better off on the dole; at least you've got your health.

Pickard: You've always worked in the shipyards?

Bob: There's nowt else man. The doctor advised me to pack it in. He said, 'Get off the welding with your bad chest, and gan somewhere else.' I said, 'It's very easy said, but there's nowhere else to gan.' I said, 'There's nowt round here at all.' I'm getting slowly poisoned.

Alf: And if they close down we'll be in a bad way. It's not just the shipyards, it's all the little surrounding things outside; shops, pubs, all them places. Dundas Street, up Monkwearmouth, they pulled it down when J. L. Thompson's shut. Pubs, the bakeries, the fish-and-chip shops, the wet-fish shops, things like that, the fruiterer's, they all stop. We used to send men out for bait, dinners: they used to keep all those little businesses going, and they get stuff from other people so it gans all the way down the line. There's thousands outside our industry affected.

nationalisation

Geordie: This yard was very successful until it got nationalised. I think it made a six-million-pound profit the year before it got nationalised. The following year it made a three-million deficit. The manager blamed the workmen. I said, 'How can you do that? You must take some of the credit?' We had a situation here with a managing director at the time, in this year when the profit turned into a deficit. There was a steel strike imminent, if you remember, at the time with Bill Sirs. He gave everybody six months' warning. When the strike come round, within three weeks we were laid up, and that was more instrumental in the deficit coming about than anything else. Anyway he was allowed to stop here for another two

259

years after that, that's what beat nationalisation. Nationalisation is the best thing that's ever come out: it's the silly bastards that run it.

the meeting with Thatcher

Tommy: The government says they're going to close, they are also saying there's twenty million pound available, so the bloke from the city council says, 'I've got to go and try to get my hands on the twenty million pounds.' In a sense, it's fair enough. But I would like to see a bit fight put up, then you fall back and try to get what you can out of the twenty million. You don't go and ask for what you can get straightaway. At the end of the day that's your fallback: you fight like fuck and then say, 'Well, there's twenty million pound there, I've done what I can do, the fucker [Thatcher] is not ganna do nowt so I'll get me hands on the twenty million.' But twenty million is pence, isn't it? There's ganna be a fight on, because he hasn't got his volunteers for redundancy. There's four hundred to gan by October. It could come to us all by October, because if there is no order, we're all fucked anyway. There's no two ways about that. You don't know what to do, do you? You daren't go to the town and buy anything, literally. You dare not take any commitments on. You don't have time for your holidays. It's fucking crackers, man.

14/7/86

in the left lug

Pickard: What would happen if a socialist government was elected into power?

Paul: You wouldn't be allowed to take power, you know what they would do to them.

Pickard: What? They'd either subvert, or corrupt?

Paul: They use the state, the police and the army.

Pickard: Don't they belong to Parliament?

Paul: But they'd use it. Look, who's the type that's in power? All your positions within the army, your generals, your fucking majors, your colonels, you name it. Where do they come from? What is their background? The system's not geared up. All right, they believe in democracy, the mother of parliaments, 'as long as it's working for us': that's what they say. They don't mind if the Labour government is elected or not, they couldn't give a fuck, they're going to be all right. 'OK, there'll be a few of our people get replaced, but ninety-nine per cent of us will be OK. The Labour government knows which side their fucking bread is buttered on, they'll look after us. All right, some of us might go to the wall and the workers get a little bit more, but what the fuck, that's the chance you take.'

Catwalk: Tom doesn't know which side his bread's buttered on at the minute.

Pickard: How do you make that out?

Catwalk: Well you mix with them, if you mix with them you get the chop just the same.

Pickard: Oh, I see. You think I might be for the chop, do you?

Paul: A .38 revolver, the left lug, boomf.

Pickard: Do it in my right lug, I'm deaf in the left.

Catwalk: Sit down and Danny'll be able to do it.

Paul: Drown the royal babies.

Pickard: Put them on a council estate.

261

Paul: Too good for them.

George: Put them in Barclay Court.

Paul: Our day will come and we'll get our own back on them bastards, hopefully.

Pickard: You could only do that if you were in control. If Rab was in control he wouldn't let you.

Paul: That's what we're just talking about. Rab would be OK in control. He's got very little ideological differences than what I have.

Pickard: Danny would be there and he'd be slapping you about. Danny would be putting you in order.

Paul: Put me in order for what?

Pickard: Keep you in fucking order so you wouldn't run rampaging all over the fucking place.

Paul: He's fucking worse than me, that cunt, he's fucking evil.

Catwalk: Danny would see to the Royal Family.

Paul: I fucking hate the bastards.

Catwalk: He'd hang them all.

Paul: The fucking Queen Mother, fucking oldest Social Security scrounger in the bastard country, that cunt.

Pickard: I think you should keep a royal family.

Paul: Fuck off.

Pickard: Yes.

Paul: Fuck off.

Pickard: What you should do though, is elect them every year, so you have Mrs Johnson from fucking Barclay Court and her family as the royal family for one year. Stick them in Buckingham Palace with all her bairns. Supply the people with what they really need, a royal fucking family. Something to look up to. But you elect the bastards every year.

Paul: Why do you need a royal family? It keeps the fucking patriotic fucking jingoistic fucking ... it gives it all on a plate ... all that fucking kind of situation. They'd use it against you all the fucking time, with all the daft fucking working-class people taking it in.

Catwalk: Who is to say when they get in they wouldn't use the power they've got to screw you into the ground again.

Pickard: Not Mrs Smith from Barclay Court.

Catwalk: Like Mr Kinnock, he was a hero of the left, fucking three or four year ago.

Paul: No he wasn't, man, not our left. He might of been the hero of the centre-left.

262

Catwalk: He was one of the lads though.

would you shoot a poet?

Jake: I wandered lonely as a cloud.

Danny: I think six months of you, Pickard, instead of fucking three, every alternative week, we would have been in the fucking madhouse.

Pickard: I don't mind doing three weeks on the stot [continuous] as your fucking apprentice.

Danny: We know you've been a hell of a grafter, we know that.

Jake: You'll not be saying that when you see the end product. He'll do a good job, Tom.

Pickard: There you are, coming from the horse's mouth. He says that you're the one that's going to have to shoot me when the revolution comes.

Tony: Would you shoot a poet? I would never shoot a poet.

Pickard: He says that I'd have to kneel down so that little Danny could shoot me.

Danny: I'll thump you, you clever fucking bastard, Catwalk. You can never keep your fucking mouth shut, can you? You four-eyed gissy!

Catwalk: Watch me lugs.

Danny: Never mind your fucking lugs, you fucking swine that you are. You never fucking stop.

Pickard: You do worse than fucking shoot poets, you – you put their fucking poems in the drawer out the way.

Tony: What poems?

Pickard: The song I wrote about the contractors.

Tony: Where is it, like?

Pickard: I sent it to you but you fucking shoved it in the drawer out of sight.

Tony: No, I'd just give you a job of work. That's what I'd do to poets.

Pickard: What kind of work?

Tony: Manual work; digging holes or something like that. Then you'd be able to compose all the poetry you like, while you were digging fucking holes.

Danny: Fuck off, fuck off, fuck off.

263

Pickard: That rhymes.

Danny: It rhymes better than anything you've got, you cunt; 'wings in your ear'!

Pickard: I'm really touched the way you know my poems off by heart.

Jake: Not been feeling creative today? On strike, are you?

Pickard: Thinking.

Jake: Thinking about the pamphlet?

Pickard: Pamphlet?

Jake: Is there to be no pamphlet now?

Tony: Yes, you've fucking conned us, you fucker, for the last six months.

Pickard: What a twat you are.

Tony: That's right, you've fucking conned us, you bastard, getting hundreds and hundreds of pounds and done fuck all.

Jake: Thousands.

Pickard: Not weekly.

Tony: You still did all right, you cunt. Just get dug down into the Northern Arts money and buy us a fucking drink next fucking week. You've got your ticket for the old men's do. Don't bring your car.

Danny: We might even get you up to give a reading.

Pickard: Trying to kill the old buggers off?

Danny: There'll be a mass exodus.

Pickard: I don't know what you'd do without me for a scapegoat. You'll not be short of them: pick on the weakest bastard.

Jake: If you'd wrote any shipyard poems while you've been here, we could maybe do one to two of them and they might be appreciated. Especially if there's some humour in them and they fucking rhymes.

Pickard: I don't want to fucking embarrass you.

Jake: 'Let's sing songs to my cock!'

Brian: You see, they all know your poems, they've all got your work off by heart.

Pickard: And my book hasn't been here for three months. Fucking burnt into the memories.

Paul: '*Tongue-cup of come*', you fucker!

Brian: You see, there's another one.

Danny: '*Almost perceptible*', you fucker.

Pickard: I tell you, I'm honoured.

Paul: You bullshitting bastard.

264

Tony: How many converts have you made to poetry?

Pickard: I don't know, was that my job?

Tony: Part of it.

Jake: He's in the top ten.

Danny: There's only fucking nine.

Tony: Surely he's a fucking socialist poet. The whole idea was to waken latent fucking poets amongst the fucking working class. And how many have you fucking released?

Pickard: Morgan, Mick, Jim wrote a fucking poem.

Danny: He could write one in two minutes better than any one Pickard could fucking write.

Pickard: But I get paid for mine.

Danny: I know, you fucking bullshitting bastard.

Pickard: Well, what do you want me to do? Fucking starve or what?

Tony: You've got the connections.

Pickard: You don't need many connections to starve.

Danny: He was a paper lad. He had a paper round when he was twenty-seven.

Ronnie: He'll be worth a few bob when he's dead though.

Brian: You need some nude models for your poetry.

Jake: I'm all right when I've got me knickers off.

Brian: Why should the artists have all the fun? Poets should have the same.

Bluey: He made a derogatory reference to your height, Danny.

Mick: I didn't. You know that little conversation we had just before...

Danny: *Little* conversation, eh?

Mick: There was nothing malicious about it at all, Danny.

Brian: Why did you do it when he was on the phone and he couldn't do anything?

Mick: It doesn't matter what you say, some bastard will pick up a negative point.

Jake: Mick, if you went out with your mate to a party and you got pissed, really pissed, blacking out, and you woke up the next morning sleeping next to your mate, and your case was really sore, would you tell anybody about it?

Mick: No.

Jake: Do you want to come to a party tomorrow night?

Pickard: Is a welded ship stronger?

Brian: A riveted ship is a hell of a lot stronger, no shadow of a doubt. The weight of the steel alone made it impractical.

Dodds: You never saw ships cracking in half then, like. Design has a lot to do with it.

Pickard: So the riveters were still the bosses when you were apprentices?

Brian: A lad served his time the same time I did and he was a riveter.

Pickard: Did you think riveting was going to gan on for ever or did you know it was going to change?

Brian: The riveters thought it was going to go on for ever but it was obvious to every fucker else.

Dodds: If you look at the history of shipbuilding, and you gan to the Liberty boats that the Americans were making, there was quite a few of them cracked up. They were fetching them over here, riveting extra bands on them to strengthen them. They were all going at the same place. OK, it was a design fault, I'm not just saying it was because it was welded, plus the proper grade steel hadn't been used, they found out after that. And the temperatures they were getting made in, the ones that were doing the investigation, the old riveters were saying there was hundreds of them fucking smashed up. There wasn't, you know, there was about a dozen. They had come from the northern yard where they had been built in fucking cold weather, the welding techniques weren't as good as they are now, plus they never had a different grade of steel, the high-tensile steel round the hatch corners. And that's where they started that.

Pickard: How do they get high-tensile steel? Is it from different kinds of ore or a different process?

Dodds: Different process . . .

Brian: Different additives, they put more carbon in it and things like that.

Dodds: It's got greater strength and it will bend, give. These ships here are high-tensile. Because of the length of the ship and the narrow beam they need to be a lot stronger on the deck area. Your sheer line, that's where it takes all the movement. I've been out on trials with boats, all welded boats, and I was out on one in particular, the *American Star*, and it was rough weather, and I had a storm line, a lifeline on the deck. When you walked along, and got a hold of it, you could actually see the ship flexing. The wire would be taut one second and she's like that, she's hovering, then when she went down the wire would gan slack. They bend. They are designed to fucking bend, there is no fucking question about it.

If you look at Hitler, and how he broke the convention by building bigger ships, it was mainly through the welding technique. *Bismarck*, and all them, *Graf Spee*, all welded.

Brian: It reduced the weight of the ship. So they got a bigger ship for the same weight. They had a code of ethics on fucking tonnage. They weren't allowed to build them over thirty thousand ton or something. So, because they were making a welded ship, they were reducing the amount of steel involved drastically and getting a bigger ship for the same weight.

Dodds: When you look at them and you read the history of it and the punishment they took, that shows you how good the welding was. *Bismarck*, the fucking stuff they hoyed at her, the Germans actually fucking opened her up and started to scuttle her themselves. She was hit by about twenty-odd torpedoes and fucking hundreds of fucking sixteen, fifteen, fourteen-inch shells. And they still had to open the cunt up to scuttle her. The *Scharnhorst* was the same in the battle of the North Cape when that one got caught with the *Duke of York*. It took a long time to fucking gan down. Again, it was design as well. The Germans went into barracks, ours had mess decks right across, all the different messes and the mess deck was right across the ship, and obviously that is a fucking weakness. That's how the fucking HMS *Hood* and the likes of them went straight down. Like the *Repulse* went straight down. But it wasn't the men's fault, it was a design fault. They didn't learn off the First World War. The first battle I think was the Battle of Dogger Bank when Fisher and them caught a few of the German ships which had been shelling Scarborough, they actually come in and shelled Scarborough, and the next one on the list was Sunderland. They were gan to bombard Sunderland. Fisher come down and they caught them. Admiral Jellicoe caught them on the fucking Dogger Bank. The Germans realised they were coming and they made a run for home, and there was a battle there and some of their ships nearly went down. It was a design fault in the gun turret cordite room. They'd go into the cordite room and the doors gave a flashback. There was the *Derfflinger*, and another one called the *Seydlitz* got it like that. And the *Derfflinger*, after they'd got to the Jade River she was awash. When they opened the cordite room, the blokes that was in there was just dust. The Germans realised then that there was a fault in the ship and they put it right, and when they come out a few months later for the Battle of Jutland their ships was all right. The British ships, four or five of them, blew up, just blew to pieces. And fucking Admiral Beatty says, 'There's something the matter with our ships here. Twenty-thousand-ton ships blowing to fuck.' That's what it was, and it still hadn't been put right even in the Second World War: HMS *Hood*, which was laid down in 1916 but not completed until after the war, her first action was sinking the fucking French Fleet at Oran. That's when her first shots were fired in anger. But again the fault was still there, and within five minutes of open engagement she was gone. Only three men left. It was the biggest ship in the Royal Navy. Biggest ship in the world with the *Bismarck* and them. But again the fault was still in there. No cunt would put it right. I mean obviously it was a battlecruiser. It had the punch of a heavyweight but with a glass jaw.

16/7/86

selective overtime

Dodds: He hoyed a paper out, saying, 'For our state of health we'll be working selective overtime.' We all just picked it up and hoyed it back at him. Jake says, 'Shove your fucking shipyard and shove your fucking job up your fucking arse! That's what our members have telt us and that's what they have voted on.' They voted on it: 'We don't want the job at any price, and if that's the way, well shut the fucking gates.'

Pickard: What was the paper?

Danny: He put a paper out on selective overtime, and we had to fucking work selective overtime by 11 August. We said to them, 'If that is the case, shove the fucking shipyard up your fucking arse, we are not working it.'

Bluey: When P— first come here, Tony asked him, 'Are you here to do a job of work or are you just here on an ego trip?' He didn't know what to say, did he?

Danny: F— says he is the most unscrupulous bastard he's ever met in his life.

Bluey: Tony is clever when he starts, isn't he, Dan?

Brian: A lot more clever than these cunts.

Bluey: I'm sure he is.

Brian: They're educated but by God they're not intelligent.

Pickard: How is that? Does he see through their strategies?

Bluey: Like looking through a fucking string vest.

Danny: A two-year-old bairn could see through these cunts, man. They are not even fucking clever with it. Selective groups, selective little deals for selective people.

Pickard: Is that what he said or is that what he implied?

Danny: That's what he fucking said.

Brian: He's doing it.

Pickard: Did you say DS— has got the sack?

Danny: He's finished. The senior production manager, he was.

Pickard: Was he a prat?

Danny: No, as a matter of fact he was one of the better ones. At least he is a practical man, he was a plater by trade. He served his time as a plater and he worked his way from the shop floor.

Pickard: Has he actually left?

Danny: No, he's got a job counselling the redundancies.

Bluey: Is that the job he was offered?

Danny: They telt him on the Tuesday he was finished and S— had him in on the Wednesday for three hours talking about production. DS— said, 'What are you talking to me about production for, I'm finished?' S— said, 'That's no attitude to take. That's a poor attitude that.'

Pickard: Do you think he would give me an interview?

Danny: You still don't understand the difference between management and manuals, do you?

Pickard: I know there is a class divide which is insurmountable.

Danny: You don't understand that when they gan on that side of the fence, how they are brought up, and how it is instilled into them that they are a management team, and they become a different animal.

Pickard: Yes, but he's finished though, isn't he?

Danny: He's only forty-nine year old . . .

Pickard: And he'll get another job?

Danny: That's what he'll be thinking even if he doesn't. He wouldn't have nowt to do with you. He is still management team.

Pickard: But, if he thinks he has been ratted on, he might want to talk.

Danny: He's quite clear. He's quite clear what he said. He telt W—, 'I've been finished for being incompetent, yet I reached the ninety per cent target figure for erection, I received a letter from the financial director congratulating me for getting £4,500,000 for getting the launch on time. Our production is higher than SS, our quality of work is better than SS, and you are bringing a man here who is eleven year older than me to do my job. Can you give me any answers?' W— didn't answer him. He just sat there.

Pickard: So why are they doing it?

Danny: Quite simply: there is seventy-five per cent of the steelwork going to be done at A&P, so he is going to fetch his steelworking team over here. He's shoving our lot out and bringing his own in.

You see it all the time. They've already got the paint manager in and the joiners' manager in, they've got a steel preparation manager: they've all come from over there. They've got a maintenance manager from over there. They've got a welding manager coming at the end of the month from over there. And now we've got B— coming to take SD's job, and you see the whole strata of fucking management at that level coming in and taking over.

Pickard: What's going to happen to P—?

Danny: P— is number one.

Pickard: I thought it was W—?

Danny: No he's number two to P—. That's why W— is doing it, because W— is complaining to BS that the upper strata of management, the top fucking board, are coming out of BS and A&P. And A&P and BS mafia are moving in. So he wants to get his mafia in here. They are at each other's throats at top level. P— is the managing director of the company (NESL). W— was number one at SS, same as P— was over here, when they set the company up, they made P— number one of the whole group, and W— was made number two. You see what happened this morning with the burners, W— is saying, 'You've got to use arc air in the shed, you've got to use iron powder, further subcontracting of staging, fucking take the platers off the Kamags, it should be a fucking labourer doing it.' And all the fucking things has just been piled in.

Bluey: The yard is just like a volcano, eventually it is just going to erupt. Before eleven o'clock I hope.

Danny: Tony said, 'The shop stewards here are like firemen, that's what we are, at the moment.'

Pickard: Is there any chance of me getting a word from any dissident manager or director?

Danny: The only bloke that I've ever known that's come out and said what he thought about it after he finished was the previous chairman to Day [Sir Robert Atkinson]. All they done to him was brush him aside and called it sour grapes. What they said was: 'Why didn't you say it when you were chairman?' Same argument could apply to SD—. He's known us a lot of years.

Bluey: As a manual he was sacked from Laing's for playing cards. He was foreman plater, then preparation manager, then he went to assembly manager, then he moved to steelworks manager, and then he took over as senior production manager.

Danny: That's what he was saying, he was in charge of all production

271

in the yard. All steelwork production was under him. That's his argument: each stage of the ship he got it on time, and launched it, got the four and a half million quid. Why is he being replaced by a man who hasn't got as good a record as him?

Bluey: Not only that, you could see what was happening a few months back when they got N— from across the water, and our control of preparation was took out of SD—'s hands and was placed in N—'s control.

Danny: The director responsible to W—.

Bluey: We've got managers over here that are not responsible to our directors. All they are is W—'s spies.

Danny: W— is the production director for the two yards. All production in every area is directly under W—. And everybody is accountable to P—.

Bluey: What a bastard.

Danny: When you get a man like F— who has been in the game for more years than you care to remember, and he must have dealt with different industries and different people up and down the country all his trade union life, he turns round and says P— is the most unscrupulous man he's ever met in his life. Because he is not only unscrupulous, he is such an egotist he brags about being unscrupulous.

Pickard: What is the basic issue that Micky was telling me about?

Bluey: It's the contaminants in the process. They are saying, 'Fair enough, but why not do it in the dinner hour when nobody is about?' But the shit gans all over the place. You open the fucking door and it's still in the atmosphere, that's what we are on about.

Brian: S— has called a meeting and it all depends on what his attitude is. If he's dogmatic, there will be trouble.

Pickard: If he's dogmatic what would Mick do?

Brian: Mick has got a mandate from their department that if P— fucking insists that he wants arc air in the shed they want a meeting. They'll be away up the bank.

Bluey: He'll gan straight to the members, they'll take their decision and he comes back and asks for our (confed) support which he'll get, no bother.

Alf: One time down here everybody knew each other and they were all Picky's hands, like. Now it's like the United Nations, they're from all over the place. I keep seeing the demise of all the old hands: they are just getting squeezed out like blackheads. It's only an open prison with the doors on, you come down and work here for eight hours a day. While you are in here, you don't know what's going on outside. They could drop a fucking bomb and you wouldn't know.

Pickard: They'd probably drop it on here.

Alf: No need to, the government's done it for them. It all comes down to what these people say: 'If you want a job and you want to work here, you have got to do as you are told.' You've got contractors coming in to put up staging and all sorts. That wouldn't be allowed at one time.

You see where the extractor machines are, there used to be a mini fog hanging in this fucking shed. It was thick enough so you couldn't see through it to the side of the shed. It just used to hang there. And that was only about eighteen foot or so to the machine, and that used to be there. When you came back after your fortnight's holiday these three bays used to have at least an eighth of an inch to a quarter of an inch of fucking settled dust all over, like a blanket. And the labourers used to get on and have to sweep all the fucking bays down to get all the fucking stuff off, the dust. It was settling on you, all the time. We didn't know anything, we'd ignore it. Up there now, they are new windows that have been put in, and the roof had all the painting. You see all these girders that's rusting a little bit, they have all been painted. They were all green and fucking grey and the fucking muck was standing off. It's a wonder we aren't all in a fucking mental home down here. Caulking inside a fucking unit, four or five bays, and they are only fucking narrow, and you are inside and he sends a fucking caulker on the outside. In here! The mind was absolutely blanko. It's an impossibility to think. We had to do all this, fucking ridiculous.

Pickard: How could you do your work in that situation?

Alf: You either did or you didn't. If you didn't, the gaffer would want to know why. It was only later on that we started to rebel. These conditions just weren't good enough. I've went home on a nighttime and me fucking head has been ringing that much it has

273

knocked me out. I fell asleep. How shall I put it? The magnitude of the fucking noise in your head! You know when the wife is talking to you, the fucking noise is going whzzzzzzzz. You were blanko, man, it was no good. We worked down there on a shell panel, seventeen welders, one of them was a shop steward. Seventeen welders, one burner and two caulkers. And we were using five-sixteenth welding rods on the seams. That's a big rod. When you get a flash off one of them,[1] your fucking eyes are out on stalks. I had a flash. In them days, you either came to work and got drops in or you went to the eye infirmary. I had this flash and to come to work was a long way for me because I didn't live near the yard, and to gan to the eye infirmary was a long way away, so you know what I done? The old remedy is to pour tea leaves in the eyes, the essence of tea in the eye, and then a bowl of cold water and keep cooling your eyes down. It's just like hot sand. That would be three o'clock in the morning. Not long after I started doing that, the fucking water was steaming! Your fucking eyes are that red hot that when you put the sponge back the water is getting warm and there was actually steam coming off it.

morale

Pickard: What do you think of these lot that's coming round and asking why you've stopped the job?
Alf: That's just another form of harrassment. That's to make the lads who are working sick as fuck so they'll eventually get what they want, all the redundancies that they want. It's a prelude to which way they are going to run the industry. Apart from that, you don't get the best results out of people by harrassment. The best results you can get is by getting that person interested in what they are doing, and them saying, 'I'll get stuck in and do it.' But if you find some of them, which you know and I do, they wouldn't work if they could help it, and you can give them a job a million times and they still wouldn't do it, they are the people that should have been weeded out. But they are not. What they have done here is they haven't cut the dead wood out, they've cut a hell of a load of

1. The flash burns the skin off the eyeball. The effect of the flash doesn't come on until the evening or night, several hours after the incident.

fucking good workers out of this yard, I'll tell you. Have they not! Better welders than me, you know what I mean? They might of been harder but they were fucking good at their jobs. They whip along no bother. But they did it in the knowledge that they were going to get well recompensed and they were doing it for the shipyard. It's fucking gone that, finished! I wouldn't be standing here talking to you now, you know. I would be on my fucking job, because I would know that the ones I was working alongside were working, and I couldn't bear the thought of them working and me standing watching them. But it has all changed. You say to yourself, 'They are working and I am letting the side down.' You always get some goons, though.

Pickard: So do you see this purge as a way of forcing redundancies? That lad that was just saying, 'Close the whole fucking place down,' is that a result?

Alf: Of course it is. He couldn't give two fucks about what he is doing. He's got no pride in his job. There is no job satisfaction, as the Americans would put it. The harrassment is the wrong way round, they have got it wrong. It's not up to me to tell them how to do it. You see they haven't gained the men's confidence for a kick-off. What they have done is, they have destroyed all the confidence the men had in the management, because they fucking blew the management out, Picky's management. There is nobody left off Picky's management, you know.

Pickard: Were they any good?

Alf: How can I put it? They were prepared to negotiate on a basis of man to man, talking to the shop stewards, they used to fucking negotiate ... it was like a little family. But it doesn't work like that now. Isn't that right, John? The management have lost the confidence of the men in this yard? Everybody used to work together at one time?

John: Everybody is sick of them now. The daft little things they are getting you for. As long as they harass us, they'll not get no work done.

Pickard: I know they are sick in the ship, not being able to leave until it's on the dot. The gaffers standing on the gangplank watching their clocks.

John: I know they take a few minutes here, we've always done it, but we work in between. We work hard here. These fellahs, you just cannot be bothered to work for them, that's the top and bottom

275

of it. They are treating us like schoolbairns now, but we'll not have it.

Alf: I wouldn't treat me bairns like they treat us down here.

John: My lad would flatten me he would. He's twenty-four year old and he wishes he was out, now.

Alf: He was lucky to get a job in Sunderland with the high rate of unemployment.

John: He stopped on in college to get his HNCs. They are no good, they want to finish him the first chance they get. There is fuck all for the young lads, is there?

Nissan again

Alf: There's a thing gets right up my fucking back. They've got to bring a car factory from Japan and operate here in this country. What's wrong with operating your own car factories and that? You cannot tell me they can't do it. I think it is a load of shit. There are other companies that are coming here and there are goods that used to be made in this country that are now made on the Continent. It's a disgrace. The same way they are abandoning merchant ship-building to the Japanese and the Koreans. We beat the Japs with the SD14. There was no competition, we were just the outright winners. They brought out the Freedom ship and we brought out the Liberty ship replacement, and we beat them fucking hands down, easy. They couldn't whack it.

John: The last SD14 that was built was in this company, no word of a lie, we were doing the funnel down here: me, little Charlie Roker with Jimmy Whitty. There was a manager, foreman, and two platers came down from Scotland asking Jimmy Whitty how to make the funnel. Fucking old Jimmy just looked at the drawing: he said, 'Are you a plater?' He says, 'Aye.' Jimmy says, 'That's what I work at. If you cannot read them, you shouldn't be working on the job.' He wouldn't tell them.

Alf: Smith's Docks, it took them eighteen months to build an SD14. It took fucking eight weeks here, from start to finish.

John: They were building about seven or eight up here and about five down Bartram's in one year.

Alf: We built three twenty-sixes, and the tonnage for that year, compared to Bartram's tonnage, we had actually built thirty thousand ton extra. And we were building twenty-six-thousand-ton ships. We built less ships but produced more tonnage. And there was only these three fucking bays doing it.

Alf: I think it is the biggest mistake of the government's life, what they are doing to this industry, chopping it to bits. We are an island nation, we need fucking vessels, man. I'll tell you something and all, I wouldn't build that fucking tunnel, no way.

John: They are forgetting the main thing that the tunnel will cause in this country, rabies.

Alf: You know as well as I do that rats and mice and all the rest of it will be along that tunnel like a squirrel up a tree. If it was up to me I'd pull out of the EEC and all. We should have stuck with fucking New Zealand, Australia and Canada and all these African countries and that. There should be free trade throughout the world, not just the Common Market where they are screwing everybody. It's only them at the top that's getting all the profit. It proves it when they can gan and dump valuable foods, like milk and butter, and they have got storerooms of fucking meat, millions of tons of the fucker, it just doesn't get through to me. What's the point of keeping it in storage like that; sell it off. It's like the management here.

John: I'm getting wrong for not booking them. I'm a gaffer. How can I book anybody if they are not doing anything wrong?

Pickard: Are you getting a bollocking for not booking enough people?

Alf: You know the powers that be? They have been getting to the foreman and have said, 'If you are not going to start booking the men, we are going to start booking you.' Like the police force, they have got to have a quota.

subcontractors

BBC: Swan Hunter's on the Tyne is only getting one new naval order. Even though the order for a frigate is worth more than a hundred million pounds, Swan's says they won't make a promise on it, and union leaders say unless the Ministry of Defence comes up with more contracts it could lead to further job losses and the closure of one of the company's yards. Meanwhile in BS headquarters in

277

Newcastle, plans to axe around three and a half thousand jobs: two and a half thousand of them from the North-East are being discussed. The redundancies are tied in with a twelve-and-a-half per cent pay offer being made to the remaining workforce. The unions say they can't accept yard closures and job losses; BS say they can't have the pay rises without them. At this afternoon's meeting, the unions are hoping to persuade BS to separate the two issues . . .

Chris: S— pulled me. He said, 'I'm bringing contractors in.' I said, 'You're fucking not, it'll cause a dispute.'

Billy: Chris, it's the only way you can talk to them, it's the only language they know.

Eddy: The shop stewards, I'm not kidding – I'm only a little fucking cog – have gotten them the best conditions ever. I have been working forty-three fucking year from being a boy, and it is the best fucking situation that I've been in.

Chris: The terrible thing about it is, Eddy's forty-three years' commitment, Billy's done thirty-odd year, twenty-five for myself, and you have got people coming down from Scotland, the managing directors and them, and they can fucking ruin this town and they can ruin you as an individual. Put you on the fucking scrapheap, where you don't want to be, and they'll just fuck off to Scotland and retire into a nice big house or whatever and we'll be fucking left with nowt. It is fucking serious, man. There should be revolutions in here, in this yard, but we cannot get them motivated. They just think of the ten thousand pound [redundancy money] and things like that. I mean young boys, they are earning potentially about eight and half or nine thousand a year. So the young boys are walking about thinking, *ten thousand, five thousand!* And they're going to ruin my future, Eddy's future. In the plumbing department, all the boys could take their redundancy, create an imbalance. So what does he do? Contractors. Just through young boys taking four thousand pounds to buy a bastard brand new car and you were in thirty-three years, or forty years! It's fucking sickening.

Eddy: Where do *we* gan? There'll be nowhere for us, I mean the steelmen might say, 'Well, come with us,' if they've got anything. They might not be allowed to do it.

Chris: I think all the tensions will close this fucking yard.

Chris: Say Tom, one day maybe you'll be famous, and I'll say to the grandbairns, 'I know that lad.'

Pickard: You can say, 'That bastard picked my fucking brains and stole my lines.'

Chris: I knew that man, Pickard.

Eddy: You'll see the television come on with 'Face To Face', or one of them, and there's Tom sitting there, grey hair and a fucking multimillionaire.

Jim: 'And how did you start?'

Chris: 'Well, er, actually it was all through the flap that it all happened.'

George: 'Through the flap,' I think that's the term they use down there.

Eddy: 'Chris B— was a great influence.'

Chris: 'And in fact I now own three feet out of every four that comes out on Betamax.'

Pickard: Anyway, I don't want any fucking letters from you afterwards saying, 'That was my fucking joke!'

Chris: We've got to get some money out of it.

Pickard: Get fucked!

Tommy: I know all my jokes, mind.

Chris: Tony telt a joke yesterday.

Pickard: I don't believe you.

Chris: Tony telt a joke when he was singing going across the yard.

Pickard: When confronted he said he was talking to himself, but I think he was singing a Max Bygraves song: 'Singa longa Max and the revolutionary struggle.' Is the company saying get rid of the plumbers and just get contractors in when they need them?

Eddy: Oh aye, that's what they want. The whole outfitting department; plumbers, blacksmiths ... what they do then is fetch short-term contractors in. When the job's done, you'll be out. You'll be paid off by the company you're working for. And when the work comes up again, they'll take you on. That's what they want.

Pickard: What effect does that have on working conditions?

Eddy: Crap! Safety is out the window. And if they tell you to gan on staging where there's only one plank and you ask for another one, you've got your card marked. And at the first opportunity you're out. But having said that, you could say nowt, gan on one plank, say you fall, injure yourself. You're off work and sue the company. They'll turn around and say, 'You shouldn't have gone on

279

one plank. You should have known different.' But if you complain there's only one plank there, they mark your card. Safety gans through the window. It's like a dollar in the matchbox; it's the same thing.

Kenny: Dollar in the matchbox, told a tale on you...

Eddy: Dollar in my matchbox gets my overtime. Why, I've heard of fucking blokes man, only a few year ago, hanging round the gaffer's arse, we used to call it feather-plucking. You know when you kept pigeons when they feather-pluck them to hant [train to return home] them? Well, we used to call these fellahs feather-pluckers. You'd never see the manager, it was only maybe one manager of a fucking big area, not managers like you've got here – managers of fucking inkwells and things like that. You used to have to feather-pluck the foreman: we didn't. You used to see them out of a weekend with their wives, the wives would be better dressed maybe than your wife, they'd have a car and you'd have no car. They used to get all the gash [spare] overtime that was gannin', and you used to get fuck all. You got nowt. Anyway, say the work peters out, what they do is, they put you on short-term because they don't have to pay holiday pay, they don't have to pay stamp money or fuck all. No insurance or nowt.

someone jumped off the bridge

Tommy: We went round, just grabbed his overalls and lifted him up on the stretcher. Picked him up on to the stretcher and into the fucking thing. Dead.

Eddy: Chris Evans just went out the back for a piss and coming in he heard bump bump. He shouted of me, and I ran along and I looked out, and he was lying on the deck, stretched out like that. And he looked up, and then down his fucking head went. He jumped off and hit our roof, like a rail off the roof, and then boomf.

Tommy: Couldn't do nowt for him.

Eddy: There was a woman jumped off and she went through our roof, her legs were sticking through. She landed on the heater and she melted. The smell of melted fat!

Chris: We couldn't ask any other cunt to take her down so we had to put on face-masks to take her down.

Eddy: I went to the ladder to take her down, and for a fortnight

everything that I was eating came back. You see she was sticking there, and it was winter, and the heater was on. Big industrial heaters. Anyway, I'm away over. We'll see you, Tom. Arrividerci.
Chris: He's only gannin' to London, not Spain.

17/7/86

the purge

Harry: If you've got a job to do, they're saying, 'Just leave it, gan to the ship at twenty to eight, and stand on the ship, see the gaffer if you want to and come back.' You've got one gaffer in the shop, he's chasing you out, 'Round the ship,' you see the gaffer on the ship and tell him that you've got to gan back and do a job in the shop. So you come back and do a job in the shop and you get fucking chased again, telling you not to fucking do it, you have to gan on the fucking ship. Anyway, they had a job on the deck to do the hatches, the painting was stuck, they couldn't get it out. And the only way to get it out was with the jack. So they had to gan round the millwrights for a jack, well, that's what they were supposed to have done anyway. They went and seen the gaffer in the shop and told him that they wanted the jack out the millwrights. He says, 'We'll send the labourer along to get the jack. Anyway, in the meantime you'll have to get back to the ship. Stand there and do nowt, just stand, and if anybody says owt to you, say you're waiting for gear.' They waited two days for a jack. They could have done it in ten minutes by walking along and getting it. The job would have been done. The lad says, 'You's are barmy, you're getting nowt done, two days we stood waiting for this jack that we could have got in five or ten minutes ourselves,' just cause they wouldn't let them off the ship. He's says, 'Aye, that's the way we want it to happen. I couldn't give two monkeys if you do nowt all day as long as you are on the ship the times you're supposed to be.'

The next one was the cherry-picker. There's about three cherry-pickers on the ship and none of them work, broken down. They've gotten one off and sent to the millwrights to get fixed. Well, this day, they wanted a cherry-picker, because they have to get in under the hatches from underneath. So he went and seen the foreman and he says, 'We want a cherry-picker in this hold.' So the foreman says, 'Aye, well, you'll have to gan and see the manager.' So they went and seen the manager, the manager says, 'Aye, right oh, you'll have to gan and see the foreman shipwright.' So they gan and see the foreman shipwright and foreman shipwright says, 'Oh, you'll have to gan and see the manager.' This went on for about an hour, they kept gannin' round each one, nobody would make a phone call or nowt to tell the lads to come out from the garage to fix it, or nowt. Anyway, they phoned up the garage eventually after two hours, and the garage lads went straight over and started to do the job. The head foreman said, 'It's not your job to get it fixed.' Because the lad had to phone up the garage in the end, himself. He says, 'It's not your job to do that, what you've got to do is stand on the deck and tell the manager or the foreman on the ship that you want the cherry-picker and it's up to them to do it.' And the lad says, 'I've already done that, man, for two blinking hours.' He says, 'I want the cherry-picker now and I've had to gan and phone the garage up meself.' And he says, 'Well, that's not your job, it's our job to do that.' But the lad said, 'But nobody'll take it on their own back to do it.' So they stood about for nearly a day waiting for the cherry-picker.

There was a welder, he got a flash on the night before. Flashes are bad like, they make your eyes water like hell, you feel as if you've got grit in them. Anyway, he come down to work on the morning, at half-past seven, and he went to the ambulance room to get his drops, to get his eyes seen to. You have to gan two or three times a day. Anyway he didn't get on to the ship until quarter to eight, so his foreman booked him. Took his name and number. 'But,' he says, 'I've been in the ambulance room, getting drops in me eyes. It's marked down in the ambulance room book, if you want to check.' The foreman went round and checked, and he says, 'Fair enough.' So he went round and seen the manager and the manager says, 'Still book him.' So the foreman went back to him and says, 'I've been told by the manager that I've still got to book you.' The lad says, 'Well, it's crackers that.' He says, 'I don't care, you can gan round the ambulance room and stop there all day if you want, but be on the ship for twenty to eight.'

The lads are not carrying nowt. Before they used to maybe stop in the shop and do whatever job we had to do and carry it round to the ship. Now what we are doing is, we don't bother doing no job in the shop, just get our overalls on and when the buzzer gans

283

walk down to the ship and get on there for twenty to eight, and then come straight off to gan to the shop. It's a hell of a waste of time.

poets

Tony: What about Buddhist monks? Just gannin' around with a fucking bowl and saying, 'Well, this is my job, I'm a disciple of the fucking religion, and I'm a priest of the religion, and so can you spare a couple of grains of rice for me cause I'm fucking starving to death?' That's what you'll have to say, 'I'm a poet and...'
Pickard: Buddha, can you spare a dime?
Jake: Are you fucking glue-sniffing, or what?
Tony: If his output as a poet depends on how he lives and so he gans to a person and says, 'Well, I'm a poet and I'm ganna read you a bit of my poetry, and whatever you think of it, just give us a few bob.'
Danny: For a start he'd starve to fucking death.
Jake: I'm telling you, it's not a fucking go at you, it's just that unfortunately the people that you've got to communicate with, all right I might be thick but there's one thousand of us thick down here.
Pickard: How can you judge the cultural aspirations of your entire fucking membership?
Jake: Everybody I've talked to says, 'I don't understand what he's on about, what he's fucking saying.'
Pickard: I've fucking said fuck all to anybody.
Jake: We've had your books around the yard, man. 'Singing to your cock!' People think you're a fucking weirdo.
Tony: Who's got that book then? Couldn't even take it home, could ya?
Jake: That's the way the working class speak, man. Tell your lasses to 'fuck off and is me dinner ready, you bastard? Come here and I'll give you a good fucking clubbing'.
Tony: You couldn't take that book into a good Catholic home.
Pickard: I heard you cracked a joke the other day, Tony.
Danny: That little cunt, Ronnie, was gassing when you were away, telling them all about you ganin' round the yard singing and cracking jokes and that.

284

Jake: Pickard, you'll get wrong before you gan, I'm telling you, you'll end up bruised.

Tony: Is he on fucking drugs, this cunt?

Jake: Glue-sniffing. It's the end of term, man, isn't it? Hols coming up.

Tony: They're all on fucking drugs, the middle classes.

Jake: I hope he doesn't break down tomorrow and start crying. Mind you, no speeches tomorrow, thanking the shop stewards.

Tony: Just say goodbye, gratefully.

Pickard: Well, I wish I could say it's been a pleasure, but I have to be honest … But, look, what I'm proposing is to get a sub every week, like ten pence a week to support a poet.

Tony: They tried to do that you know.

Pickard: For a poet?

Tony: No, they called them the industrial chaplains. And what their idea was, with the church being in decline, and divorce, and a lot of vicars, et cetera, not being able to find fucking parishes to keep themselves, they decided on the bright idea of non-denominational industrial chaplain who would be adopted by certain groups of workpeople who would pay half a crown a week for their fucking upkeep. Good idea, son. They got good ideas, son, off me!

Pickard: I thought you had a religious bent?

Jake: If the bloke had been a Catholic it would have been all right.

Tony: That would be different. If it wasn't for you blue-nosed bastards, there wouldn't be any trouble in the world. If we were all Catholics we'd all be happy. It's only you blue-nosed cunts that causes all the trouble.

Pickard: Are you a blue-nose, Jake?

Jake: I'm an atheist.

Tony: He was baptised a fucking Protestant. A Methodist or fucking something like that.

Pickard: You defended your religion?

Jake: Me? I wouldn't defend any fucking religion.

Tony: You defend yours by saying, 'They're all the same, they're all a load of shite.'

Jake: They are a load of shite.

Eddy: He's got an each-way bet on, Tony.

Tony: You've got to. Aye, The Queen'll fucking sort all these cunts out.

Jake: Did you see that interview with Powell, 'My Sovereign'? He

285

was asked if the Queen won't intervene if Mrs Thatcher doesn't impose sanctions on the South Africans. He says, 'Of course she can't intervene, she's a constitutional monarch. She's my monarch, she's our monarch, and she serves us and we serve her.' But the BBC bloke says, 'Do you not think, if there is no intervention, there is a possibility that the Commonwealth will break up?' He says, 'What Commonwealth? Most of them's republicans. And she's got no say whatsoever, because she takes advice from ministers, ministers give her advice, and in the republics, as I say, she's got no say at all in there. Lots of people in this country would look forward to the breaking up of the so-called Commonwealth, because it doesn't help us one iota, and we'd be better severing our ties with them.' He was just this close to getting his shotgun out and saying, 'The black bastards should be fucked.'

Tony: She'd not intervene in that situation, but I'll tell you a situation she would fucking intervene in.

Jake: What's that?

Tony: She'd intervene if they fucking elected a real socialist fucking government and started to take the fucker over.

Jake: Then she'd use the Churches again.

Pickard: What could she do?

Tony: Appeal to the fucking people for national unity, to defeat the socialist government. Same as they did for Harold Wilson. The administration was elected, and they were going to do a tricky Dicky, fucking Mountbatten; he had meetings with the top industrialists, and fucking King and them from Fleet Street.

Jake: They'd put the Americans in charge, and troops on the streets, martial law.

a Trot or not

Tony: I see that comedian was ganna come up and do our festival.

Jake: I know he was ganna come up, so the paper said. The arsehole also attends Tory Party conferences. It's no good trying to put yourself right now, man.

Tony: It's not me, it was fucking Stoppard said it.

Jake: It was you, you bastard, it was you. 'He's a good socialist, mind: he gives lots of money to the miners' groups.'

Tony: You exaggerate on it. Stoppard telt me he was a bit of a fucking Trot, that's what he said.

Jake: It was you, man.

Tony: It wasn't me. You can ask Stoppard now.

Jake: Because you've conditioned him that it was him.

Tony: He just says fucking anything, Stoppard.

Jake: You get these fucking romantic ideas man and away you gan.

Tony: But I've never liked the fucker.

Jake: Telling people that he was a fucking raving Trotskyite.

Nissan

Ronnie: Did you see that TV programme on Nissan? They're getting loads of overtime. They're not getting paid for it, but they're getting loads of it.

Tony: Creeps.

Jake: I deliberately didn't watch it. I watched fucking 'Newsnight'.

Ronnie: It was disgusting.

Paul: One of them was an ex-welder or a driller from here.

Jake: What did he say?

Tony: He left the yards because the trade unions had a stranglehold.

Paul: He said they were too entrenched in their ways.

Jake: So we're all fucking Trotskyites, eh, like your mate the famous comedian.

company jokes

Tommy: It's right: these lads get jokes. He says they get a joke every morning, and they fucking gan down and they get all the foremen together and they say, 'This is this morning's joke.'

Ronnie: Never in the fucking world.

Tommy: And the foremen then go and tell them. He says it's a fact.

Pickard: Where's this?

Tommy: Sunderland Shipbuilders. It's a fucking fact. 'Joke of the day! This is how we've got to get the men. Take a joke in. Today's joke.'

Pickard: Who tells them it?

Tommy: Well, the fucking managers must.

287

Cal: 'Hello hello hello, as I was coming into work this morning a chap came over here and says...'

Eddy: It's fucking terrible, it is lad. You fucker, Hitler must be laughing his cock off.

24/7/86

the last riveter on the Wear

> Conversation with Joe Henderson at the 'Old Men's
> Party', an annual party given to honour the old men of
> the river.

Joe: I worked fifty-one year in the shipyards. I served me time at
Short's but I first started at Doxford's. In 1930, I was there when
the Duke of York was there – that was the Prince of Wales. When
the Prince of Wales got married to Mrs Simpson. Then they closed
down in August 1930, and I started up at Picky's, that was the old
Picky's in 1931. They used to build a boat on spec, hoping somebody
would buy it. So I was about six months there and they closed
down, then I went down Laing's and worked on the old dock at
Laing's. Laing's had their own dock then because 1933 was a bad
year for the Wear because there was that many yards closed down,
and I started serving me time at Short's as a riveter. Well I left
Short's in '48 and I went to Swansea, worked Swansea six months,
went to Cardiff and only worked there a week, come back, went to
Doxford's, from Doxford's went to Short's five weeks, left Short's,
went to Picky's, was there five year from '49 to '54. Now then, from
there I went to Gell's, from Gell's to Greywood's, from Greywood's
to Laing's, from Laing's to Doxford's; from there down to
Greenwell's, from there to Greythorp, from Greythorp to South
Bank, from South Bank back to Greenwell's, from there down to
Immingham. Now when I come back last time from Greythorp I
went to Bartram's and I was sixty-four, worked there eleven year
and finished up at Picky's in 1980 and I'm seventy-one now so that's
the finish.
Pickard: Why did you travel so much?
Joe: For the money.
Pickard: Was it better at different yards?
Joe: Now wait a bit: you would have been getting seven pound a

week here, you'd go for nine pound there. You'd just go for the money. When you were working in a shipyard you got poor money, but when you worked at Greenwell's you got a big overtime and usually it would boost it. That was how you went for the money. So you could give the wife your board money and have a bit pocket money for yourself. I'd work all night for five quid; six hundred rivets and twelve-hour shifts for five quid. And that's all you got. You give the old tart three quid and keep the two quid as pocket money, extra on top of your full week.

Pickard: Easier for young men to do than older blokes?

Joe: Oh, they wouldn't do it. What we had to gan through: we had to gan down there and work all day, then they'd come along: 'Will you work all night tonight?' You had no money to buy any bait at the canteen. There was no canteens. You'd work straight through with nowt to eat. Work all night, till the next morning, twelve hours.

Oh, aye. There's many a time you wouldn't have a pair of boots on, and standing in the wet, working in the dock down there at Greenwell's. There was a spring there that was leaking all the time.

Pickard: What were labour relations like? What was management like in those days?

Joe: Very poor. They were at the top and they kept you down. We couldn't get our ten o'clock, we had to get our ten o'clock on the dock bottom. It was that way for years. Oh aye, it was years later before we got a cabin on the top. And you were bloody soaking, you had no bloody boots. Later on you got industrial boots, dollar a week, got a pair of them. It was bloody good if you had a good pair of boots for standing in. But you had to have a good pair of boots in the dock bottom because they were all clarts [mud] then in the shipyards. But now they've got tarmacadam down the sides. Every plate then was one plate at a time, now it's all fabricated. You had to drag every plate down and drag it up. And when they got it up, our trade, riveting, they just took it up – they were on piece and we were on piece – they stuck it up with – we used to call it – chewing gum. They stuck a plate on to the side of the ship with it where they put bolts in to make it safe. They just put a lead bolt in the coat. We had to screw all that up and make it watertight, presentable for riveting, then we had to pay that man.

Now there's one thing and one thing only about riveting: they said that there was not such a thing as nothing. I said, in our trade, the riveting trade, there was. I tell you why. We got a job, went down to the job, we'll say to do the double bottom. Now there they used to leave the tank top off. The tank top was off. When the tank top was off you were down the bottom, you lost two shilling a hundred off your rivets, you got nine and a penny a hundred. Now if your tank top was on you got eleven and a penny a hundred. Now the tank top off, now you went down – I'm talking about before the war, like – I'd screw her up with hand tool, roll up and put the rivets in – you'd sent the heater for the rivets, you've got to have the rivets in, everything – now then you'd done that, it took you nearly half a day to get prepared: it started to snow. You were sent home: not one rivet in. You didn't get a ha'penny, not one ha'penny. Now this man that's heating for you, you had to pay him half a day. Now that's less than nowt, isn't it? That's the God's honest truth. Now it didn't happen till 1943 that we got a fall-back rate. We were the first ones to get a fall-back rate, twenty-six shilling a day. There's a fellah here, our young 'un, Doxford's, a married man with four bairns, couldn't make it pay, got fourteen shilling, and he had four bairns.

Doing the lower deck you got six and ten pence a hundred, for putting up the lower deck. You had to prepare that job, screw it up, then you had to get a hundred rivets in and three shared that – well, two of you – but you had to pay the heater. I mean it went on, and if you didn't make it pay, what would he get? The lieu rate on the boilermakers was thirty-five shilling then before the war. Now we got a fall-back rate, that's if you couldn't make it pay, at Short's, at twenty-six shilling a day.

There was fifty-four shipyards on the River Wear at one time. My grandfather, he served his time, and we've still got the old credentials – *1865, Shipwright* – now my father was a shipwright, and I went into boilermaking. He got a shilling a day for seven year, as a bound apprentice. On that sheet it says, 'This man is duty bound' – cause they were all Quakers them, like, that was off the beer, see – duty bound for to serve your time. Now then, he was duty bound for to make a man of you, like, serving your time. You had to do everything your maister telt ya. They hadn't to play cards, you hadn't to go out gambling, you hadn't to go here, you hadn't to go there, you hadn't to drink, you hadn't to masturbate, you know what I mean? I can assure you, everything. And you had to have that seven-year apprentice, he's duty bound to make you a

291

good apprentice. Now he got a shilling a day, that was the old man's father, 1865, and it's in linen, it's not on paper, and when he come out his time at twenty-one he got the princely sum of ten shilling. I was the last riveter on the Wear. But you had to follow the money.

AFTERWORD

tell them in Gdansk

All through 1988, North East Shipbuilders Ltd (NESL) was under threat of closure for lack of orders. The shop stewards, with their MP Bob Clay and supported by the Labour council and all other parties in the town of Sunderland, mounted a vigorous campaign to keep the yards open. Towards the middle of 1988 the government said that the only hope was to privatise. They invited bidders. Foreign owners obviously saw the value of the most modern yards in Europe and their highly skilled and committed workforce even if the British government didn't. One of the earliest bidders for the yards was a consortium set up by Peter Zacci which included the West German shipping company, the Egon Oldendorf line. Oldendorf was prepared to bring to the consortium an order for six 33,000-ton bulk carriers which he was on the brink of placing in Korea. He was offering to pay a higher price too, but was rejected out of hand in the same way as the Cubans were later, with a much larger order. The Cubans are one of the biggest shipping nations in the world and have a massive and expanding fleet, many of whose ships were built on the North-east coast. They wanted to continue that association and tried to place an order for ten SD15s with NESL. The then Minister of State (Kenneth Clarke) denied the existence of the order until, several months later – forced to admit that there was an order – he dismissed it out of hand saying the price offered per ship was too low. The Cubans were never invited to the negotiating table to discuss prices and specifications. They were also willing to negotiate a five-year co-operation agreement with the yard to market their ships in other parts of Latin America, Africa, and the Far East where they have extensive contacts. It was later admitted that the DTI were aware, from July 1988, of the Cuban willingness to have co-operation agreements.

The government were due to announce their decision on the private bids for the yards in early November, but obviously thought it prudent to postpone it until after Mrs Thatcher's visit to Poland where controversy was raging over the Polish government's threatened closure of the Lenin shipyard in Gdansk. It was said the British government were seeking more time to consider the bids, but subsequent events suggest that there was never any serious intention of keeping the yards open at all, and that they merely sought to protect Mrs Thatcher from the hypocrisy of her position when expressing solidarity with the shipyard workers of Poland.

Another consortium, brought together so imaginatively by Bob Clay and the shop stewards, was told that the fundamental problem they faced was that the consortium had not organised sufficient financial backing; not in terms of the bid itself, but as a financial cushion to fall back on. Both the DTI and BS argued that a new owner would need substantial financial reserves in order to risk a contract as large as the Cuban one. There is a savage irony in that argument, given that a year earlier the yard was having to close because there were no orders: then the goalposts were moved again and the yard was closed because it had too large an order.

It was obvious from the outset that the government had no intention of allowing the yards to remain open. The privatisation process has to be seen as a sham. If they were genuinely interested in the sale of the yards they would not have damaged their reputation as Kenneth Clarke did in Parliament, and they would have made sure that orders were secured before privatisation. We only have to look at their habit of fattening the cow before taking it to market where the government is serious about privatisation: BP, British Gas, writing off four billion pounds of Rover's debts before selling it to British Aerospace (whose chairman is advised by Norman Tebbit), the water industry, etc. NESL was starved of work, its facilities run down, and its reputation criticised by the government minister then responsible for its sale. The workforce had every reason to be demoralised but they showed great tenacity and solidarity with the shop stewards who were so actively fighting in defence of their jobs. Peter Callaghan, chairman of the shop stewards in 1988, speaks of the determination inspired by the 'collectivity and camaraderie' of the workforce.

With Mrs Thatcher back from her photo-call in Poland she could safely forget about the plight of the shipyard workers there. Leaks began to appear in the press to the effect that the government was set to reject all bids for NESL. After the charade was over Bob Clay was told by the chairman of British Shipbuilders (the parent company): 'NESL is not a free-standing shipbuilding company in the market place.' How anyone was expected to buy it in that case is a mystery.

Although some MPs on the opposition benches thought that Tony Newton, Minister of Trade and Industry, had a conscience they also believed that he had inherited a course of events set by his predecessor, Kenneth Clarke, and that the only way to avert that course of events was to reverse some aspects of government policy. But Lord Young was not to be opposed.

On the 7th of December 1988,[1] with a growing volume of orders in world shipbuilding, the government finally made their devastating announcement which brought more than six hundred years of continuous shipbuilding on the River Wear to a close. The immediate effect was to make 2,400 highly skilled shipyard workers redundant with a further 4,000 in dependent industries following them onto the already long dole queues of Sunderland. Two weeks later the former chairman of British Shipbuilders, Graham Day, was rewarded for his services with a knighthood.

January 1989

1. See *Hansard* 14/12/88 for a more detailed account of the attempted privatisation.